ISRAEL

PRAEGER COUNTRY PROFILE SERIES

BURMA: *A Profile* by Norma Bixler
BOLIVIA: *A Profile* by William Carter
TANZANIA: *A Profile* by John Hatch
ROMANIA: *A Profile* by Ian M. Matley
MONGOLIA: *A Profile* by Victor P. Petrov
PUERTO RICO: *A Profile* by Kal Wagenheim

ISRAEL

A PROFILE

Israel T. Naamani

PRAEGER PUBLISHERS
New York • Washington • London

To Zehava—for obvious and wonderful reasons

PRAEGER PUBLISHERS
111 Fourth Avenue, New York, N.Y. 10003, U.S.A.
5, Cromwell Place, London SW7 2JL, England

Published in the United States of America in 1972
by Praeger Publishers, Inc.

© 1972 by Praeger Publishers, Inc.

Library of Congress Catalog Card Number: 78–173284

Printed in the United States of America

Contents

A SECTION OF PHOTOGRAPHS FOLLOWS PAGE 86

Introduction

The caravan of Jewish history has made a globe-circling, multi-millennial round trip and is back home now. It was not a planned journey, and not all of the travelers have returned. Some chose to remain in the Americas and in West European countries. Others, perhaps unwillingly, stayed behind in the U.S.S.R. and in its satellites. Small groups of Jews continue to live in North and South Africa, Australia, and New Zealand, and smaller remnants are to be found in India, China, and other remote corners of the world.

From Apion to Zhdanov (the former a Stoic philosopher of the first century b.c.; the latter the ideologue of the Russian "cultural revolution" in the 1940's), historians and theologians, political scientists and sociologists have considered the fate (as well as the faith) of the Jewish people. This was not and is not an exclusive occupation of non-Jews. Marx, Trotsky, Freud, Bergson—to name a few —had some dark thoughts about their ancestors and about the future of the descendants of Abraham, Isaac, and Jacob. But neither statistics nor casuistics, neither expedience nor logic has stopped the caravan of Jewish history from the compulsive return to its origins. Thus Israel is one of the very few countries, perhaps the only country in the world, where the triumphs of its present match the glories of its past.

In Defiance of Definition

Mention Flanders, Normandy, the Yalu, or Hué, and they will not mean much to most Americans, although hundreds of thousands of their compatriots lost their lives there in World War I, World War II, and the Korean and Vietnamese conflicts. But indicate Galilee, Jordan, Jerusalem, Bethlehem, Nazareth and the names will evoke a set of emotions in the vast majority of the people in the United States. Pick up a newspaper in any part of the world and it will invariably have some item regarding Israel and its neighbors. The mystique, the élan, the fertile ground of the eastern shores of the Mediterranean are a constant source of attention from theologians, sociologists, political scientists, economists, and belletrists.

The expulsion of the Jews from their homeland after the Roman conquest in A.D. 70, the aberrant impulses of the medieval world toward the destruction of Judaism, the memories of the crematoria, and the cleverly veneered anti-Semitism of modern days impelled them—the Jews of the Diaspora (Dispersion)—to keep pace with history and to deal creatively with their problems. They developed physical, spiritual, and cultural staying power by summoning the past as a promise for the future. They created a dilemma for the social scientist who tried to categorize them into a psychoreligious sect, an ethnonational group, a sociolinguistic offshoot, or even a politico-economic entity. The Jews remain *sui generis,* defying definition and analysis both in the Diaspora and in their old-new home of Israel.

Uniqueness and Anomaly

The one-time Prime Minister of the United Kingdom, Harold Macmillan, was asked in 1968 what future he envisioned for Great Britain. Devoid of empire, did it lie along the lines of another Sweden or another Athens? The English statesman pondered a while, then replied: "No, the future I hope for Britain is more like that of Israel. In the time of Elizabeth we were only two million people. In the time of Marlborough, only five or six millions, in the time of Napoleon, only ten millions. The other day, while the world debated, Israel's three millions imposed their will on their enemies. They had what many great people need—resolution, courage, determination, pride. These are what really count in men and nations."

The rich religiocultural protoplasm of the eastern shores of the Mediterranean is an invitation to greatness. Some Israelis, haunted by history and convinced of manifest destiny, walk and talk as though they are the sole inventors of justice, morality, compassion, and the other great human values. But their future, the future of their country, is at least as manipulated as it is ordained, and, contrary to what the Israelis themselves believe, their solutions of problems are not always Sinaic or millennial. Nevertheless, it would be myopic to disregard the uniqueness of the new state.

Long before the British "splendid isolation" at the end of the nineteenth century, Balaam, the biblical soothsayer, who was sent to curse the Israelites, ended up by blessing them. "Lo, it is a people that dwelleth alone," he said. The singularity of the Israelites of the past and the Israelis of the present is that they were not overwhelmed by surrounding cultures, no matter how imposing or glittering. Receptive at times, yes. Influenced frequently, yes. Overwhelmed, never.

Jewish leaders—Abraham, Moses, the prophets, the rabbis, and even the contemporary secularists in Israel—exerted all their efforts to combat destructive incursions and to preserve the "Jewish heritage." Babylon, Assyria, Egypt, even Greece, with its dazzling culture overflowing into Europe, Asia, and North Africa and enveloping the entire civilized world, only modulated but did not swallow up the Jews.

This perhaps is a basic problem in the Middle East today—the desire of Israel to maintain distinctiveness and not to be engulfed by the "Semitic Idea." Israel is determined not to abandon or even weaken its identification with the Jewish legacy, on the one hand, and with the Western world, on the other, in order to become part of a new amalgam (binational or confederate) of Arabs and Jews. We shall return to this matter in later pages of this book.

This attachment to roots was evidenced in the only instance in history when a seemingly dead tongue, a language of the books, became a language of the streets, when Hebrew was revived as a vehicle for everyday expression in Israel. Another manifestation of the Jewish rootedness is the neo-Messianism of the kibbutz (the Israeli collective settlement); although impregnated at times with impeccable Marxist maxims, the kibbutz is imbedded in the social conscience of ancient Judaism.

World Workshop

Israel, as in its distant past, continues to be one of the great workshops for human ideas and affairs. Having ingathered since 1948 a million and a half people from the primordial caves of the Atlas Mountains and from the hallowed halls of learning at Heidelberg, Harvard, Oxford, and the Sorbonne, Israel succeeded, with much pain and patience, in molding these culturally, socially, and psychologically diverse elements into a nation capable of warding off its adversaries.

The Histadrut, the General Federation of Labor, is a workers' institution the like of which is not to be found in any other land. Developing countries in Africa, Asia, and South America look to the Histadrut, to the government, and to private institutions in Israel for technical help, scientific aid, and agricultural and educational guidance. Even in the most highly developed lands, there are those who seek the counsel of Israel—for instance, some black cooperatives in the United States.

Again relying on its usable past, Israel offers a solution not only to the problem of Jews in a hostile environment but also to Judaism in hospitable climates. A contemporary Jewish historian notes: "In terms of distance, Israel is a suburb of the Diaspora; in terms of historic Judaism, the entire Diaspora is a suburb of Israel."

How many Jews are there in the world? In 1972 they were approaching the 15 million mark. Of these, 6.3 million lived in the United States and Canada; 900,000 in Latin America; 4.5 million in Europe (3 million in the U.S.S.R., 570,000 in France, 460,000 in Great Britain, 470,000 in other European countries); 75,000 in Australia and New Zealand; 200,000 in Africa (mostly in South Africa and Morocco); 100,000 in Asia (excluding Israel); 2.6 million in Israel.

While Israel is a spiritual and cultural center for world Jewry, it is also, because of its geographical location, an international bridge for the traffic of ideas between East and West and a target for imperialist, colonialist, and nationalist ambitions. Should Israel succeed in maintaining its independence and distinctiveness—and at present there is no valid evidence that it cannot—its potential as a distributing center of science and culture is unlimited. Although rooted in its heritage, Israel (with the exception of the political sphere) is one of the world's most rapidly changing countries. Its permutations are dramatic and of long-range significance. Suffice it to compare the Israel of 1948 with Israel of today.

The self-confidence and the sense of destiny of the contemporary Israeli, sometimes offensively excessive, are not conditioned by territorialism. The Jewish people came into being before it had a state and then survived statelessness for almost two thousand years after the Roman conquest. It never worshiped the state *per se*. Between nation and land, nation always took precedence. As Thomas Hobbes put it: "The Jews, who being a peculiar kingdom of God, thought it unlawful to acknowledge subjugation to any mortal being or state whatsoever."

The following chapters will deal with the homecoming of the caravan of Jewish history, its deployment and the institutions it built, the socio-economic patterns it developed, the political moods it displayed, and the implications of all those phenomena for the Israelis themselves, the Middle East, the Jews of the Diaspora, the United States, and the world at large.

ISRAEL

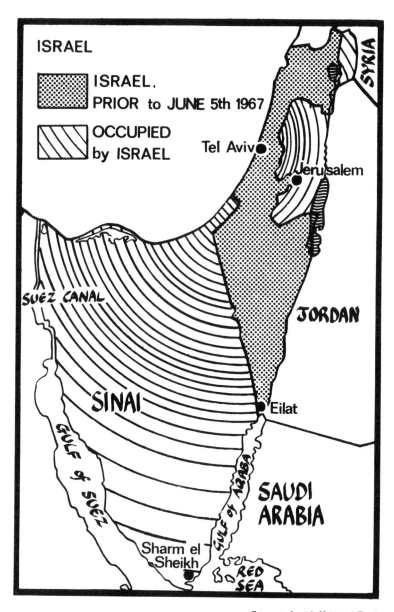

ISRAEL

ISRAEL,
PRIOR to JUNE 5th 1967

OCCUPIED
by ISRAEL

SYRIA

Tel Aviv

Jerusalem

SUEZ CANAL

JORDAN

SINAI

Eilat

GULF of SUEZ

GULF of AQABA

SAUDI
ARABIA

Sharm el
Sheikh

RED
SEA

Courtesy Jewish National Fund

1 Lay of the Land

Israel is a meeting point of Asia, Africa, and Europe, physically as well as culturally.

Always at the mercy of history, it was and is a battleground of empires and peoples: Canaanites, Hittites, Egyptians (at various periods), Hebrews, Philistines, Assyrians, Babylonians, Persians, Greeks, Syrians, Romans, Arabs, Mongols, Crusaders, Turks, Frenchmen, Englishmen, Jews (again), Arabs (again), Russians, and perhaps, in the future, Chinese and Americans. In fact, the first military engagement of significance took place in that region in 1878(9) B.C.

The locus of the country was meaningful as a link between the great civilization on the banks of Tigris-Euphrates and that of the Nile Valley; the wellspring of several religions, it is a Holy Land to Judaism, Christianity, and Islam. In the twentieth century, it is still a basin for a confluence of Western civilization and Eastern culture and a testing ground for new ideas and unique life patterns. Thus, from the very beginning of recorded history the area was pre-ordained to the harsh existence of a volcanic buffer state.

Comparable in size (before the 1967 Six-Day War) to Massachusetts or Wales, Israel covered an area of about 8,000 square miles: 50 zigzagging miles bordered Lebanon; about 48 wayward miles bordered Syria; 335 miles of alternately straight and looping boundary faced Jordan; and about 165 bristling miles separated Israel from Egyptian-controlled Sinai. The Mediterranean provided nearly 160 miles of shoreline. The length of the country from Metulah in the north to Eilat on the Aqaba Gulf was 280 miles. At its widest, from the Gaza Strip through the area immediately south of Beersheba in the Negev to the Dead Sea, Israel was 70 miles across. At its narrowest, just north of Tel Aviv, it was 12 miles, and at the southern edge of the Negev, between the port of Eilat and the port of Aqaba in Jordan, only 9 miles. This small stretch along the Red Sea gave access to Africa and the Indian Ocean.

The "promised land," biblically described as "flowing with milk and honey," did not look too promising to the Hebrews of old even after forty years of wandering in the wilderness. Contemporary Israelis like to say that Moses did not live to enter the country because, when he stood on Mount Nebo and surveyed the waste and desolation of the land to which he led his people after centuries of enslavement in Egypt, he had a fatal stroke.

A country of many contrasts, its limited physical assets could be cruel to inhabitants who tried to carve a living out of the rocky desert of the Negev, the sand dunes of the seashore, and the malarial marshlands of the north. But it also could inspire prophets and psalmists with the mystic majesty of the Galilean hills around Safad and Nazareth. Israel cannot boast the loftiest mountains (its tallest, Mount Meron, is only 3,692 feet high), but it can show off the world's cellar. The Dead Sea is about 1,300 feet below the sea level, the lowest spot on the earth's surface. The rapid descent from Jerusalem's mountain peaks (about 1,800 feet) to Sodom on the Dead Sea is breathtaking.

Overlooking the Mediterranean, Mount Carmel (1,789 feet), "God's Vineyard," as the name connotes in Hebrew, is of haunting splendor. The author of the Song of Songs, speaking of the beloved Shulamite, exclaims: "Thine head upon thee is like Carmel." Mount Tabor (1,929 feet), of the Galilean range was crowned with altars dedicated to heathen gods in remote antiquity. Later its slopes were the scene of the triumphs of Deborah and Barak as well as the defeat of the Jewish defenders against the Romans in A.D. 66. It is also referred to as the Mount of Transfiguration, where, as Christians believe, Peter, James, and John beheld that the face of Jesus of a sudden "did shine as the sun" and that Jesus's "raiment was as white as the light."

Valleys in Israel are hardly less cherished, for sentimental or economic reasons, by people inside and out of the country. Jezreel (Esdraelon) is the largest. It lies between the Galilean Mountains and the Samarian Mountains in the south, reaching out diagonally to the Valley of the Jordan. Some of the great battles of the ancient Middle East were fought here. One of history's earliest recorded campaigns, that of Thutmose III in 1878 B.C., took place at Megiddo, a hillock on the edge of the valley guarding a strategic passageway. It was here that King Ahaziah and later King Josiah were killed. It was through this passageway that the British troops in World War II pushed northward to Lebanon and Syria. Christian tradition proclaims that the final battle, that of Armageddon, will be fought here. It is also here, in Jezreel, that the modern kibbutz (collective settlement) and moshav (cooperative settlement) developed new socio-economic patterns now emulated in many parts of the world.

The coastal plain along the Mediterranean begins with the Valley of Zevulun, is interrupted by Mount Carmel, and resumes its southward course as the Plain of Sharon until it reaches Tel Aviv, where it continues as the Plain of Judea all the way down to Gaza and the Sinai Peninsula. The coastline south of the Carmel is a continuous stretch of sand dunes, but it is also now the most thickly populated part of Israel, dotted with some of its major cities.

The arid Negev wilderness is a triangle spreading out of the coastal plain eastward and southward. At the Negev's widest, the northern area, it starts slowly from its Mediterranean border tip to climb up awesome cliffs and crags overlooking precipitously the Dead Sea and the Valley of Arava. The Negev's western boundary, with the Sinai Peninsula, and its eastern boundary, with the State of Jordan, come together at the Gulf of Aqaba. In the midst of this vast triangular expanse are high and fantastic multihued mountain ranges with gouged mile-wide craters. Further south at Timna are the reddish and regal high-rise Pillars of Solomon. Around 900 B.C. the king's men dug copper in this area. Some three thousand years later the mines still yield copper and manganese.

It is this wasteland that Israel is beginning to develop, startling unsuspecting visitors with wondrous green patches of tilled soil, a budding frontier settlement, a nuclear reactor. Israelis call it the "desert of destiny."

Israel can hardly boast of mighty rivers, only of the fame of some of its streams. The Jordan, the largest, flows a mere 157 miles. The Kishon, the third largest, memorialized in the song of Deborah, rolls along for only eight miles! The celebrated Sea of Galilee (Lake Kinneret) is 63 square miles. The Dead (Salt) Sea (so called because hardly any living thing can survive in it) is 360 square miles. Yet the historian Josephus, during the "wars of the Jews" in the first century A.D., replied to the emperor who was trying to win him over to the Roman side: "Whatever thou givest me, Imperator, thou canst not give me a spring like that in Galilee."

To get the waters of Galilee to flow to the Negev has been of primary significance to Israel. An integrated national distribution system was launched in recent years, enabling the country to increase its irrigation area almost sixfold—from about 75,000 acres in 1949 to approximately 500,000 acres in 1969. The largest undertaking in the system was the Kinneret-to-Negev, a ninety-mile-long project, which draws water from the Sea of Galilee to the south via a national carrier. Its annual capacity was initially 320 million cubic meters. Hydrological studies indicated that utilizing the Jordan River, the Sea of Galilee, ground water, springs, hillside runoffs, reduced evaporation, reclaimed wastes, and seeded clouds, the yield would be almost 2 billion cubic meters, for both human consumption and industrial needs.

Even full tapping of all resources could provide only 40 to 45 per cent of water needs for irrigable lands. Nevertheless, under current circumstances efficient use has made it possible to produce most of Israel's agricultural food and to grow new industrial crops.

The climate in this small land ranges from temperate to tropical. The north-central part of the country is affected by the Mediterranean. Consequently it does not share the aridity of interior Arabia, and October to March is the rainy season. However, the southern part of Israel, barred from the sea and boxed in by Sinai and Africa, is largely sapless and barren. It is warm and humid along the shoreline of Tel Aviv (average daily minimum and maximum temperatures in the winter are 47°–65° F., in the summer 71°–88°). Fresh and invigorating breezes prevail in the Galilean Mountains and in Jerusalem (winter, 40°–50°; summer, 67°–84°). It is hot and arid in the Negev and in the Dead Sea area (winter, 47°–50°; summer 79°–103°). In the north it rains in winter but hardly ever in summer. The south is dry the year round, with sudden, unexpected downpours forming the famous "dry-streams," the wadis of the Negev.

The flora in Israel naturally follows the variegated physical, climatic, and seasonal features of the land. Symphonies of color and intoxicating scents abound in the north and along the Mediterranean, the Sea of Galilee, and the Jordan in the spring, but only yellowish, stunted growths appear in the Negev, occasionally relieved by clusters of date palms. Some 2,500 species of plants have been identified in the country, among them the evocative lily of the valley, rose of Sharon, hyacinth, gladiolus, carnation, narcissus, anemone, bougainvillaea, cyclamen, iris, daisy, and tulip.

In primordial days, the area was thickly covered with forests of oak and unique pine. Only a few of the oaks now remain. In biblical times, the tamarisk, carob, poplar, palm, oleander, fig, grapevine, pomegranate, and olive flourished. The eucalyptus prospered in Palestine toward the end of the nineteenth century. Since the establishment of the State of Israel, some 35 million trees have been planted—mostly pine in the north and acacia in the southern dunes—by the Jewish National Fund and the government, in large measure with money contributed by benefactors the world over. Aesthetic in effect but practical in purpose, the trees grow where no other crops would do well; they prevent erosion, provide shade, and promise raw material.

Banana groves were evidently introduced during the Middle Ages, as were the citrus trees that have attained a pre-eminent position in Israel's agriculture. Growing along the coastal plains, the orange, especially the Jaffa variety, has gained world esteem. The grapefruit and the clementina are also attracting attention. But it is the cactus fruit (sabra) that gave its name to indigenous Israelis. Immigrant parents pointed to their native born children and proudly pronounced: "Prickly on the outside, but sweet and savory within."

Gazelles, hyenas, jackals, shrews, lynx, wild boars, porcupines, badgers, cheetahs, and occasionally wolves are still to be found, and camels in the Negev continue to be reminders of an ancient past, but around Tel Aviv even donkeys, mules, and horses are a rare sight.

About 400 species and subspecies of birds have been identified at one time or another in Israel. Of these, some 150 are still around, either as permanent residents or seasonal visitors. Eagles, wild duck, quail, bulbul, hoopoe, white stork, gray crane, swans, pelicans, gulls, ravens, herons, buzzards, kites, vultures, and sparrows are among the characteristic birds in the land.

Snakes, scorpions, spiders, grasshoppers, locusts, and many species of insects make their intrusive presence felt in the country. Bees, on the other hand, despite their sting, are welcome in Israel for their economic value.

Israeli cities are as picturesque and as diverse as the history of the country. Tel Aviv was founded in 1909 on the sand dunes along the Mediterranean, but it now encompasses Jaffa, which according to some accounts is one of the oldest (if not the oldest) seaports of the world. It was from Jaffa that the prophet Jonah sailed on his ill-fated boat. The largest city in the country, Tel Aviv proper has a population of about 400,000 and a surrounding metropolitan area with another 400,000. It is a miniature of New York, Los Angeles, and Paris. Most of all it is like Sandburg's Chicago—dynamic, noisy, slummy, imaginative, creative, avant-garde. It is the entertainment and art center of Israel.

Jerusalem (including the Old City, in East Jerusalem, taken by

Israel in 1967) has a population of close to 300,000. King David conquered it around 1000 B.C. and made it his capital. It continued as a seat of Jewish government as long as the last vestiges of Jewish autonomy remained in the land. In the War of Independence of 1948 Israel succeeded in occupying only the modern New City. In time, Israel proclaimed the part it controlled as the capital of the new state, although some governments had not recognized the legality of the act. Believers as well as nonbelievers succumb to the city's history, charm, and spirituality. Sacred to several faiths, especially Jews, Christians, and Muslims, Jerusalem has more holy places than one can justly and fully enumerate: the Western (Wailing) Wall of the Temple Court, Mount Zion (where Jewish tradition points to King David's tomb), the Church of the Holy Sepulchre, Via Dolorosa, the Mount of Olives, the Tomb of the Virgin, the Dome of the Rock, and the el Aqsa Mosque, the last two on a site sacred to all three religions. It was here, many believe, that Abraham prepared Isaac for sacrifice. It was in this area that Solomon built the First Temple and King Herod reconstructed it as the Second Temple. It was here that Jesus had a major confrontation with the "establishment" by throwing out the money-changers. It was from this spot, Muslim tradition holds, that Muhammad made his nocturnal trip to heaven on the white charger Baraq (Lightning). In Jerusalem are also situated Hebrew University, museums, and new government complexes.

The main port of Israel is Haifa (population: 230,000), perhaps the country's most beautiful city. Spread out on the slopes of Mount Carmel, it most resembles San Francisco. Haifa, too, is a holy city. It is the world center of the Bahai faith, whose gold-capped temple rises from resplendent Persian gardens. It was in this area, long before the city was founded, that the prophet Elijah hid in a cave from the tyranny of Jezebel, and it was through the harbor near that cave, some 2,800 years later, that tens of thousands of Jewish refugees from Nazi terror streamed into the country after World War II. Haifa's bayside now is a prime industrial center, with oil refineries, textile factories, glass foundries, fertilizer plants, automotive assembly lines, cement works, and quarries. The city also is the site of the Israel Institute of Technology (Technion) and a new university.

Cities that excite religious fervor in millions of people are Nazareth (35,000), where Jesus grew up and had his ministry; Tiberias (25,000) and Safad (15,000), where Jewish learning and mysticism flourished for many centuries; Beersheba (80,000), Abraham's city, now capital of the Negev and a university seat; and Acre (35,000), important as a Phoenician port, a crusader stronghold, and site of Napoleon's defeat. Among the cities occupied by Israel in 1967 are Bethlehem (32,000), near which the matriarch Rachel was interred and where Boaz, the forefather of David, dwelt, and Jesus, according to Christian tradition, was born, and Hebron (40,000), famous for the Double Cave (Machpelah), burial site of Abraham, progenitor of the Hebrew people (through Isaac) and the Arabs (through Ishmael), and the other two patriarchs, Isaac and Jacob (Israel).

Cities of economic significance are Ashdod, a new deep-sea port south of Tel Aviv, founded in recent years and already past the 40,000 population mark; Eilat (15,000), on the Gulf of Aqaba, terminal of oil pipelines and trade outlet to Africa and Asia, and a year-round skin-diving and fishing resort. Kiriyat Gat (20,000) and Arad (more than 8,000 and growing) are new development towns in the northern Negev designed as agricultural and industrial centers. Rehovot (40,000), an older settlement, takes pride in its famed Weizmann Institute of Science.

The problem of Israel's natural resources appears "hopeless but not critical." The country does not have an abundance of the treasures of the earth or of raw material. Among the chemicals of the Dead Sea, potassium salts are important for fertilizer; magnesium salts, lighter than aluminum, are especially significant in the infant aircraft industry; and sodium salts are basic for multipurpose manufacturing. Silica sand or quartz for glass-making is found in the Negev.

For building materials the country has almost inexhaustible sources of stone, cement, and lime, and some marble is available in the north. Copper and manganese are found in the southern Negev desert. Despite many drillings, only a limited quantity of oil and natural gas has been discovered (about 10 per cent of current needs). Fish are available in moderate quantities in the Sea of Galilee and in the Red Sea, but sweet water has always been a problem. More than half of the country is arid, and a third is at present non-irrigable.

When a UPI reporter asked an Israeli on the campus of the Tel Aviv University, "Do many college students cut classes?" the young man was incredulous: "Don't you see that our main resource is here, in our heads?" Similarly, a professor at the Hebrew University once pointed to his head and said smilingly: "Since we have no natural resources we are developing supranatural resources."

The combination of the expected extraordinary brain power with unexpected extraordinary physical exertion made the "promised land" a land of promise. "A land of wheat and barley and vines and fig trees and pomegranates, a land of olive-oil and honey," the Bible coaxed. Modern Israelis have added oranges, other citrus fruits, bananas, avocados, tomatoes, apples, mangoes, pears, guavas, dates, tobacco, cotton, ground nuts, sugar beets, and medicinal herbs. Israel has become a hothouse for agricultural exports to many foreign lands. Its fruit and flowers are in ready bloom early in January; hence its orange juice appears in the breakfast menus, and its blossoms on the dinner tables, of European hotels and homes while the snow still covers the ground outside.

Wine-making is as vital today as it was in antiquity but has a more balancing effect on the domestic economy, and the edible oil industry (olive oil, peanut oil) also helps lubricate the Israeli economic machinery. Jams and fruit preserves sweeten slightly a distasteful imbalance of payments.

Israel also exports diamonds, textiles, wearing apparel, chemicals and fertilizers, tires and tubes, light machinery, plastics, plywood, pharmaceuticals, cement, books, and religious articles. But its imports still are far greater than its exports, mainly because of the burden of defending the country.

Continued harnessing of the Jordan River, desalination of water, and maximum use of knowledge in nuclear, medical, and computer sciences would, however, in a period of peace, compensate for the country's lack of natural resources.

2 The Ever Present Past

Some Hebrews arrived in the area that is now Israel about four thousand years ago. Whether heeding the call of God, as the Bible has it; the clamor of "manifest destiny," as nationalists term it; the compulsion of economic determinism, as Marx-oriented thinkers argue; or the interaction of "correlates," as the current political behavioralists compute it, they came from the city of Ur of the Chaldeans (in what is now Iraq), under the leadership of Abraham, and from other eastern regions. Evidently they were one of many such groups that at intervals, but continually, pushed westward toward the seashore.

The numbers of the early arrivals were swelled by kinfolk who also forded the Jordan to get to the land of Canaan and who alone were called the "crossers-over" (Abiru or Habiru, hence "Ivrim" and the Anglicized "Hebrews"). A famine later drove some of them —Abraham's grandson Jacob (also known as Israel, hence the Israelites) and his twelve sons—to Egypt, where they experienced both glory and exploitation. Joseph, who preceded his father Jacob, became viceroy, but when a new pharaoh "who knew not Joseph" assumed power, the Hebrews, or Israelites, entered a long period of bondage, stirring up in them dormant tribal memories of the cousins they left behind. Under the tutelage of Moses they began a forty-year march back to the land of Canaan.

The long wanderings in the wilderness were intentional—to dim the servile past in the conscience of the older people and to afford time for a new, freeborn generation to sprout. As the Israelites approached their old-new land, they had been forged into a nation possessed of a strong, centralizing monotheistic faith and a functional, binding cult. In the meantime, the Canaanites, a mixture of earlier Semitic and later Aryan (Armenoid) strains who suffered much from successive invasions by the Hittites of the north and the Egyptians of the south, lost much of their cohesion. When the Israelites appeared on their western horizon, the Canaanites succumbed to, and coalesced with, the returnees, forming a large Semitic base in the land, with some non-Semitic elements. Thus the prophet Ezekiel, as late as the sixth century B.C., could say of his people: "Thy father as an Amorite and thy mother a Hittite."

Another non-Semitic element was the Philistines, who appeared from the Aegean basin shortly after the Israelite return and settled along the Mediterranean coast of the country, spreading inland southward and spasmodically occupying large areas in the north. It was the Philistine threat that reawakened the Israelite sense of national unity, lost in part because of tribal preoccupation with daily chores and the attraction of local deities.

The challenge of the Philistines occasioned the Samsonian epic and brought forth leaders like Samuel, Saul, and David, who checked and finally dispersed the lurking danger. Although they ebbed into history, the Philistines left a residual effect—their name. The Romans, a millennium later, having conquered Judea, sought to erase Jewish association with the land and renamed it Palaestina.

King David (end of eleventh and beginning of tenth century B.C.), after subduing his adversaries, consolidated his domain and made Jerusalem his capital. It was during his reign and the reign of his son Solomon, who built the First Temple, that the country reached its political peak, extending its influence virtually from the Euphrates to the Egyptian border and sending its merchant vessels to the far ends of the Mediterranean and into the oceans of the Far East. Upon the death of Solomon (*ca.* 920 B.C.), the realm was split into the northern kingdom of Israel (Samaria) and the southern kingdom of Judea.

As the political power of the Hebrews contracted and deteriorated, their moral and religious insights broadened and deepened. One hardly need elaborate on the lasting influence of the prophets on the mind and conscience of Western man. In the ninth and eighth centuries B.C. the Assyrian empire thrust westward and in 721 swept away the northern kingdom of Israel. Most of its population was exiled and resettled by foreign elements. Babylonia, the imperial successor of Assyria, conquered the southern kingdom of Judea in 587–86 B.C. Solomon's temple was destroyed, and large sections of the population were carried off into Babylonian captivity.

Some fifty years later, King Cyrus of Persia, after putting down Babylonia, permitted the Hebrews to return to the "land of Israel." A Second Temple was built in Jerusalem, and a small religious Jewish state, governed by a high priest, began to take shape around it. For about four centuries the country enjoyed self-rule and varying degrees of independence under watchful Persian and later Hellenistic eyes. During the latter part of that period there was a heavy influx of Greek culture into the country, mainly from the northern regions. When Antiochus IV, the Syrian ruler, attempted to impose the Hellenistic way of life on the Jews to the detriment of their religious observances—going so far as to order a change in worship in the Temple—the Jews rose in rebellion (167–65 B.C.). Under the leadership of the Maccabees they regained control of the Temple, cleansed it, repaired the altar, and rekindled the "eternal light." This struggle for their cultural identity and freedom of conscience is commemorated by Jews to this day in a Feast of Lights, Hanukkah.

Rivalries among the Hasmonean successors to the Maccabees led to Roman intervention a century later, in 65 B.C. Although Jewish kings continued to rule the land nominally, and at times the country even enjoyed outward prosperity, as during the reign of Herod, 37 B.C. to A.D. 4, Rome held sway over the area. Upon the death of Herod, however, the country became a subprovince of Syria, governed by procurators, the best known of whom was Pontius Pilate. So long as Roman rule was tolerant, the Jews contained their deep-seated, long-endured hatred of overlords, but when it became blatantly despotic and offended their religious sensitivities they swelled the ranks of the normally small group of Zealots and struck in retaliation. In A.D. 66 the Romans were compelled to marshal significant parts of their vaunted imperial power to put down the uprising. It took them four years to achieve victory, but in A.D. 70 Jerusalem fell and the Second Temple was burned. The last rebel stronghold, Massada, overlooking symbolically what later became better known as the Dead Sea, held out for three more years. The drama and the heroics of its defenders, who perished in a suicide pact, according to contemporary historian Josephus Flavius, were uncovered and verified in recent archaeological excavations.

Another attempt at freedom was made in A.D. 132 by Simon Bar-Kokhba, despite admonitions from more moderate elements. Again Rome had to fight savagely for three years, with heavy loss of life on both sides, to subdue the insurgents. Jerusalem was recaptured and named Aelia Capitolina. The Temple grounds were plowed over and an edifice to Jupiter was erected on the site of the Temple. Jews were forbidden, on pain of death, to appear within sight of their holy city.

This last defeat sealed off an era in the history of the Jews. Their independence was lost and was not reclaimed until 1948, almost two millenniums later. Again, symbolically, it was an Israeli military-commander-turned-archaeologist, Professor Yigael Yadin, who recently uncovered letters in the Dead Sea area bearing witness to the last struggles of the other commander, 1,800 years ago, Simon Bar-Kokhba.

While the Jews were in the throes of political agony, Judaism sprouted new religious and cultural shoots. The Jews could not come to terms with the destruction of their state, so they pushed its horizons to the far ends of the earth. They could not govern their past, so they grew determined to control their future. Ever since Ezra, who returned from the Babylonian dispersion in the fifth century B.C., the study of Torah* became the basis of Jewish life. This relentless and pious occupation with learning first transcended the political difficulties at home, later mitigated the miseries of the long Diaspora, and finally substituted a meritocracy of scholarship for the political power of a state. This was not an easy process in the complex comings and goings of history. During the Second Temple period there were three major and contesting divisions in Jewish life. The Pharisees were a small group closed to the masses but directed toward motivating them to the holiness of traditional Jewish teaching. The Sadducees, an aristocratic and nationalistic movement, were at odds with the Pharisees, on both political and ritualistic grounds. The Essenes, although closer to the Pharisees than to the Sadducees in religious outlook, found spiritual fulfillment in physical withdrawal from the "sham of modern civilization." It was at that time that Christianity made its appearance. When the Romans burned the Temple in A.D. 70, the Sadducees and the Essenes slipped out of history, and Christianity separated itself from its Jewish parentage to set up its own more prosperous existence.

At this most critical moment, when Judaism faced disintegration, one man erred on the side of optimism. Rabbi Yohanan Ben-Zakkai escaped from the beleaguered city of Jerusalem and with the permission of the Romans established a yeshiva—an academy—at Yavneh. There he mobilized the remnants of Jewish hope and faith for his people's future. Deprived of the Temple, its spiritual center, and shorn of political power, Judaism, stimulated by Yohanan Ben-Zakkai, made the Torah and its derivatives the foundation for survival. Thus, out of weakness and defeat, Judaism emerged as one of the most vital and creative forces in the Western world. An oral law, interpreting and extending the written biblical text, was developed to meet new contingencies at home and abroad. In time the corpus of these rulings was set down in an encyclopedic work, the

---

* "Torah" sometimes is restricted in meaning to only the Five Books of Moses, but in broader interpretation it is the sum total of Jewish religiocultural experience.

Talmud, which since about A.D. 500 has become the instrument for the preservation of traditional Judaism.

The Roman conquest and the attempted eviction of the vanquished did not quite dislodge all Jews from their homeland. Many of them clung to their birthplace, especially in Galilee. Throughout the years, until the mass return in modern times, there were always some Jews in Palestine. But after the reign of Emperor Constantine, at the turn of the fourth century, the country bore the stamp of Christianity—with a few momentary blot-outs by the Persians—until the Muslim Arab conquest in 636. From the seventh century until 1948, the Arabs constituted a majority of the population in the country they called Falastin.

Under Muslim rule Palestine as a whole enjoyed comparative peace and prosperity. Although expected to pay heavy taxes, Jews and other non-Muslims were allowed to retain their possessions and to maintain autonomy in religious matters. Jews increased their numbers and established cultural centers in the country. Arab political (but not numerical) supremacy in Palestine came to an end in 1071 when the Seljuks overran the land. Then the Crusaders, fired by religious fervor, wrested the country from the "heathens" in 1099 and occupied it or, more specifically, Jerusalem and environs, until 1187.

The power of the Crusaders was broken by a Kurdish monarch of Egypt, Saladin, and despite repeated efforts by the Crusaders to regain control, the last shadow of Western rule was dispelled in 1291, as it was forced to give up the famed fortress in Acre. During the latter part of the thirteenth century and all of the fourteenth, Palestine was ravaged by the Mongols. In the fifteenth century Egypt still held out tenuously, but in 1517 Palestine, Syria, and Egypt itself fell into the hands of the Ottoman Turks.

Early under Ottoman rule, which lasted some 400 years, the Jews were treated with favor, so that on the death of Suleiman the Magnificent in 1566 their position in Palestine was stronger than it had been for a thousand years. Safad, with its 15,000 Jews, became one of the most significant religious centers in Jewish annals and had profound and abiding influence upon world Jewry. However, during the seventeenth and eighteenth centuries, Safad and other cities in Galilee, exposed to constant raids of marauding tribesmen from the north, degenerated into poverty—stricken and dispirited communities in which the Jewish population depended mostly upon pious benefactors from abroad. There were only 12,000 Jews in Palestine in 1845. Only 25,000 Jews (in a total of 8 million the world over) lived in Palestine in 1881, when modern Zionism, the movement for Jewish self-determination in the ancient homeland, assumed a more practical character.

The deterioration of the Ottoman Empire provided an occasion for Western expansion—this time economic and political rather than theological—in the Middle East. A Napoleonic adventure in 1799 at Acre, a key city in the French designs to take over this area, brought Palestine once more into European focus. But the walls of the city withstood Napoleon's assaults. "The fate of the East hangs on this town," cried the Emperor as he beat a retreat. It was World War I that wrenched the land from Ottoman control and shortly thereafter put it in the hands of England as a League of Nations mandate. In 1947, unable to cope with the problems inherent in the country, Great Britain gave up the mandate to the United Nations, which wanted to partition the land into two independent states, Jewish and Arab.

During the 1,800 years following their banishment by the Romans, the majority of the Jews wandered in exile, coming into contact with many civilizations on all continents. Puzzled occasionally during the nearly two millenniums by the peculiar eternality of Jewish destiny—prophets who are timeless and a Messiah who never comes—they nevertheless clung to the hope of a return to Zion. Floating wisps of glory from the distant past held out a promise of ultimate redemption. The same tribal memories that compelled the Israelites in Egypt to come back animated the Jews during their long years in the more modern Diaspora. A British Royal Commission reported in 1937: "Small though their numbers were, the continued existence of . . . Jews in Palestine meant much to all Jewry."

Multitudes of poor and ignorant Jews in the ghettos of Eastern Europe felt themselves represented, as it were, by this remnant of their race who were keeping a foothold in the land against the day of the coming of the Messiah."

Jewish spiritual attachment to the Holy Land found its echo in countless prophecies, prayers, sayings, poems, and mystic contemplations. Deutero-Isaiah's supplication during the Babylonian captivity is among the first of such expressions: "For Zion's sake will I not keep my peace and for Jerusalem's sake I will not rest."

Practically every festival, ceremony, and observance of the traditional Jews is connected with Eretz (the Land of) Israel. Their literature is permeated with longing for the Holy Land. "Let our eyes behold Thy return in mercy to Zion. Blessed art Thou, O Lord, who restorest Thy Divine Presence unto Zion." "Sound the great horn for our freedom; lift up the ensign to gather our exiles, and gather us from the four corners of the earth. Blessed art Thou, O Lord, who gathered the banished ones of Thy people Israel." Also, "Return in mercy to Jerusalem, and . . . rebuild it soon in our days as an everlasting building."

The various pseudo-Messianic movements were another manifestation of Jewish yearning for Eretz Israel. In the thirteenth century Abraham Abulafia drew many credulous disciples in Sicily by predicting that 1290 would see the end of the Diaspora. In the sixteenth century another "redeemer," David Reubeni, arrived in Egypt with news of prosperous Jewish kingdoms in the Far East and stirred the wildest hopes among his coreligiozionists by gaining the ear of Pope Clement VII and King John III of Portugal for the purpose of Jewish restoration to Palestine in exchange for military help from the "Jewish states in the Far East." He was exposed by Emperor Charles V of the Holy Roman Empire and thrown into prison. In the seventeenth century, Sabbatai Zevi, the most famous of the pseudo-Messiahs, attracted, despite rabbinic excommunication, tens of thousands of Jewish followers from Holland, Poland, Germany, Moravia, Morocco, and other countries to his headquarters in Smyrna. The Ottoman government, uneasy over this mass movement, decided to put the "Messiah" to a test. Zevi was arrested and threatened with death unless he embraced Islam. He converted, but even this inglorious act did not stop the Sabbatean movement. Regarding the conversion as one of the "tribulations of the Messiah," thousands of Jews imitated their master and became Muslims. Many others, disillusioned and disheartened, started out for their places of origin, only to perish on the way back.

Thus, their ethnic idiom audible in every prayer, their psalm-singing plucking their own soul-strings, their bent yet defiant bodies carrying the "yoke of exile," the bulk of the Jews moved among the hostile Christians of Europe. Observing the Sabbath on Saturday, not on Sunday, and celebrating Passover, Yom Kippur, and Rosh Hashanah instead of Easter, New Year's Day, and Christmas sufficed to render them offensive to the general population in the Middle Ages and to subject them to persecution. When mysterious pestilences occurred, the strange and suspicious-looking Jews were likely to be held responsible, especially because the preventive hygiene of their dietary laws kept many of them from falling victim to epidemics. They were denied the right to own land, till the soil, belong to craft guilds, or to engage in many other occupations. When they prospered in the fields to which they were restricted, such as trading, they excited envy. Herded into ghettos and compelled to wear identifying labels, they became fair game for sanctimonious inquisitors, political tyrants, and blatant bigots from Iberia to Siberia.

3 The Rise of Political Zionism

The miasma of medieval hostilities persisted into modern times, although with less pungence and less obvious lethal residue. Indeed, the French Revolution held out many promises to the Jews, but its moral credit was limited and its "liberty, equality, and fraternity" were highly selective. The attempts of some Jews at complete assimilation into French and German culture were mostly rebuffed. On the other hand, the fires of nationalism kindled by Napoleon also ignited flashes of political awareness among the more Europeanized Jews.

Judaism's strivings for Zion up to that time were mostly Messianic and introspective. Then Moses Hess (1812–75), reared in an "emancipated" German environment remote from things Jewish, nurtured in left-wing Hegelianism and befriended by Karl Marx (with whom he later quarreled), found himself, toward the end of his life, betrayed by his own ideology. Looking around him, he saw Heinrich Heine, who in order to get his works published had to be converted to Christianity, at least for appearances' sake. Hess came to the conclusion (as later so many in other minorities did) that legal equality does not make for social acceptance. Emancipation, he wrote in his *Rome and Jerusalem,* was detaching the Jew from his legacy without giving him entrance to European culture. Only in his own homeland could the Jew function as a free and an uninhibited human being. Many years later, a spiritual descendant of Hess and a noted Jewish anarchist, Hillel Zolotarev, taunted by his colleagues for his pro-Zionist attitudes, silenced his friendly detractors by declaring: "If I am to be hanged, I would rather be hanged in my own country."

Among the religious Jews as well, the Messianic idea took on more practical aspects. Rabbi Zevi Hirsch Kalischer (1795–1874), quoting many biblical and Talmudic sources in support of his views, contended that it would be easier for Jews to wait for the Messiah in their own land. He thus founded in 1870 the first Jewish agricultural school in Palestine. Another rabbi, Samuel Mohliver (1824–98), organized in 1881 in Warsaw the first society of Hovevei Zion (Lovers of Zion), a colonizing movement which had a tremendous sentimental and even practical impact on the Jews of Eastern Europe. Mohliver also helped convince Baron Edmond de Rothschild and Baron Maurice de Hirsch of the need for Jewish pioneering in the "land of their ancestors."

The Russian pogroms of 1881–82, subjecting 200 Jewish communities to murder, rape, arson, and pillage, while the Tsarist authorities did nothing to stop the atrocities, gave further impetus to Jewish nationalist stirrings. An Odessa physician, Dr. Leon Pinsker (1824–91), wrote a pamphlet, *Auto-Emancipation,* in which he said that anti-Semitism is a disease, "the fear of a bodiless spirit." The Jew, a "stranger everywhere, wanted nowhere, and having no home of his own," was to many such a spirit. "Men are afraid of disembodied spirits." Terror breeds hatred.

But the founder of "political Zionism" was an assimilated Jew from Western Europe, Dr. Theodor Herzl. Born in Budapest, Herzl (1860–1904) in his youth was hardly aware of his ancestry, but he was endowed with keen social intelligence. Although trained as a jurist, he became a noted journalist working for Vienna newspapers. In 1894, while in Paris, Herzl came face to face with the Jewish problem. Alfred Dreyfus, a young French Army officer of

Jewish descent, was found guilty of treason at a public trial to cover up the misdeeds of his non-Jewish superior officers and was sentenced to Devil's Island. This flagrant miscarriage of justice in a country regarded as the very flower of Western culture left Herzl disillusioned and depressed. He shuddered at the implications for all his coreligionists. Unaware of much of Jewish history, Herzl was struck by an idea: a Jewish state! In 1896 he wrote *Judenstaat*.

An activist as well as a dreamer—"If you will it, it need not be a legend"—Herzl started a flurry of diplomatic efforts among the ruling heads of Europe and the leaders of the Ottoman Empire. The wealthy, would-be assimilated Jews, the extreme orthodox, and the radical left opposed and ridiculed him. Erect, majestic, with square black beard and blazing eyes, he looked like a character of the Bible. He captured the imagination of the Jewish masses the world over: old and young, East European and West European, religious and secular. In August, 1897, he convened the first Zionist Congress in Basle, Switzerland. This marked the beginning of modern political Zionism. Hundreds of delegates and numerous visitors from many lands met for the first time in Jewish history to discuss and fashion their future.

The congress asserted in a newly acquired political idiom that the Jews were a nation and that Palestine was the center for their self-determination. The Basle Program, as it became known, declared that the "aim of Zionism is to create for the Jewish people a publicly and legally assured home in Palestine" through the following means: strengthening Jewish consciousness; organizing Jewry in local, national, and international institutions; obtaining governmental consent to the attainment of Zionist goals; and intensive colonization of Palestine. At the conclusion of the Congress, Herzl wrote in his diary: "Today I founded the Jewish state."

Herzl died in 1904 at the age of forty-four, exhausted by his gigantic effort. His political work was carried on and intensified by his successors, notably by Dr. Chaim Weizmann. A native of Eastern Europe educated in Western universities, Weizmann was a rare combination of Jewish small-town folksiness and the cosmopolitan urbanity of the European man. "A Jew must believe in miracles if he is a realist," he said characteristically. Another time, reacting to pessimistic moods, he observed that "the impossible takes longer."

World War I presented Zionism and Dr. Weizmann with a real opportunity. Living in England since 1904 as a member of the chemistry faculty of Manchester University, Weizmann gained the acquaintance of many leading statesmen in the country. His scientific contributions (especially new processes for producing acetone) helped tremendously the British war effort. The then Prime Minister, David Lloyd George, later wrote in his memoirs that the famed Balfour Declaration was in gratitude for the services rendered by the Jewish chemist. The document, issued on November 2, 1917, and bearing the name of the British Foreign Secretary, stated:

His Majesty's Government view with favour the establishment in Palestine of a national home for the Jewish people, and will use their best endeavours to facilitate the achievement of this project, it being clearly understood that nothing shall be done which may prejudice the civil and religious rights of existing non-Jewish communities in Palestine, or the rights and political status enjoyed by Jews in any other country.

While Weizmann's services were no doubt appreciated by the British, there were weightier reasons for the issuance of the Balfour Declaration. England wanted to stir sympathetic public opinion for its war effort from American minorities working for the self-determination of their brothers abroad: Czechs, Poles, Jews. At the same time, it was seeking to neutralize the Russian minorities. Besides, London had heard of diplomatic overtures from Germany and Turkey to the Zionist Organization. Great Britain, looking ahead to the implementation of secret agreements with its European allies giving the British control over the area, saw a way of breaking into the almost solid Arab bloc along the Suez Canal by the reintroduction into the region of a European element. Finally, there was a genuine desire to atone for the injustices perpetrated by the Western world against the Jews for many centuries. "Oh, what wonders will come again from these hills of Judea," exclaimed Josephus Daniels, Secretary of the Navy in Woodrow Wilson's Cabinet, when he heard of the Balfour Declaration.

Past masters of diplomacy, the British purposely worded the document ambiguously. What is a "national home"? What is the significance of the establishment *in* Palestine of a national home for the Jewish people, as compared with the establishment *of* Palestine as a Jewish national home? Did it mean, as some Englishmen later interpreted it, Jewish self-determination in a *part* of Palestine?

But the "much promised land" was also equivocally pledged and later unequivocally denied by the British to the Arabs. During World War I, Sir Henry McMahon, then High Commissioner in Egypt, communicated with Hussein, Sherif of Mecca, about the latter's revolt against the Ottoman Empire. The Sultan declared the hostilities a "holy war," so that his soldiers would fight bravely and the Muslims on the side of the Allies would desert. Hussein, who wielded great religious influence over the Arabs, was ordered to confirm the Turkish declaration. The Sherif refused. He cherished the ambition of becoming the *khalif,* the religious head, of all Islam, a title which the Sultan held. The refusal aroused the ire of the Turks, and they cut off the provisions sent to Mecca by the Hejaz railway. Then England stepped in, dispatched its "food ships" to Jeddah, the port of Mecca, and gained Hussein's support.

In a letter dated July 14, 1915, to Sir Henry, Hussein, who decided to take up arms on the side of the Allies, requested that England, in return, acknowledge the independence of all Arabia— including Syria-Lebanon, Iraq, and Palestine. McMahon, who suspected that his government had made secret pledges to France and Russia, replied on October 24, 1915, undertaking in principle to recognize Arab independence, in the event of a revolt, and making reservations with regard to the boundaries of the would-be state. The reservations excluded some provinces where Great Britain was "not free to act without detriment to the interests of France," and those territories "lying west of the districts of Damascus, Homs, Hama, and Aleppo."

It is contended by the Arabs, but refuted by the British, that Palestine was included in the area in which Sir Henry promised Arab independence, and therefore the pledge antedates the Balfour Declaration and takes precedence. The Arab view is that Damascus is the most southerly point mentioned and that Palestine cannot be properly regarded as lying west of Damascus. A look at the map does not help much—Palestine is southwest of Damascus. The Jewish claim is that, regardless of the geographical considerations, if secret agreements have legal standing, then earlier concealed pacts among Great Britain, France, and Russia, dating several months before the McMahon pledges (the Constantinople Agreement of March, 1915, for instance) and disposing of the areas along different lines, must be given recognition. Thus to this day adversaries from time to time air their legal, economic, historical, humanitarian, and political arguments in the academic world, as well as in other areas, including the United Nations.

The initial Arab response to Zionist aspirations appears to have been positive. Hussein, who later became king (only in part of Arabia, around Mecca), declared in March, 1918: "We saw the Jews . . . streaming into Palestine from Russia, Germany, Austria, Spain, America. . . . The cause of causes could not escape those who had the gift of deeper insight; they knew that the country was for its original sons, for all their differences, a sacred and beloved homeland."

Hussein's son, Feisal, future king of Iraq, who represented the Arabs at the Paris peace talks, issued a statement in January, 1919, that "all necessary measures shall be taken to encourage and stimulate immigration of Jews into Palestine on a large scale. . . . In taking such measures the Arab peasant and tenant farmers shall be protected in their rights, and shall be assisted in forwarding their economic development." He made his statement conditional, however, upon fulfillment of the big-power pledges of Arab independence.

Then, in February, 1921, Winston Churchill, on behalf of the British Government, recognized Emir Abdullah, another son of Hussein, as "Administrator of Transjordan [the east side of the river]" in final settlement of the McMahon pledges, thus detaching two-thirds of the original area of Palestine and transferring it to Arab rule. (To this day there are small elements in Israel who consider the east side of the Jordan as irredenta—an area to be "redeemed" at some future date.) In 1922 Great Britain formally declared that "the whole of Palestine west of the Jordan was thus excluded from Sir H. McMahon's pledges."

Initially, neither the McMahon promise nor the Balfour Declaration was taken too seriously by the Versailles peace negotiators. At the end of World War I, the victors demanded the complete crushing of the enemy and full rights to as much of the spoils as could be obtained. The Allies were in possession of certain Turkish and German territories. The former included Syria-Lebanon, Palestine, and Iraq—all of them chiefly inhabited by Arabs. When the problem was brought up for discussion at Versailles, an intense struggle ensued between the masterminds of the political world: Lloyd George, Clemenceau, and Italy's Orlando on one side, and Wilson on the other. Lloyd George proposed that the territories be divided up even before the European boundaries were outlined. Wilson was strongly opposed. He had another plan (based on an idea by Field Marshal Jan Smuts of South Africa). He suggested that the conquered territories be placed under the tutelage of a future League of Nations, which would then "delegate its authority" over any given area to a specific state "whom it appoints as its Mandatory."

While the American President espoused the cause of the "helpless parts of the world," a fascinating idea dawned upon the Europeans. Direct annexation would give the enemy grounds for demanding to subtract the cost of the annexed territories from his indemnities. Would it not be beneficial to exercise direct control of the "helpless parts of the world" under the guise of Wilson's League of Nations mandate plan? So a resolution was passed endorsing the President's draft in principle. The next step was allotment.

In May, 1916, Mark Sykes and Georges Picot, political agents representing Great Britain and France, met and worked out an agreement under which France obtained full sovereignty over southern Armenia and part of the Syrian-Lebanese coast, together with a sphere of influence over Aleppo, Damascus, and northern Iraq. Great Britain secured southern Iraq and the north Palestinian ports of Haifa and Acre. Palestine proper was to be internationalized.

And so the Allied plenipotentiaries came to Versailles on the one hand with secret agreements among themselves and on the other hand with idealistic avowals and half-hearted promises to various peoples and national groups. Needless to say, the allotments were based on the secret treaties. Thus, on the basis of the Sykes-Picot agreement, Syria-Lebanon came under the French mandate, Iraq and Palestine under the British mandate. Iraq became fully independent in 1932. Separated, Syria and Lebanon gained their respective statehoods immediately after World War II. Transjordan, detached from Palestine, added some areas it occupied after the 1948 Israeli War of Independence (including the Old City, or East Jerusalem) and became the Hashimite Kingdom of Jordan.

The British mandate for Palestine (at that time still including Transjordan) was approved by the Supreme Council of the Principal Allied Powers at San Remo in April, 1920. It incorporated, with some amplification, the Balfour Declaration, which by that time was countersigned by more than fifty nations, among them the United States. After the San Remo conference, the terms of the mandate were drawn up and approved by the Council of the League of Nations in July, 1922, and became effective in September, 1923. The preamble again contains the Balfour Declaration, thereby giving "recognition to the historical connection of the Jewish people with Palestine and to the grounds for reconstituting their national home in that country"—excluding Transjordan. The other key stipulation stated:

The Mandatory shall be responsible for placing the country under such political, administrative, and economic conditions as will secure the establishment of the Jewish national home . . . and the development of self-governing institutions, and also for safeguarding the civil and religious rights of all the inhabitants of Palestine, irrespective of race and religion.

Additional articles provided for facilitating Jewish immigration by the Mandatory; insuring the rights and status of the other elements in the community; encouraging settlement of Jews on the land; enacting a national law to enable Jews in Palestine to acquire citizenship in the land; guaranteeing the sanctity of holy places; granting freedom of worship to all religious groups; recognizing English, Arabic, and Hebrew as the official languages of Palestine; maintaining schools of the respective national groups; and proclaiming the holidays of the respective communities as legal days of rest for these entities. (There would be three weekly days of worship—Friday for Muslims, Saturday for Jews, and Sunday for Christians.)

While Hussein, Feisal, and even Abdullah, recipients of the McMahon pledges in 1915, initially were favorably disposed to a Jewish return to Palestine, that was not the case with the Palestinian Arabs. Moreover, Feisal later insisted that his 1919 declaration was valid only as long as the Arab demands for independence were met as promised.

Thus, stereotyped British officials undertook to rule two history-laden groups possessed of not only a holier-than-thou but also a wiser-than-thou attitude. In 1940, the Palestine Mandate authorities refused to admit 1,771 Jewish "illegal" immigrants to their "homeland" on the ship *Patria*. On November 25, Jewish resistance forces blew up the "boat with no port," resulting in the loss of some 250 lives. Similarly, in 1947 the *Exodus,* with 4,554 Jewish refugees aboard, was turned away with less tragic consequences, but with more "uneasy feelings" at 10 Downing Street and even greater worldwide repercussions.

This and growing Arab unrest indicated that England, with all its cumulative experience of colonial administration, and despite its various inquiry commissions and White Papers, was helpless in attempting to meet a mid-twentieth-century problem of two militant movements for national self-determination. Its failure in Palestine marked the beginning of the deterioration of Britain's imperial power. In despair, the United Kingdom gave up the mandate for Palestine, writing an awkward finish to a preposterous situation.

On November 29, 1947, the United Nations voted to partition the country into two states, Arab and Jewish. Although the new state was truncated to some 5,600 square miles (from 10,000) the Zionists accepted the decision. The Arabs would not or could not acquiesce. Armed conflict ensued, and from it an independent Israel with an enlarged area of about 8,000 square miles emerged, the culmination of one era and the start of another, an era of misery and grandeur.

4 Ingathering: From Caucasus to Casablanca

The Jews began returning to Palestine in significant numbers following the Russian pogroms of 1881. Years later, the Russian-born and Russian-speaking second president of Israel, Itzhak Ben-Zvi, was asked amiably by the Soviet Ambassador in the new Jewish state why he, a socialist, had left his Russian fatherland. The President smiled and said: "It appeared that the Tsar and I could not live in the same country. One of us had to leave." The ambassador, somewhat undiplomatically but still affably, persisted: "Why, as a socialist, didn't you work for the expulsion of the Tsar?" Ben-Zvi replied gravely: "But the Tsar had no place to go."

Ben-Zvi and his Jewish predecessors in Russia thought they had a place to go, although it was difficult to reach and resettle. In 1882, fifteen years before the formal inauguration of political Zionism by Theodor Herzl at the Basle Congress, a group of students met at Kharkov and launched the first pioneering movement— Bilu, the Hebrew initials of *"Bet Yaakov lekhu v'nelkha"* (O House of Jacob, come ye and let us go). The first contingent of men and women reached Jaffa in the summer of 1882, and others came later that year, constituting the vanguard of the First Aliyah ("ascent," or immigration wave).

After having waited for the "return of the exiles," Palestine, a desolate district in the wobbly Turkish Empire, was not very hospitable to the Bilu pioneers. As a matter of fact, it was none too kind to its other inhabitants. The Arab population of about 400,000 remained stagnant for many years. It was kept that way by disease as well as by the harsh Ottoman system of conscription, which picked the ablest men for the Sultan's armies. The much smaller permanent Jewish community of close to 25,000, called the Old Yishuv (Old Settlement), was made up, in part, of pious individuals who spent their time in study. Many were the descendants of those who arrived in the Holy Land in the sixteenth and seventeenth centuries from Central and Eastern Europe (Ashkenazim). Impelled by religious feelings, they settled mainly in the "four sacred cities": Jerusalem, Hebron, Tiberias, and Safad. They came to await the Messiah and to bring about redemption by fasts, self-affliction, prayers, and lamentations. Their livelihood depended on *meshulahim,* emissaries to the Jewish communities abroad who collected funds (Halukkah) for the sustenance of their Palestinian coreligionists. They spoke Yiddish, a medieval German dialect strongly embellished with Hebrew words and written in Hebrew characters. Immersed in their devotionals, they remained throughout the centuries virtually apolitical.

Another element in the Jewish community at the time of the Bilu arrival was the Sephardim (Spanish Jews), some of whom were the progeny of the victims of the Spanish Expulsion in 1492 who immigrated either directly or at a later time—after a sojourn in North Africa, Turkey, and the Balkans—to Palestine. The Sephardim brought with them another jargon, Ladino, a medieval Spanish also strongly embellished with Hebrew words and written in Hebrew characters. The Sephardim spoke Arabic as well, and some were conversant in Turkish. During the Ottoman rule of Palestine the Turks recognized only the Chief Rabbi of the Sephardim as the spiritual and administrative head of the Jews in the Holy Land. The significance of this will be apparent later. The Turks called him Haham Bashi, but the members of his religious community named him Rishon LeZion (First in Zion or Primate of Zion). Of the two Chief Rabbis in Israel today, the Sephardi and the Ashkenazi, the Sephardi still retains the title of Rishon LeZion.

Like the Old Yishuv, the Bilu immigration had no political aspirations. Contact between the two groups was tenuous. Most of the new arrivals were middle-class intellectuals with rather hazy ideologies. They too courted funds from abroad, but for the purpose of establishing Jewish agricultural villages, schools, and their own religious institutions. Unaware of the difficulties awaiting them, and lacking agrarian experience, the settlers were rudely shaken by the realities of malaria and desperately disappointed in the stinginess of the soil. Will power and tenacity were not enough to withstand a hostile environment, but they did evoke the interest of several wealthy Jews in Western Europe.

Baron Maurice de Hirsch and Baron Edmond de Rothschild, responsive to the needs of their fellow Jews who sought refuge from East European persecution, organized two rescue efforts. Baron Hirsch headed a philanthropic movement mostly for the settlement of the escapees in South America, especially in Argentina, whereas Baron Rothschild turned to Palestine. Large amounts of money were invested in the projects. The experiment in the Americas, lacking the emotional appeal of Palestine, was a failure. Nevertheless, remnants of Hirsch's agricultural settlements are still visible in Argentina, where in 1940 there were twenty-five Jewish colonies with about 25,000 settlers. The number dwindled down to about 5,000 in the 1970's.

Baron Rothschild, on the other hand, found his efforts better rewarded in Palestine; he visited the Holy Land in 1887 and was deeply moved by the colonists who tried to "square their shoulders" in productive physical labor. Thus, some of the older colonies were helped and a series of new settlements, Moshavot, were established by the Baron. By 1904, when the Second Aliyah began, there were about 5,000 Jewish "colonists" in Palestine, in addition to the Old Yishuv. Most of them were hard-working small planters who in time became prosperous enough to employ outside labor, mostly Arab.

The ideological range of the First Aliyah settlers was rather limited and somewhat archaic even for the 1880's. Despite their ardor, spirit, and perseverance, they were merely transplanting old socio-economic forms from Russia to Palestine. To be sure, for them, as Jews who were excluded from the East European value system, there was innovation and challenge. They were in "their own land" rather than in the Diaspora; they had become farmers rather than merchants, but their mold was petit bourgeois, and their concepts were rather myopic.

Theodor Herzl was a Joshua rather than a Moses; he did not come up with a political theory or with a "grand design" for a new social order. He had the capacity to identify Jewish needs and hopes and to politicize them into pragmatic collective action. Fundamentally, Herzl's Zionism was also bourgeois, "like unto all the other nations" of his time.

The second Aliyah, begun after the Kishinev pogroms in 1903 and after the death of Herzl in the following year, was agitated by new ideas and sought new patterns of social behavior. The driving force of the Second Aliyah was a new Jewish labor movement, Poalei Zion (Zionist Socialist Party), founded in 1901. Its major theoretician was Ber Borochov, who for a number of reasons— mainly party strategy—did not himself settle in Palestine. Borochov's contribution was a Marxist analysis of the economic structure and social reality of the Jewish people.

Borochov pointed out that the Jews in their forced roles as petit bourgeois were employed only in the last stage of production and distribution. As long as the Jews occupied these restricted positions without too much outside competition, they were for the most part unmolested. The moment non-Jews began moving into these positions, the Jews, being a minority everywhere, lacked the strategic basis to withstand the pressure. In most countries, farmers and industrial workers formed the foundation of the population; the Jews, for a variety of reasons, were detached from these primary occupations. To remedy the situation, Borochov claimed, the Jews had to create a terra firma for a new social structure, which pointed to the physical inevitability of territorial concentration in Palestine. Sensing new economic crises in the capitalistic system, with Jews as marked victims, Borochov argued that the Jewish middle class, especially, must mobilize its capital to develop Palestine, creating a demand for Jewish labor as a step in the occupational redistribution and economic normalization of the Jewish people.

It is in the light of Borochov's socialist Zionism that one must view the efforts of the Second Aliyah pioneers. Like the Bilu of the First Aliyah, they came to a country miserly, marshy, and miasmic in the north, and rocky, craggy, and dry in the south. But they were captivated by the beauty of its wilderness and touched by the muted spirit of its past. One cannot understand the achievements of the Jews in Israel without an inquiry into the minds and souls of these 40,000 immigrants who "ascended" to Palestine from 1904 to the end of World War I, with the idea that their efforts there would be a first step in establishing a new social order not only for themselves but also for other peoples. After all, that land was the cradle and the workshop of new religiomoral patterns in the past. It was the Second Aliyah, introducing the kevutzah-kibbutz idea and the "religion of labor," that determined to a large degree the character of the embryonic State of Israel.

Among the initial Second Aliyah pioneers—*halutzim,* as they were called in Hebrew—was A. D. Gordon. Born in Russia to a well-to-do Jewish family, he had held prominent positions in the business world. In 1904, at the age of forty-eight, he arrived in Palestine and immediately engaged in agricultural work, something totally alien to his bourgeois background but necessary for his personal fulfillment.

Gordon regarded physical toil as fundamental to human existence, as a remedy for society's anxieties. Labor, he maintained, confers rights. Thus, Jews would have claim only to the soil they personally settled and tilled. There were vast stretches of wasteland in Palestine, which the Arabs did not work. Those, he affirmed, could be justifiably used by the returning Jews. Labor, Gordon explained, was a psychological and spiritual necessity for the development of the Jewish personality. The evils of an acquisitive society and its passion for possessions had to be avoided, hence work tools could not be the property of the individual. In Gordon's view, it was necessary not, as Marx claimed, to "change the mechanics of economic life" but to nurture a new attitude to work and negate the "push for power."

Also unlike Marx and the "world citizens" of his and other eras, Gordon felt that the concept of a nation, cleansed of its predatory aspects, was extremely useful—until such time as technology and rapid communication would break down the geographical and the cultural barriers among states. The primary source for the individual's creativity is his national culture, and it is only through his immediate social surroundings and the wider national patterns that the individual can reach out for universality. These, because of the obvious limitations of man, are the vehicles by which he can make contact with the world at large. Eloquence in advocating ideas is not enough. Everyone—philosophers, toilers, theologians, farmers— must seek self-realization. Only by example—work, not words—can one influence others.

The fact that Gordon practiced his preachments had a tremendous influence on his fellow *halutzim* of the Second Aliyah. They, too, began manipulating tools instead of slogans. Gordon's "religion of labor" eventuated in a concrete physical rather than a metaphysical accomplishment—the kevutzah (the group, the collective, later broadened into the kibbutz).

True to the Gordonian concepts, which extolled the dignity of labor and the baseness of the acquisitive society, the *halutzim* of the Second Aliyah were naturally reluctant to hire themselves out to the landowners of the First Aliyah. Relations in some instances became strained between these two groups. In 1909 a small contingent of newcomers instituted a cooperative agricultural project near Tiberias without benefit of owners and foremen. This successful venture was emulated by another group of ten men and two women, who founded Deganiah, the first kevutzah, in 1910.

The basic principles of the kevutzah envisaged a collective of people settled on land granted to the group by national or state authorities. The soil was tilled conjointly, and production and purchases were communal. Consumption was determined by the needs of the membership and the means of the collective. The kevutzah comprised the land under cultivation, all public buildings and institutions, and the living quarters.

Being a social laboratory, the kevutzah sprouted variants, ranging from small, selective units to larger and more permissive communities, from pure collectivism to scaled ownership of property. Underlying them all is the precept that labor in the field, in the workshop, or in the kitchen is done by all men and women in rotation; physical ability and unique skills are taken into account but are not accorded special status. The highest authority of the kevutzah is the general meeting of the members, but day-to-day administration is handled by an elected secretariat. No wages are paid and no outside workers are hired. Meals are eaten in common. The children from infancy to adolescence are raised in communal quarters. In some settlements, the children are taken home overnight by the parents, while in others, parents merely spend the evening hours with their offspring.

Hard labor—clearing marshlands and fructifying soil perverted by centuries of misuse—coupled with the psychological problems of adjusting to unfamiliar life-patterns, wrought a different Jewish type, the agricultural worker, who attained a new dignity in the eyes of the Jewish community itself and the world at large. The kevutzah not only served as a social workshop and as a remaker of the Jewish image but also contributed to the solution of another problem: self-defense, first against marauders, later against incipient Arab nationalism, which could be better coped with on a collective basis. Moreover, as the defense problem became more complex, people bonded by common ideals and sharing a common fate were more easily induced to settle in hostile frontier areas than were separate individuals. The kevutzah and its later variant, the kibbutz, took economic risks that private investors would not or could not take. The dedication of the *halutzim* often turned high-risk undertakings into most successful projects.

One other achievement, sometimes overlooked, should be credited to the kevutzah—the revival of the ancient and dormant language, Hebrew, as the national tongue of a people renascent. Isolated pioneers made it their life's work to resuscitate the venerable tongue of the prophets into a viable day-to-day vehicle of communication, but it was the kevutzah that lifted the words out of books and put them into the mouths of their children.

As Jewish immigration into Palestine increased during the Third Aliyah (1918–23), the economic problems of the Yishuv became more complicated, necessitating the creation of large workers' aggregates to occupy more extensive tracts of land and to undertake contractual projects. The concept of the kevutzah was broadened to include industry, wage work, and membership expansion. Thus the present-day kibbutz ("ingathering") is an elaborate kevutzah with some unavoidable murking of the kevutzah's pristine purity. One old-timer of the First Aliyah, a hardened "colonist" and a rugged individualist, who had observed intently the struggles of the newer pioneers, mused: "The trouble with this darned collectivism, this misguided idealism, is that *it works!*"

Not everyone who came to Palestine in the Second Aliyah went into a kevutzah. Some of them joined the Bilu Moshavot (colonies). Many more made for the towns, Jerusalem, Jaffa, Haifa. In 1909 they built Tel Aviv on the sands of the Mediterranean, laying the foundation and the example for future urban development in many parts of the country. They also instituted a different form of village life, moshav ovdim (workers' settlement)—for example, Beer Yaakov and Ein-Ganim—although the best known of these settlements, sometimes erroneously referred to as the first, Nahalal, was founded in 1921.

The moshav ovdim is a village of smallholders who do not own the land as their private property but who maintain it under a hereditary lease. The land is national property. Each settler has his plot, which he and his family till, and his rights extend to livestock, buildings, and tools. His cooperation is mandatory in all matters affecting the general economy of the community, such as the purchase of massive equipment and seed, the sale of produce, and the maintenance of central institutions. In some instances livestock is also owned in common. The employment of wage labor is avoided in principle. This form of settlement was a reaction to the more socialist kevutzah and kibbutz. It, too, developed many variations and figured prominently in the defense of the Yishuv and the revival of the Hebrew language. Since the establishment of the State of Israel, the moshav ovdim has become the most popular form of workers' settlement, possibly because it retains individual ownership in a cooperative mold.

The moshav shitufi is an organization midway between the moshav ovdim and the kibbutz. On the economic side, with its communal production, marketing, and management, it resembles the kibbutz, but family life is organized along more traditional lines, as in the moshav ovdim.

The Third Aliyah, which produced the kibbutz alongside the kevutzah, was marked by a youthful and mildly socialistic element, mostly from Russia. However, a substantial minority of craftsmen and middle-class immigrants also entered Palestine at that time. The Jewish population had declined during World War I, and in 1918 it numbered only 55,000. By 1923, at the end of the Third Aliyah, it had grown to between 85,000 and 90,000. It was this aliyah that brought the intensification of Jewish agriculture, new agronomical experimentation, the organization of the Histadrut (the still powerful labor federation), and the inception of new industry (under Ottoman rule, industry had been restricted to wine, soap, and olivewood articles for religious use). The newcomers built an electric power station in Tel Aviv, a salt plant at Atlit, and a flour mill in Haifa. They also inaugurated a centralized network of schools, from kindergarten through elementary and secondary to higher education. The Yishuv, the general Jewish community, as distinct from the Old Yishuv (which continued to live on Halukkah money, collected by its emissaries), became aware of the need for mobilizing its resources for self-government and initiated the Asefat Hanivharim (elected assembly) in 1920 and many other quasi-governmental institutions.

The Fourth Aliyah (1923–31) brought 80,000 more Jews, the majority of whom were middle-class Polish emigrants with some capital. They flocked to the larger towns but also founded new agricultural settlements on private land, which in time grew into small towns and even cities: Bnai Brak, Herzliyah, Kfar Ata. Thus they reinforced the previously rather weak private sector in the mixed economy of the land.

The bulk of the Fifth Aliyah came from Germany. During the earlier days of Nazi persecution, up until 1935, about 150,000 Jews entered the country, importing with them West European scholarship and highly sophisticated know-how. It was during this period that Youth Aliyah, the rescue effort to save children from the Nazi atrocities and to educate them in Palestine, was mobilized. It operated until the end of World War II. By the mid-1940's some 30,000 youngsters were snatched from destruction.

But 1936–40 coincided with an economic depression and Arab riots. The British Government, first for fiscal reasons and then out of political calculations, restricted immigration. Somehow more than 50,000 Jews managed to get into Palestine in 1937–38 by legal means; 15,000 illegal (without government permission) immigrants succeeded in eluding the turbulence and terror of Europe and the diligence of the Mandatory authorities in Palestine to slip into the country. In 1939 a British White Paper limited Jewish immigration to a five-year total of 75,000, in accordance with the "absorptive capacity" of the country. Moreover, the White Paper indicated that future influx would depend on Arab acquiescence. In view of what was happening in Germany, the British policy elicited bitter protest against the "illegal and lethal document" not only from the Yishuv but also from Jews and non-Jews the world over.

Between 1941 and 1948 (sometimes called the Sixth Aliyah) only 60,000 Jews were allowed into Palestine. This period witnessed a titanic struggle between the Yishuv, mostly through its underground, and the British Government for the rescue of the escapees from the Nazi inferno, with such tragic incidents as the aforementioned *Patria, Exodus,* and also *Struma,* another "boat without a port," carrying 769 refugees and denied entry to Palestine. Seeking a friendly harbor, *Struma* foundered in the Black Sea in February, 1942, and all aboard were lost. Despite British vigilance, about 30,000 "illegal" immigrants were ingeniously and heroically smuggled into Palestine. On several occasions they were literally fished out of the sea in the dark of night. It was during this stormy period that David Ben-Gurion, later Prime Minister of Israel, issued his dramatic declaration: "We will fight Hitler as if there was no White Paper, and we will fight the White Paper as if there was no Hitler."

After the establishment of the state in 1948, the Law of Return was passed by the Israeli parliament, allowing all Jews the world over free immigration into Israel. The survivors of the Nazi rule in Europe, the detainees on Cyprus, virtually the entire Jewish communities of Yemen and Iraq, and most of the Jews of North Africa flocked into the country, straining the truncated state to its utmost economic and human capacity.

There were some 75,000 who were delivered by the Allies at the end of the war from the crematoria and put in DP (displaced persons) camps; 24,000 contrived to escape from the clutches of the Nazis even before the end of the war and were within reach of Palestine, only to be intercepted by the British Navy and sent to the island of Cyprus for detention. The Jewish underground found ways to get to them and to train them in Hebrew, history, and agriculture for eventual relocation in Palestine.

The Arab-Israeli hostilities after 1948 seriously affected the position of the Jews in the Arab countries. In March, 1949, more than 5,000 Yemeni Jews, who had sought refuge in Aden and had undergone there indescribable ordeals, arrived in Israel. In May, the Imam of Yemen permitted all the Jews of his country to leave. In a fantastic "Operation Magic Carpet," more than 45,000 deliriously happy human beings were crowded into makeshift transport planes and brought to Israel "on the wings of eagles," in the words of one exuberant evacuee. In 1950, more than 100,000 Jews from Iraq were "ingathered." Other multitudes reached Israel from Persia, Turkey, Libya, and Egypt. Still others arrived from Poland, Romania, Bulgaria, Yugoslavia, and Czechoslovakia. By the end of 1951 close to 700,000 immigrants staggered into Israel to double the 1948 Jewish population of Palestine! But this was not the end. Hundreds of thousands continued to converge on the country in the late 1950's from the localized miseries of Algeria, Morocco, Tunis, and, again, from Romania, Poland, Hungary, and Czechoslovakia.

At the time of the Israeli declaration of independence, there were 650,000 Jews in the country, most of them of European origin. By 1960, the number of Jews from the Oriental and North African communities constituted about 45 per cent of the total Jewish population of 2 million. In 1971, because of larger immigration and a higher birth rate, the non-Western element was more than half of the 2.6 million Jews in the state. Non-Jews—Muslim Arabs, Christian Arabs, other Christians, and various smaller minorities—numbered close to 450,000.

The efforts of accommodating the newcomers—first in camps, then in maabarot (transit villages), and finally in absorption areas—defied human ingenuity. One of the true wonders of Israel is not its brilliant military victories but its remodeling of the ghetto minds of hundreds of thousands of people, welding into one nation the Jewish Ph.D.'s of Heidelberg, Cambridge, and Harvard, on one hand, and the Jewish cave dwellers of the Atlas mountains, on the other.

Welded? Almost.

5 The People of the Land

An Israeli-born Jew is called a sabra. He is different from his parents, grandparents, or any other adults who came into the country bearing the "yoke of exile." Those immigrants arrived displaying every conceivable type of pigmentation—Ethiopian black, Yemeni brown, Chinese yellow, and East European pallor—every shade of religious belief, every nuance of nonbelief; they talked a torrent of dissonant tongues and imported strange, staid, exotic, and intractable customs. The sabra is, in effect, a new breed, without inhibitions, eager, until recently, to forget the past miseries of his forefathers, willing to skip two thousand years of Jewish history; to tie his genesis with the Joshuas, Davids, Maccabees, and Bar-Kokhbas; to ignore Yohanan Ben-Zakkai, Moses Maimonides, and the other great Torah and Talmud luminaries of the intervening years of dispersion. The sabra is interested in archaeology because it means uncovering glories of the past, and he looks upon the Bible not merely as a holy book but as a constitution, a national record, the very essence of Jewish peoplehood.

Secluded and apart from other Jewries, the Oriental communities have, on the one hand, kept their Judaism more intact. On the other hand, they have fallen behind modern sociocultural behavior. To the newcomers from North Africa and other Arab states, the sudden change of pace in Israel was unsettling. They were cata-

44

pulted into a small country and housed in tent camps or transit villages (maabarot) in makeshift dwellings with leaky roofs in winter and suffocating heat in the summer. At first they were settled by country of origin, so that they would feel more comfortable with their own language and peer group, but that kept them out of the mainstream of Israeli life. Some were put up in abandoned Arab houses in Jaffa, Haifa, Safad, Jerusalem, and elsewhere. There, they were soon spilling over into the streets, but more immigrants kept on arriving, resulting in serious socio-economic dilemmas. But how could Israel shut the gates of virtually the only and last haven for the troubled?

The government and the Jewish Agency, representing Jewry outside Israel, launched a Samsonian effort with the financial help of coreligionists abroad, mainly in the United States. Each maabarah was hooked up with a well-established neighboring settlement. The idea was to link the "transients" with a smooth-functioning local community. Labor exchanges were augmented, social services extended, and medical clinics expanded. The Housing Department of the Ministry of Labor began feverish activity to build permanent dwellings. In the meantime, an increasing number of newcomers were put to work on the new projects: road-building, the national water conduit, and other essential public enterprises. In 1952 immigrants were induced to purchase their own homes in new development areas with a very low down payment and, when needed, interest-free loans. In a later phase the newcomers were offered the opportunity to settle along the borders and in isolated areas and were provided with a plot, housing, livestock, and instruction in farming. Many who took up the challenge later quit, defeated by the hardships, the loneliness, the double burden of daytime work and nighttime defense, and jealousy of the "luckier ones" who somehow had managed to locate in urban centers. Also, because they were different in ideological denomination and cultural background from the socialist *halutzim* of the Second Aliyah, many of the Oriental newcomers drifted back to the maabarot or to city slums.

The stories of the difficulties spread abroad among the North

African Jews, deterring many, especially the educated and well-to-do, from migrating to Israel. They either remained in their own countries, or, when possible, went to France. The authorities in Israel acted swiftly and constructively. They built new roads to the isolated settlements, installed electricity and telephones, arranged for temporary relief of the frontiersmen by employing them in afforestation and other development projects, assuring them of a much more tolerable existence when their "crops came up." The youths of older settlements volunteered for part-time or full-time service in the villages, and soldiers were allowed to serve part of their compulsory military duty in the frontier hamlets. Social and artistic programs were initiated—films, ballets, and concerts by mobile units specially organized for frequent visits even to remote areas. Counseling to housewives among the culturally underprivileged was expanded, and vocational education was supplied.

On the whole, compulsory elementary education served as an effective integrating catalyst for all newcomers throughout the land, although it, too, had to face problems of language, caste, discrimination, and incompetence. But the army was, and still is, the most powerful instrument of unity for young adults, particularly the Oriental citizens who arrived illiterate. At the age of eighteen, both males and females are conscripted. Although defense is the primary aim, not far behind is the goal of galvanizing the antagonistic tribes of Israel into a national entity. They are put through accelerated courses in Hebrew and are imbued with a sense of historic values, beliefs, self-esteem, and will to self-sacrifice for the security and survival of others. They are made equal partners in a national experience. The psychological impact is obvious.

The housing shortage was more or less solved temporarily by the early 1960's. Education and the concomitant socio-economic problems were of much more concern to the Israeli authorities, because the Orientals were not as motivated intellectually as the Occidentals— even after serving in the army. They lacked the consuming desire for schooling that marked the East European Jews. Leaders of the country worried that two Israels would develop, one a white European elite, and the other a Second Israel of "hewers of wood and drawers of water." Not that there was equality among the Westerners: the "kibbutznik," mostly European, had become a status symbol (about one-third of the Cabinet membership since the founding of the state is of kibbutz origin, although the collective settlements make up only 4 per cent of the population). The older German Jews, forgetting Dachau and Auschwitz, recall fondly Goethe and Schiller, and some still refuse to learn that "barbarous language," Hebrew. It is said, not facetiously, that the Russians browbeat the Poles, the Poles look down upon the Hungarians, the Hungarians will not associate with the Romanians, and the Americans and the British talk only among themselves. The Germans merely bow to one another: *"Danke schoen!"* and *"Bitte schoen!"* Nevertheless, all of them share a common passion: education for the children.

However, compulsory education in Israel tore the social fabric of the Oriental Jew. For instance, it undermined the authority of the father. The father wanted his sons to go to work and his daughters to stay home and help their mother with her chores. "Have I come to Israel to be robbed of my dignity?" His expectations of Israel as the Land of the Fathers was woefully unfulfilled. He had come to the new state to escape the disabilities of exile, to find personal as well as religious salvation. Instead he encountered in Israel in some ways the same indignities as in the country he had left: superior airs, misunderstanding, unemployment—manifested in social discrimination, preference for the more efficient Occidental, lower income in less valued occupations, and inferior housing. Thus the North African had tended, in some instances, to get along better with the Israeli Arab, whose language he spoke and whom he resembled in pigmentation and custom.

The European Jews were also baffled: "Look at these Orientals! Are these bedraggled, cunning, primitive Jews the 'People of the Book,' as Muhammad called them?" And the Occidentals felt both abashed and sorry. They put forth a mighty effort to provide vocational training for the children, only to discover that the articulate leaders of the Orientals accused the Westerners, the "master group," of a conscious attempt to perpetuate the less educated in a Second Israel, in a second-class citizenship. Aware that they were compounding errors, and in near despair to find ways to avoid the calamity, the government strained its resources to provide additional hours of after-school instruction to slow learners and offered proportionately more scholarships to North Africans than to Europeans.

There was increased alarm among the intellectuals that the influx of so many non-Europeans would turn Israel into a provincial, comatose Middle East society.*(There are some in Israel who maintain that this would be a desirable underdevelopment—bridging the psychological, economic, and cultural gap between the dynamic, avant-garde Jewish state and its belligerent neighbors.) This concern was intensified by the additional fact that nearly 50 per cent of the population was sabra, lacking much contact with the great cultural resources of the West. Thus there was much rejoicing in the Establishment, and among Occidentals in general, when the Orientals began shifting their complaints, at times giving them physical substance through minor outbreaks: "Why shouldn't my children go to school? Why shouldn't they attend the university?" It was not merely "my son," but "my children." Daughters were now included!

Thus the real miracle of Israel. (But in the 1970's, it needed another one.) The bulk of a million people, weighed down by a cruel past, inarticulate and culturally destitute, almost overnight turned into a positive, productive element in a different unfamiliar, challenging, high-standard society. By 1970 some of the "bedraggled" people of the 1950's had established nearly thirty new towns and several hundred new villages; many of them are in the Negev—Dimona, for instance, where one of the Israeli atomic reactors is located. If the *halutzim* of the earlier aliyot dried the swamps in the north, many Orientals rolled back the desert in the south. But not all of them.

Only 15 per cent of the Sephardim were in Israeli institutions of higher learning in the late 1960's. While the number indicates an appreciable increase, there was still a cultural gap at the top between the Easterners and the Westerners. North African, Yemeni, and Iraqi Jews could be found in the Knesset and in the Cabinet, as well as in laboratories and in computer centers, but their number was still comparatively small.

In the early 1970's, with the influx of olim (ascenders) from the West, especially the United States and Latin America (because of unsettling conditions) and from the Soviet Union (because of Jewish difficulties), the situation was aggravated. The newcomers, a desirable element because of their higher educational levels and superior technological skills, were accorded preferential treatment —immediate and better housing, employment in well-paying positions. These were the people Israel hoped for. They had more cultural and political affinity with the leadership of the country.

Some Orientals, about 20 per cent, who did not quite "make it" socially, economically, and politically, felt betrayed. Assurances that, if an Easterner and a Westerner with the same qualifications were applying for the same job, the position usually went to the former did not placate the Oriental slum-dwellers. On the contrary, it pointed to their inability to compete, to their frustrations, to the hopelessness of their situation. Thus, emulating American patterns, some darker-skinned Orientals organized in 1971 a Black Panther movement, staging demonstrations, hunger strikes, and mini-riots to the embarrassment of the government and the majority of the population, both the Sephardim and the Ashkenazim.

The Black Panther leaders accused members of their own community of being Uncle Toms. "Unmask Yourself!" a placard demanded of Shlomo Hillel, a Sephardi member of the Cabinet. Another placard in the same demonstration proclaimed sarcastically, "Golda, Teach Us Yiddish!" referring to the Prime Minister's occasional use of the language spoken by the Ashkenazim.

Spurred by these and similar protests, the government has intensified its efforts to provide more economic opportunities and better educational guidance to the deprived among the Orientals. At the same time it has cast an anxious eye on the American and Russian arrivals, who themselves present a unique problem of polarization. The former thrive on economic competition and the latter find it difficult to adjust to a "profiteering" society. For example, a newcomer from the Soviet Union may be set up by a public agency in a shoe shop. Several weeks later he would burst into the government office complaining vociferously that he can't make a go of his business. "Where is the list of customers assigned to me?" When told that he has to get his own customers, he becomes even more indignant. "Do you expect me to hustle for buyers, to submit to degrading commercial competition?" In contrast, the newcomer from the United States in a similar shoe shop would work day and night, cut prices, make private visits, and may even drive a competitor out of business.

On the other hand, to the embarrassment of the left-wing labor parties in Israel, many of the Soviet Jews join the rival right-wing, ultra-nationalist movements, such as Herut.

Whether as a result of Sephardic protests, which grew louder as more Occidental Jews arrived in Israel, or from other causes, in the June, 1971, elections for the most important post of the most powerful party in the land, that of Secretary General of the Labor Party (Avodah), Yisrael Yeshayahu, a leader of the Oriental Jews, was chosen.

While there was and still is the quandary of "two Israels," there is also a "third Israel"—the more than 400,000 Arab citizens, apart from the Arabs in the areas occupied by the victor in the June, 1967, war (but including the Christian Arabs in Israel).

Untouched by time until World War I, the somnolent Arab community of Palestine was living very much as it had for centuries in the same square huts of clay and mud, sometimes painted blue to ward off evil spirits, and in houses carved out of the rocks in which they nestled. Practically the same forms of agriculture, trade, and customs prevailed in their villages as in the Middle Ages. Some 30,000 nomadic Bedouins roamed the wilderness of the Negev, and in manner they were not much different from the biblical Abraham and his sons Ishmael (whom the Arabs consider their progenitor) and Isaac (from whom the Hebrews have descended).

Arab society in the settled part of Palestine had an elite, the effendis, some of whom were educated in Europe or had traveled abroad and had about them an aura of cosmopolitanism. They thoroughly dominated the bulk of the Arab population, some 400,000 *fellahin*, small farmers who sometimes owned their little plots of land but more commonly paid an absentee landowner for the privilege of raising crops on the rich man's estate. In other instances, the Arabs of Palestine practiced an economy much like the open field system in feudal England, where all the property in the village was held in common, and each villager had a right to till a parcel of land in annual rotation. This system was not conducive to effective cultivation. Who would devote his time and energy to a piece of land later to be transferred to another *fellah?*

Thus, like many of the Jews, the Arabs were victims of cruel circumstances, which robbed them of creative self-expression and stereotyped them in the eyes of the world and in their own eyes. Under the British mandate they made some headway. Reforms mitigating the open field system were introduced. More tenant security was provided. Housing improved. Hygiene measures were expanded. More schools and clinics were built, penetrating the paralyzed and mystifying existence of the inhabitants of the land. The small group of professionals and businessmen was enlarged and encouraged to make contact with the outside world. Little by little, the idea of self-determination began motivating the increasing Arab middle class. Jewish successes both attracted and repelled them. The Arab population had grown most quickly in and around Jewish settlements, which brought employment, higher pay, public health services, and general prosperity to the Arabs. But Jewish immigration into the country aroused suspicion and fear among the budding Arab intelligentsia, on one hand, and the feudal lords, on the other. There was a genuine intuitive uneasiness among the politically unsophisticated masses of the *fellahin,* who benefited most from the Jewish presence. Assurances from the newcomers that there was room in the country for both "cousins" did little to allay the anxiety of the Arabs that in time the Jews would become a majority in the land.

The British were at a loss. It was easy enough at the early stages of their administration, but it became tougher later, to treat the Arabs as they had treated other "natives" in their empire. It was much more difficult and psychologically more disturbing for the average British official to relate to the Jewish immigrants from Europe, who were often better educated and more efficient than the English civil servants. The sweeping winds of nationalism in the post–World War II period whipped up waves of newfound patriotism among the Arabs, who until then had not heard of a Palestinian Arab entity—much like the African nations that suddenly discovered a new and undreamed-of political identity for themselves as their colonial status ended. In the meantime, the Nazi holocaust proved, if proof was needed, that the only solution to the problem of the Jews was a return to their birthplace.

The ensuing three-sided conflict among the Jews, Arabs, and British wound up at the United Nations. In 1947 partition of Palestine into two states, Jewish and Arab, was voted; it was grudgingly accepted by the Jews and totally rejected by the Arabs. An armed conflict eventuated in which the Jews emerged victorious, with an enlarged area.

As is inevitable in war, many innocent people suffered. Hundreds of thousands of Arabs fled the new Jewish state. Whether they were moved by propaganda from neighboring countries to leave, for fear of being destroyed by the same bombings that would annihilate the Israelis, or whether they were actually driven out by the Israelis as a security measure is a question that will be debated for a long time. The fact remains that only about 200,000 Arabs, Muslim and Christian, remained in the state after the war of 1948–49 subsided. Their number in the early 1970's more than doubled through the natural birth rate, the admission of refugees under a small-scale plan for family reunification, and the virtual annexation of East Jerusalem with its 65,000 inhabitants.

The declaration of Israeli independence promised that the state would "maintain complete equality of social and political rights for all its citizens, without distinction of creed, race, or sect." It also appealed to the "Arab people dwelling in Israel to keep the peace and play their part in building the state of Israel on the basis of equal citizenship and due representation in all its institutions."

The Jews submit with considerable pride that the country has the best-educated, healthiest, and most prosperous (in mean income rather than per capita income, where Kuwait, for one, would surpass it) population in the Middle East. But there is no denying the ambivalent feelings on both sides that the Arabs constitute a somewhat unequal, if not underprivileged, ethnic and religious minority in a country where they or their parents once constituted a majority. The Jews cannot help but have an uncomfortable thought that the Arab minority is a potential threat. Regardless of the fact that during the Six-Day War the overwhelming majority of the Muslims openly identified with the defense of the country and volunteered as blood donors and as replacement for laborers who were called up to the front, it is only "natural" that basically the Arabs would hope for the triumph of their brothers in the neighboring countries.

Israel does not seek to assimilate its Arab citizens. Arabic is one of the two official languages of the country and is used in the Knesset (parliament) by those who care to speak it. There are simultaneous translations of either of the two tongues. Arabic is officially employed in the courts and appears on paper currency, coins, and stamps. Arabs have held from three to seven out of the 120 Knesset seats in each of the parliaments elected since the establishment of the state. In 1971 an Arab attained the post of Deputy Minister of Health, and his cousin at one time had been a Deputy Speaker in the parliament. Another Arab, a Druze, later in that year became Deputy Minister of Communications. The Arabs have full local autonomy in cities, towns, and villages where they constitute a majority. In the 1969 elections to the city council of Jerusalem some 8,000 Arab citizens of the newly annexed East Jerusalem participated in the voting, in the face of threats from Arab commandos. Before 1967, under the Jordanian regime, only 6,000 Arabs in the city had polling rights. The Israeli Arabs have their own political parties, or they may affiliate with the larger Jewish parties.

Most of the initial security restrictions banning unauthorized travel by Arabs from their villages or changes of jobs and domiciles have been rescinded. The only official serious handicap now suffered or enjoyed by the Arabs is their inability to join the military forces or to settle in border villages that are exposed to enemy fire or sabotage. The per capita expenditure by the Israeli authorities is higher for the Arab population than for the Jewish population. Guided by the government, there is now the beginning of a movement for cooperative settlements. This is an extremely difficult task because of two seemingly "negative" elements, family loyalty and individualistic tendencies. Nevertheless, about 125 agricultural co-ops, some rudimentary in nature, were established in the last several years. The General Federation of Labor, the most powerful single institution in the country next to the government itself, in the early 1970's had close to 50,000 Arab members (half of the Arab labor force), and they were entitled to all the substantial privileges and benefits of membership in the organization.

The government also introduced into the Arab village modern irrigation and reclamation schemes and mechanized farming. These raised the Arab agricultural output per acre in many cases two to five times over. Hamlets and villages that never before had roads now have them, as well as electricity, piped water, and other modern conveniences. Even the Bedouins, who for centuries roamed the wilderness of the Negev feuding among themselves over water holes and yellowish stretches of pasturage, were induced to fold their tents and move into the twentieth century, as represented by model villages surrounded by green fields. By 1970 they had their own Bedouin physician, a graduate of the Hebrew University in Jerusalem.

All this is in addition to the 170 kindergartens, 200 primary schools, 20 post-primary institutions (including teacher-training seminaries), with a total of 80,000 Arab students, not counting the 15,000 in mission and private schools. Some 700 are studying in Israeli colleges and universities. As in the case of other religious groups in the country, the needs of the Muslim community are provided by governmental assistance and sometimes complete maintenance of institutions, such as the building of new mosques and the repair of old ones. The life expectancy of the Arab in Israel is seventy, as compared with seventy-two among the Jews, which at this writing is the highest in the world. Before the establishment of the state it was forty-seven among the Palestinian Arabs.

What do the Arabs have to say about their situation in Israel? Most of the complaints are similar to the earlier gripes of the Oriental Jews. The older people are not happy to see the fabric of their society ripped by the swift winds of change, by the modernism and dynamism of the new state. Even more than the Eastern Jews, they resist compulsory education, especially for girls. They resent the undermining of family life and religious observance. Paradoxically, many of the older generation preferred the military restrictions, which at first kept their clans together, to the uncertainties and alien ways of democracy, to the rights and the obligations that "freedom" conferred on them. Even those who are the beneficiaries of greater economic advantage are not always happy with the price they have to pay for them.

There is, for example, the problem of "eminent domain," which requires that Arabs be moved from one district to another for security reasons—at times rather vague and dubious—by military authorities whose sensitivity is somewhat less than that of an experienced social worker. Occasionally a wealthy family in a stately villa near the border is asked to move for a "short duration" several kilometers away into much less imposing quarters. The temporary few months stretch out for well over two decades because of the uneasy frontier situation and the duration of hostilities with the neighboring country. In the meantime, the family's children grow up in the "transitory dwelling," almost within sight of what in time is exaggerated into an even more imposing and spacious stone mansion.

The Arabs who accept the inevitability of change, the compulsion of progress, have perhaps even more serious strictures. Workers, members of the Histadrut and, particularly, those who are not union-affiliated, speak of job discrimination. For a better-paying job, a Jew will be preferred to an Arab. It is the menial, the least attractive of jobs, that go to the Arab. A whole area completely barred to the Arabs for obvious "security reasons" is defense, which is the biggest employment market.

Male workers who locate jobs and rooming (another touchy problem) in the larger Jewish cities—Tel Aviv, for instance, with an average of 7,000 to 10,000 seasonal or transient laborers—find it difficult to adjust socially. What can an Arab do, or where can he go, when Jewish girls are reluctant to date him? (Again, this problem existed initially also between the Eastern and Western Jews.)

More anomalous is the position of the student, because high schools in Israel are more or less under private auspices (but under government supervision). Thus Arab secondary institutions suffer from both inadequate sponsorship and paucity of qualified instruction. When a graduate of an Arab high school (not very many attend high schools under Jewish aegis—although they are open to all minorities—because of geography and cost) enters the university, he finds it very difficult to keep up with his classmates, even with special tutoring. If he manages to overcome the scholastic handicaps and specializes in engineering or in electronics, his chance of finding a job after graduation is nil—again, for "security reasons." Most Arabs, therefore, concentrate in the social sciences and in law, which, by the way, are also "honorable professions" in the eyes of their parents, who still think of engineering or electronics as "menial labor." The job opportunities for an Arab graduate in the humanities, social sciences, and the legal field are slim in the intellectually saturated Israeli market. The only really free area is teaching, but as this means tacit approval of everything the government does, it is, as one Arab student put it, "against my conscience, in view of the Israeli conflict with my Arab brothers in neighboring countries."

The social problem of the Arab university student is even more acute. He cannot develop real friendship with the opposite sex for fear of either or both sides that it may lead to marriage. At dances, a girl sometimes politely refuses to dance with an Arab partner. Unlike the Jewish students, many of whom are married, the vast majority of the Arab students are single, because they cannot afford the price of a bride (purchasing a wife is still prevalent among the Muslims), or because they cannot find a female coreligionist who will meet their newly acquired social and cultural standards. Because of several terrorist explosions perpetrated by Arab students in theaters and movie houses, precautionary measures are taken by the Jews. An Arab student who purchases a ticket to a public performance is quickly identified, "as if it is carved on my forehead," and sometimes is searched. So most Arabs at the various colleges and universities stay home and smolder or move in their own circles and fan each other's fires of frustration.

Both Arab and Israeli leaders are keenly aware of the inner conflicts of the Arab citizens. The 1967 hostilities did not make things easier. Before the Six-Day War the Arabs of Israel were insulated and out of touch with their "kinfolk." In the postwar period there is greater contact between them and those who are in the occupied area. It is difficult for the intelligentsia, no matter how much they sympathize with Israel, not to associate themselves with the larger Arab cause. Hence the sporadic cooperation with the commando infiltrators, before the strength of the guerrilla groups waned.

The Arab in Israel enjoys more economic and political freedom than his brothers in most Arab countries. Yet his tragedy is that he cannot think of himself as a Jordanian, a Syrian, or a Lebanese. He also finds it difficult to call himself an Israeli. The educated Arab loses his moorings in his own society and yet does not fit into the tense Israeli democracy. While the welding together of the Oriental and the Western Jews is in sight, the Israeli Arab's problems will find solution only when peace is concluded in the Middle East. Save for preventing a few unsavory incidents here and there, Israel cannot do much more than it does now for its Arab citizens. Yet the Arabs cannot help but experience heart-rending ambivalence, mixing gratitude and animosity.

6 Religion in the Holy Land

"For my house shall be called a house of prayer for all the people." Palestine has been just that for most of the Western world and large portions of the Eastern world, but really not in the sense that Deutero-Isaiah meant it some 2,500 years ago. Part of the time, it has been an unholy, clamorous, frothy vortex of dogmas and stigmas. Moloch in antiquity devoured infants. Later, prophets were chased by infuriated mobs. The cross and the crescent clashed during the Crusades. The Western Wall silently and impassively listened to the wailings of the returning remnants of an exiled people. Christian denominations engaged in feuds of varying intensity over the Church of Nativity. Israeli Jews glared at each other: TV or not TV on the Jewish Sabbath.

Someone attempting to describe religion in Israel might start with the answer of a philosopher who was asked about time. "I know what it is," he said, "but I'll be damned if I can explain it." Palestine after the Roman conquest has had many masters. The Ottoman Empire held sway over the country from the sixteenth century until after World War I. The Turkish Government never established a general law regarding matters of faith, leaving to the various denominations in the realm the administration of their internal affairs—a large area in personal and domestic relations. For the Jews in Palestine the Haham Bashi, the Chief Rabbi of the Sephardi (more or less the Oriental) Jewish community, was the main authority, with some special privileges granted to the local Ashkenazi (East and Central European) settlements who were linked with the Sephardi group. Similarly, the Christian sects were guided by their respective patriarchs, metropolitans, apostolic legates, and the like.

The British, who took over the country as a mandate from the League of Nations soon after World War I, inherited and continued the system. An innovation, as far as the Jewish community was concerned, was the introduction of an Ashkenazi Chief Rabbi in addition to the Sephardi. To this day there are two Chief Rabbis in Israel who are equal in religious authority on a *modus vivendi* basis, which has worked remarkably well. The idea of one Chief Rabbi is gaining supporters, though. Among its notable advocates is one of the country's best-known leaders, Moshe Dayan.

What complicates the Jewish religious experience is that it is recorded in a series of sacred works beginning with the Old Testament, which includes the Mosaic Code as enunciated in the Pentateuch (the Five Books of Moses). When the Old Testament, also called the Written Law, was canonized—some time during the first century—and no subtraction or addition of other sacred writings to this collection was allowed, there arose a large body of rabbinic traditions, amplifying and interpreting (by analogy, deduction, and other forms of casuistics) the Old Testament.

This tremendous storehouse of interpretive material, plus the exposition and explanation of additional time-hardened customs and practices, were gathered in an encyclopedic work, the Talmud—itself the fountainhead of later commentaries and codes. All this postbiblical literature became known as Oral Law. Now it is in the continually growing Oral Law—which explains and supplements the Old Testament—that authority rests. This authority is maintained by scholars and teachers (rabbis) whose right to expound the law derives merely from their knowledge of, and loyalty to, it.

Thus the Talmud itself was subjected to commentaries, explanations, and enlargements, evolving new religious writings and codes of behavior. During the Middle Ages and the early modern period, several sages collated much of the Talmudic law and consequent commentaries and produced codified abstracts. The best known of these is the *Shulhan Arukh* by Rabbi Joseph Karo in the sixteenth century. Karo's work, with the amendments (gloss) of Rabbi Moses Isserless, in time became *the* most authoritative book in Jewish religious life. To this day it is the primary code of practice for Orthodox (fundamentalist) Jews.

In the nineteenth century two new movements in Judaism developed, departing from Orthodoxy. The Conservative group (in England, Progressive or Reform) holds that Judaism is a living spirit, which must undergo adjustments to new surroundings. While Orthodoxy (at least neo-Orthodoxy) has not been standing still in meeting modern life's problems, the Conservatives are inclined to take larger steps, employing modern scientific methods for the study of the Jewish past, so long as every attempt is made to preserve or conserve core-Judaism, the basic traditions. It is a movement that on the one hand recognizes the necessity of change and on the other hand avoids the excesses of radicalism. Thus, for example, most Conservative Jews believe in the observance of dietary laws—some in a strict manner, others less so—but would not insist on separate seating of men and women in synagogue worship, as most Orthodox Jews would.

Reform Judaism (in England, Liberal) admits the value of tradition, the Mosaic Code and the rabbinic law as expounded in the Talmud, but it disagrees with Orthodoxy—and to a lesser extent with Conservatism—as to the binding force of these rules and regulations. The Reform departure from Orthodoxy is more extreme than that of Conservatism. For instance, while both Orthodox and Conservative worshipers would wear some headgear, usually skull caps, during synagogue services, the vast majority of Reform Jews would uncover their heads in their temple devotions.

The most significant and pertinent differences among these three groups are in the matter of marriage, divorce, Sabbath and holiday observance, ritual circumcision and, of late, autopsy. Orthodox Jews in particular adhere tenaciously to the prescribed rules regarding marriage and divorce, insisting that the highest values of purity, sanctity, and stability are vested in the Jewish family. The family, they assert, not only has been necessary to the biological perpetuation of the Jews but also has preserved their religiomoral and sociocultural treasures. Understandably, then, the laws pertaining to marriage and divorce are constant problems in present-day Israel, since they affect Conservative, Reform, and secularist Jews.

The prestatehood Jewish population contained a very large segment of secularists, especially among the members of the kibbutzim. Thus, when Israel was created in 1948 and the suggestion of state and church separation was voiced, there was fear that insurmountable problems would arise. Wisely, then, Israel did not adopt a constitution that decreed separation of church from state, thus suddenly wrenching power from the religious authorities who had preserved Jewish continuity throughout the centuries. Nor did the constitution declare Judaism to be a state religion, which would give the religious authorities and their adherents a privileged position, implying disadvantages for nonconformists as well as for non-Jews. The system adopted by Israel follows a midway course requiring the government to assume a sympathetic attitude toward all denominational groups—Jewish, Muslim, Christian, Druze, and the like—while interfering with none. Thus the religious courts of the various faiths have exclusive jurisdiction in matters of marriage and divorce, but in all other questions of personal status applicants or litigants may have recourse either to the religious courts or to the civil courts.

Israeli laws are thus adjudicated by secular courts, except where the Knesset has legislated that religious courts have jurisdiction. The country's Supreme Court, however, has the right of interpretive supervision, with the implication that it can overrule the religious courts. The Knesset, of course, can overrule all courts by passing nullifying legislation. This is a most disturbing aspect for the Orthodox Jews in Israel and abroad.

Jewish marriage and divorce in Israel, then, with the consent of the Knesset, is based on Orthodox rabbinic law, but with many interesting regulations. For instance, it is a criminal offense in the country, punishable by five years of imprisonment, for a husband to dissolve a marriage unilaterally (permissible, at times, under Orthodox law). He must have the wife's consent or a court order compelling her acquiescence. Similarly, a widow, who according to rabbinic law merely receives her ketubah (marriage agreement, or contract) portion, is now fully entitled to a share in her deceased husband's estate. In fact, Israel has greatly enhanced the position of women by passing in 1951 the Women's Equal Rights Law, which gives them the same status in the eyes of the law as men—permitting women to own and dispose of property, and according them the same privileges concerning the guardianship of children and other prerogatives.

Even though this law is not in consonance with many Jewish, Muslim, or Christian maxims, the religious communities are expected to comply with it, unless all parties involved in a specific case are eighteen or older and of their own free will want to submit the case to a religious court.

The state forbids polygamy, which complicates matters for the Muslim, who may have as many as four wives (and as many concubines as he is able to support) according to the Koran. It also creates a problem for the polygamous Yemenite Jews. When the government was accused of interference with religious freedom, the Israeli High Court of Justice ruled that Islamic law permits polygamy but does not require it. Similarly, child marriage, practiced by some of the Oriental Jews, was forbidden, and the legal age for marriage is now seventeen.

While intermarriage and civil marriage are not possible in Israel, the courts have held that civil marriages contracted and recognized abroad are valid in Israel. Thus a Christian cannot marry a Muslim or a Jew unless one of the parties converts to the religion of the other. Nor, of course, can a Jew marry a Christian or a Muslim unless conversion takes place, or unless the couple chooses to marry in another country. Hence, Cyprus, the nearest foreign state not involved in Israeli hostilities, is doing a thriving business in mixed and civil marriages.

The various denominations in the land are guaranteed free access to, and inviolability of, holy shrines and places (which are cared for by the custodians employed by the respective religious authorities), unimpeded worship, and maintenance and administration of pertinent institutions, such as "orders" or charity and welfare adjuncts. The Ministry of Religious Affairs looks after the needs of the sects, pays the salaries of the practicing clergy, helps in the upkeep of buildings and grounds, and assists in the restoration and renovation of sacred sites.

The official holidays of the land are Jewish, but every other religious community is granted the statutory right to observe fully its own weekly rest days and other holidays. As already pointed out, matters of personal status—wills, probate, paternity, adoption, custody of children—are within the jurisdiction of the denominational authorities. Parents have the choice of sending their children to public schools, to sectarian institutions maintained or subsidized by the state, or to private institutions. Jewish dietary laws are observed in the military establishment and in government agencies.

Public transportation is halted on the Jewish Sabbath, Saturday, in most areas, although private or semiprivate taxi and jitney (*sherut*) runs continue to function. In some places, like Haifa, there is limited public transportation on legal holidays. This situation came about ironically: Under the British mandate, the "freethinkers" of Tel Aviv, out of a sense of nationalism, extracted from the English the right to observe the day of rest on Saturday rather than on Sunday. Tel Aviv was an all-Jewish City. Haifa, on the other hand, had an Arab majority, so public transportation on the Sabbath was not curbed in that city. With the establishment of the state and the attendant problem of communication, the secularists of Tel Aviv were in a dilemma: How could they ask a Jewish coalition government, in which the Orthodox participated, to restore Saturday public bus service in Tel Aviv? In Haifa, however, they preserved the *status quo*.

David Ben-Gurion, generally recognized as the founding father of

Israel, himself not an Orthodox or even a "traditional" Jew, feels that the Jewish state without the Bible and the Jewish religion is meaningless. He maintains that the ardor of the Hebrew prophets was largely applied to protect and to intensify spiritual and moral rather than political concepts. Many Israelis, like Ben-Gurion, view the return of the Jews to their homeland not only as an escape from the Diaspora and its problems but also as a prelude to the creation in Israel and eventually elsewhere of a humane society. This is particularly evident in the kibbutz movement. Nevertheless, the ideological differences between the religionists and the secularists, while at times making for bitter debate, do not allow compromise in the matter of peoplehood. However dithyrambic their utterings are in regard to observance and piety, their practical position is to conserve and to increase the viability of the Jewish people—until the social and/or religious Messianic era of the brotherhood of all men arrives.

Even to the secularist in Israel and to many of the nonreligious sabras who look with aversion at the Diaspora, which in Europe until the holocaust was immersed in Jewish learning, the Bible is very much a part of daily life. It is a revered historical or literary work, a source of creative inspiration for painting, music, drama, and dance. Some are ready to forget, as mentioned earlier, the two thousand years of Dispersion and to resume history from the last chapter of Second Chronicles. To those surrounded by living evidence of biblical events, the "book" is not Holy Writ but a cherished account of achievements and even a practical guide. Commanders during the 1948 campaign won several victories in the Negev desert by adopting biblical strategy and identifying secret paths mentioned in the Old Testament.

Even though Israel tries to dodge the issue of church-state relationship, many problems arise in regard to what and who is a Jew. The Law of Return, allowing every Jew abroad free and immediate entry into Israel with automatic citizenship, has caused several problems. One was the celebrated case of Father Daniel, born Jewish but converted to Christianity to become a Catholic priest. He claimed to be a Jew of Christian religion. There were the Beni Israel of India, who may have arrived in that Far Eastern country in the time of King Solomon, and whose customs and beliefs, especially regarding marriage and divorce, differ from the present-day Orthodox code. The Falasha, or the black Jews of Ethiopia, were in a similar situation. Recently an even more complex issue developed with the arrival in Israel, via Liberia, of black Jews from Chicago claiming descent from Falashas who were sold as slaves to North Americans centuries ago. Another problem, and the cause of dissension and political rifts between the partners in the government coalition—the Orthodox groups on one side and the Labor parties on the other—is raised by the non-Jewish wives of Russian Jews who recently have "ascended" to Israel. The insistence of Labor on lighter and briefer conversion processes has created a quandary for the Chief Rabbinate.

This problem is of special significance in Israel, because Judaism is not a proselytising or missionary faith. It does not seek conversions. It holds that each religion reaches out in its own way to the one God, that there is no special merit in being a Jew, and that the righteous of all nations may inherit the hereafter. Hence, for both theological and sociological reasons, Judaism discourages conversion. Perhaps this is a major element in Jewish survival throughout the ages. It explains the caution about taking in "dubious" Jewish clans or individuals. It also presents a problem for the Reform and Conservative wings of Judaism that do not fully accept the Orthodox code. These two movements flourish outside Israel, especially in the United States and Great Britain. It is only lately that they have begun to institutionalize their beliefs in Israel. Marriage and divorce ceremonies performed by Conservative and Reform rabbis (most Reform clergymen accept civil divorce) outside Israel and recognized in the states where they took place are also legal in Israel. However, marriage and divorce rites conducted in Israel by non-Orthodox Jewish clergy are not recognized by the Orthodox rabbinate, which claims sole authority in these matters.

Secularist kibbutz couples who are not married in an Orthodox ceremony scoff at the idea of "living in sin." But at times their status causes comic and embarrassing situations. In one such case, a kibbutz couple, after forty years of married life, planned a vacation abroad. Since their wedlock was sanctioned by the kibbutz authorities only, they were not considered man and wife by the rabbinate. Therefore, they could get only separate passports, the wife using her maiden name. This would create problems for the couple traveling in Europe, especially in the matter of hotel accommodations. So the couple decided to rewed in a rabbinic court, inviting all their children and grandchildren to the ceremony. The marriage certificate required the officiating rabbi to identify the bride as a widow, a divorcee, or a virgin. He put down "an experienced virgin."

The more serious question—Who is a Jew?—was raised by Ben-Gurion after a member of his Cabinet, Minister of the Interior I. Bar-Yehudah, drew up in 1958 a form for a new identity card, which all Israelis (Jews, Muslims, Christians, and others) were required to carry for security reasons. According to the instructions issued by Bar-Yehudah: "A person who bona fide declares himself Jewish and does not belong to any other religion will be registered as a Jew. In the case of a child whose parents are not Jewish, but where both parents declare bona fide that the child is Jewish and does not belong to any other religion, he (or she) will also be registered as Jewish."

This ruling evoked a sharp protest from Orthodox Jews, as well as from other sources. The Chief Rabbinate of Israel declared: "The new regulation, if enforced, would be likely to bring confusion to Jewish family life, encourage mixed marriage in Jewish communities outside Israel, create in Israel a 'mixed multitude,' which would not identify itself with the nation's historical character."

Moreover, the Chief Rabbinate insisted that no lay authority has the right to designate who is and who is not a Jew. Only the Halakha (religious law) must be followed in determining anyone's Jewishness. The two cardinal Halakhic criteria are, first, that the person was born of a Jewish mother, and, second, that the male has been dedicated to the faith of Judaism by the ritual of circumcision.

Also, persons converted to Judaism according to the specific rules and regulations guiding such conversions (circumcision for the males, ritual baths for the females, etc.), enjoy the same status, the same obligations, and the same rights as other bona fide Jews.

Ben-Gurion retorted that the government's ruling was based on Psalm XV: "Lord, who shall sojourn in Thy tabernacle? . . . He that walketh uprightly and worketh righteousness, and speaketh truth in his heart . . . , nor doeth evil to his fellow." Asked the Prime Minister: "Why should he that observes the Sabbath and Kashruth [dietary laws] be considered a Jew, while he who lives according to the Psalmic definition not be considered a Jew?" Ben-Gurion emphasized that the government does not deem itself an authority to decide who is a religious Jew, but only who is a Jew by nationality. In matters of ritual, marriage, and divorce, the government (as distinct from the parliament) decision would not be binding upon the rabbinate. Pointing out that freedom of religion and conscience is among the state's basic tenets, the Prime Minister argued that Israel's declaration of independence made it clear that the country would not be governed by religious law. In fact, Ben-Gurion added, in matters of religion and religious law, there is no unity among the Jewish people: "In America there are Orthodox, Conservative, and Reform Jews. There are many Jews who belong to none of these groups but are in my opinion Jews as long as they do not become converted to another religion."

Dr. Z. Warhaftig, later Minister of Religious Affairs stated: "So long as a person is born of a Jewish woman, and if male has been circumcised according to Jewish law, he is Jewish whether he fulfills all his Jewish obligations or none at all. . . . The state may designate who is a *citizen*, but not who is a *Jew*."

Dr. Nathan Rotenstreich, professor of philosophy at the Hebrew University, pointed out: "We do not have in Judaism a religious hierarchy similar to that in Catholicism or in other Christian or non-Christian sects. We have had and we now have great and learned rabbis, but none of them individually or collectively has the authority or the right to determine who is or who is not a Jew."

The secularist Bar-Yehudah amplified:

We have come to Israel to reconstruct a nation, not a religion. We want to normalize Jewish life. Religion is a matter of personal choice. What is it that the Agudah [ultra-Orthodox], Mizrahi [Orthodox], Ahdut Avodah [more or less secularist], a member of a kibbutz, and a Yeshivah [rabbinic academy] student have in common? It is the peoplehood, the nationhood of Jews. It is the same thing that unites the Conservatives, the Laborites, even the Communists of England. All these are members of the English *nation,* all of these have a common past, all of them have the task of social construction for the future.

Even non-Israelis were drawn into the controversy. Professor Mordecai Kaplan, one of the foremost thinkers in American Conservative Judaism, wrote:

It is certainly true to fact that religion, or a particular set of beliefs about God, with practices related to these beliefs, is all that distinguishes the Jews as a group from non-Jews. If Judaism is to mean that which unites Jews into an identifiable and distinct group, then it is a *religious civilization.* As such, Judaism is an ensemble of the following organically interrelated elements of culture: a feeling of belonging to a historic and indivisible people, a continuing history, a living language and literature, and common mores, laws and arts, with religion as the integrating and soul-giving factor of all these elements.

Even after much verbal escalation and a great deal of ink-letting, the casuistry was not exhausted. In the face of Arab threats to the very existence of the state, especially in 1967, the commotion subsided for a while, only to flare up again later. The rabbinic courts on both local and national levels were doing their utmost to untie the complicated doctrinal problems, easing the formalities for the new arrivals to be recognized as Jews with immediate citizenship. Father Daniel's case was referred to the Israeli Supreme Court, which ruled that he no longer was a Jew because he had dissociated himself not only from the Jewish faith but also from Jewish fate, not only from Jewish history but also from Jewish belonging. However, like all other non-Jewish newcomers, he could and would become a full and equal citizen after three years' sojourn in the country. Father Daniel did in this way become an Israeli, a citizen of Israel.

In the case of a navy officer, B. Shalit, the Supreme Court ruled in 1970 that Shalit's youngest child, born of his non-Jewish wife, could not be registered as a Jew. In another case, this one in 1972, the Supreme Court denied a different request. Professor G. Tamarin, born of a Jewish mother but a professed atheist, did not want to be registered as a Jew because, he claimed, "Jew" is a religious concept. He wanted to be registered as an Israeli. Chief Justice S. Agranat stated in his written opinion that the desire of a small group of Jews to be recognized merely as Israelis is not legitimate. Agranat reasoned that such recognition, if granted, would lead to the break-up of Jewish peoplehood and would negate the very aims which motivated the creation of the state of Israel.

Also, at a mass meeting of the 28th Zionist Congress in Jerusalem on January 21, 1972, Prime Minister Golda Meir declared that there is no difference between Jewish religion and Jewish nationhood. "An American may be an Anglican-American or a Buddhist-American, but I have never seen an Anglican-Jew or a Buddhist-Jew," she said.

Both the free-thinkers and the pious realize the potential explosiveness of religious issues when peace comes to the area. There are extremists in both camps. In addition to the problem of who is and who is not a Jew, other bones of contention are organ transplants, autopsies, and Sabbath observance. A League Against Religious Coercion, which is not addicted to understatements, publishes articles and pamphlets and organizes demonstrations "against the imposition of religious observance on irreligious people." An article by Shulamit Aloni, an attorney and former parliament member, describes the "Sabbath as a unifying force prized by every Jew. That is why it was proclaimed the weekly day of rest in Israel. However, its connotation of the Sabbatical spirituality, poetry and way of life can never be implanted by compelling the populace to stay at home in a spirit of dissatisfaction ranging from indifference, at best, to active resentment." In the same article she says: "Another subject currently debated among us is whether it is right for us, the eternal people, to live in accordance with the social and administrative concepts of the twentieth century and the Western world, or whether it would be better to shun alien cultures and changing times and lead our lives according to the precepts and customs of ancient days, whose quintessence lies in the fact of their antiquity."

The bind in which the religious element finds itself is that the rabbinic authorities may add observances or prohibitions but are not free to rescind them, only to interpret them. The extremist Neturei Karta insist on the letter of the law. There are only about 2,000 of them, and they live in the ghetto-like Mea Shearim in Jerusalem. They do not recognize the State of Israel and its authority, because it was established before the coming of the Messiah and is run by "heretics." Signs are hung across the streets of the quarter exhorting the daughters of Israel to dress and behave modestly. On the Sabbath, attired in their black silk or satin robes and large fur-trimmed headgear, they fume and fulminate at passing private vehicles. The children sometimes throw stones at moving cars.

Agudath Israel is also an ultra-Orthodox group, but it is a political party as well. Its purpose is to foster strict observance of the Halakha. At first it was opposed to Jewish political self-determination, but with the founding of Israel it reconciled itself to Jewish statehood and is now represented in the Knesset. A rabbinic group, Moetzet Gedolei Hatorah (Council of the Great Torah Authorities), composed of spiritual leaders in and out of Israel, is the informal guiding entity of the movement. The organization's relationship with the Chief Rabbinate of Israel is ambivalent. It also has its own network of schools, Talmudic academies, press, and even ideologically related kibbutzim of the Poalei Agudath Israel, a laborite-socialist but ultra-Orthodox group.

The moderate Orthodox organization, the largest of the religiously oriented movements, is the Mizrahi. Together with its laborite-socialist confederate, Hapoel Hamizrahi, it forms the Miflagah Datit Leumit (National Religious Party). Mizrahi fully accepts the authority of the Chief Rabbinate and makes every effort to interpret the law in light of modern conditions without veering away from the Halakha. Since Jewish law is permissive, for instance, in matters of personal health, or in the security of the community, it is also possible to explicate doctrine so as to allow ambulance service and necessary military operations or to expedite the re-entry of the scattered and battered tribes of Israel into Judaism's fold.

Mizrahi, the Chief Rabbinate, and other moderate Orthodox Jews were confronted with this dilemma when Israel was established: to submit to the legislative authority of a secular state (like, for instance, the Church of England), or to develop a self-contained, collective existence for the Orthodox—a community within a community. The moderates chose neither but embarked on a course that would help shape, if not determine, the future of Judaism in Israel. While they attempted—sometimes successfully, sometimes not—to evoke religious self-awareness among the Jews, they did not entirely close their eyes to the modern world and its problems. Curiously, East European religious thought, if not all customs, found a responsive chord among the Oriental Jews. (Similarly, the secularists among the Oriental Jews adopted European lines of argumentation and attack.)

One goal of religious moderates, then, was to consolidate the various "tribes of Israel," Western and Eastern, into a community of faith. Another was to return to Mosaic theophany and its moral and religious imperatives, making them a fundamental part of Israeli society without impairing the rights of the individual to freedom of conscience and personal behavior.

Even more complicated is the problem of the Arabs. One cannot speak of the Arabs in generic terms but must specify many subgroups, subcultures, and religious differentiations among them. Not all Arabs are Muslim and not all Muslims are Arabs. For example, the Pakistanis, the Turks, and the Kurds are Muslim but not Arab. On the other hand, there are many Arabs who are Christian—Protestant, Greek Orthodox, and of various Catholic denominations. Also Islam itself is split into two major divisions, Sunnis (fundamentalists) and Shiites (modifiers, reformists). There are also Arabs whose religion is a mixture of Islam and earlier Christianity.

The vast majority of the Arabs in Israel are Sunnis. Since Palestine under the Ottoman Empire was an integral part of Syria (although Jerusalem and its environs were governed by a Mutessarif, responsible directly to Constantinople), there were no over-all Palestinian Muslim authorities to deal exclusively with the area's problems. It was Sir Herbert Samuel, a British Jew appointed by London in 1920 to the office of High Commissioner of Palestine, who, motivated by objectivity, prompted the Arabs to organize a purely Palestinian Supreme Muslim Council. This body controlled the Islamic religious courts and charitable endowments. Initially it was a major factor in political affairs until weakened by inner dissension.

Under the regime of the State of Israel, the religious authorities, institutions, rights, and freedoms of the Muslim community were not diminished. In many instances they enjoy far greater privileges than in most Muslim countries. Religious courts and law authorities retained and enhanced their adjudicative prerogatives. The Muslims, like the Jews and Christians, have full autonomy in matters of personal status: marriage, divorce, legacies, testaments, and the like. The decisions of the Muslim courts are carried out by the executive powers of the state. The Muslims also exercise wide powers in their internal affairs, school administration, welfare agencies, and elections to their own local councils, of which there were close to thirty in the 1970's, with a total population of up to 200,000. Nazareth, with a population of 35,000, is the largest Arab-dominated city.

The local budgets of the Muslim communities trebled since 1960. The government has maintained in good repair about 130 mosques and has paid the salaries of more than 200 qadis, muezzins (callers to prayer), and other religious functionaries. Tens of thousands of copies of the Koran, mainly from Turkey, have been bought and shipped in for Muslim use in Israel (the economic boycott of the Arabs extends also to articles of faith). Additionally, Israel helped build the recently completed and splendid Great Mosque of Peace in Nazareth.

Perhaps the most magnificent edifice in Israel is the Dome of the Rock. It enshrines the sacred stone from which the Prophet Muhammad, in consort with the Angel Gabriel, alighted to heaven on the white charger Baraq in the "night of excellence and power," and where on Judgment Day the Angel Israfil, the Lord of the Trumpet, will sound the last blast, which will resurrect the dead to life of eternal bliss.

Architecturally breathtaking, ablaze in the sun in its multicolored and almost psychedelic appearance, the Dome of the Rock, with its smaller neighbor, the el-Aqsa Mosque (which a deranged Australian tried to burn in 1969), is the third-holiest place in Islam. The two structures were erected on what Jews believe to be the site of King Solomon's temple, of which only the outside western rampart, the so-called Wailing Wall, remains. The rock inside the large mosque, according to Jewish tradition, is part of the sacrificial altar on Mount Moriah where Abraham was ready to offer his son Isaac as evidence of his faith. Thus this is also hallowed ground for Jews and Christians.

Likewise, Hebron, where Abraham and Sarah, Isaac and Rebecca, Jacob and Leah are interred in the Double Cave (Rachel's tomb is near Bethlehem), is holy to the three faiths. From 1948 to 1967 Jews were barred from the Old City of Jerusalem and from the Wailing Wall. For some 700 years, until 1967, Jews could not go beyond the seventh step leading down to the Double Cave in Hebron. As a result of the Six-Day War, all sacred sites in the Old City (in East Jerusalem), Hebron, Bethlehem (also in Arab territory occupied in 1967 by the Israelis), and other sacred localities are freely accessible to all people, although they are administered by the respective religious groups that have had traditional custody of the holy places. Thus the Dome of the Rock and other mosques are supervised by

Muslim authorities, who set the visiting hours and other regulations for non-Muslims.

There is tension and drama in the guarded, underplayed confrontation of Judaism and Islam, with Christianity a concerned onlooker, on the soil where their respective spiritual roots are ensconced.

Among the non-Muslim Arabs in the country the largest group are the Druze, who filtered out of the mainstream of Islam in the eleventh century to form an esoteric and intriguing faith. Some of their religious practices are closely guarded secrets. From available evidence they appear to follow a modified version of Islam with strong Judeo-Christian nuances. Because of a long history of persecution and strife, the Druze practiced concealment (*taquiya*) and the doctrine of dissimulation, whereby a believer is free to profess publicly any other dogma or creed that might enhance his safety. Thus, for many centuries they passed for Muslims. However, the moment they felt free of compulsion, as happened immediately after World War I, when the French and the British occupied Syria, Lebanon, and Palestine, they asked for separate political identity and autonomous existence.

During Israel's war of independence in 1948, the Druze communities in Palestine made common cause with the Jews against the Arabs, forming their own units and fighting bravely. Their courage and loyalty won high praise from the army commanders. In fact, many of the 150,000 Druze then residing in Syria and Lebanon also were ready to cast their lot with the new Jewish state.

Arabic in language and in culture, the Druze claim as their progenitor Nebi Shueib, the biblical Jethro the Medianite, father-in-law of Moses. The annual pilgrimage to the Horns of Hittin in Lower Galilee, the reputed burial place of the prophet, is a highlight in their religious observance. Another is the study of the handwritten sacred scriptures, Kitab al-Hikmat, the Book of Wisdom, on Thursday nights, the beginning of the community's rest period, which extends into Friday afternoon. They are enjoined not to reveal the mysteries of their faith, which are known to a small group of *Aqils,* the initiated. A Druze who once leaves the fold can never come back.

About 35,000 Druze live in Israel in about twenty villages, mostly around Haifa, on the slopes of Mount Carmel. They were granted the status of an autonomous religious community, and they enjoy administrative rights in their local councils. Moreover, they, unlike the Arab Muslims, in the early days of the state can serve in the army. Two other small non-Arab Muslim groups, the Circassians, who came in the nineteenth century from Russia and now number about 2,000 souls, and the Ahmadi sect of some 600 people from Pakistan, can also serve in the army. The Druze, the Circassians, and the Ahmadians, like all citizens in the country, can vote in the national elections to parliament and be represented in it. Several Druze have taken seats in the Knesset along with other Arabs. In 1969, a Druze was chosen Deputy Speaker of the Parliament.

For Christianity the Holy Land is a magnet for pilgrimage and spiritual regeneration. After the 1967 Israeli occupation of areas that in biblical times were part of the country, the Christians were able to trace the trail of Jesus by touching the past and the present in the Church of Nativity in Bethlehem; by going up to Nazareth and gazing into the very skies of Galilee beheld by Jesus; by climbing Mount Tabor to be transfigured into another time; by drinking the swift waters of the impetuous Jordan; by returning to Jerusalem to kneel at the hallowed Hall of the Last Supper; by walking the Via Dolorosa and praying at the Church of the Holy Sepulchre.

But the story of the Christians in the Holy Land is even more confused than those of the Jews and the Muslims. Numbering only 80,000, mostly Arabs, they belong to some twenty-five denominations. Among them are the Greek Catholic, 25,000; Greek Orthodox, 22,000; Roman Catholic, 16,000; Maronite, 4,000; and Protestant (Anglicans, Baptists, Presbyterians, Lutherans), 4,000; and Monophysite (Armenian-Gregorian, Coptic, Ethiopian), 7,000. The largest Christian edifice in Israel, as well as the entire Middle East, is the new Basilica erected in Nazareth in the late 1960's at the cost of about $2 million. There are more than 200 other churches and chapels and 40 monasteries and convents in the Holy Land, with 1,500 priests, ministers, monks, and nuns. Most of the orders—Franciscan, Carmelite, Benedictine, Sisters of the Rosary, the Clarisses—built their monasteries and convents on sites venerated by Christians. Eight religious courts, like their Jewish and Muslim counterparts and in association with the Ministry of Religious Affairs, deal with matters of personal status.

The problem of guardianship of the holy places is complicated. There are claims, theological disputes, and also physical encounters. Muslim guards before 1967, and Jewish guards thereafter, frequently have had to separate the clashing clergy at the Church of Nativity and the Church of the Holy Sepulchre. The latter is claimed by the Greek Orthodox, the Greek Catholic, and the Armenians. But the Copts point to a small opening in their little sanctuary next to the Holy Sepulchre and declare reverently that it leads to the crypt itself. Ten different services are scheduled on Christmas Day inside the Church of Nativity. Most Protestants are not admitted to any of them. Four services are held on Pentecost at the site of the Assumption.

There is White Russian territory and Red Russian territory in the Holy City. The Roman Catholic Church, a comparatively late arrival, does not guard very many holy sites. It re-established its patriarchate in Jerusalem in 1847. The Protestant church also came to Palestine in the mid-nineteenth century, and it has hardly anything to guard, but its various denominations and missionary groups have developed effective controversies anyway. Of the larger sects, the Baptists have nurtured the most sympathetic approach to the Jewish state and to Zionist ideals. They have learned to speak Hebrew and have adapted themselves to the customs of the land. Near Tel Aviv they have founded a settlement, Kfar Habaptistim (Baptist Village), in which perhaps there is more of an Israeli atmosphere than in any other non-Jewish agricultural project in the country. Similarly, smaller contingents of Dutch, Swiss, and German orders have come to Israel to help build the land.

Aside from the Jews, Muslims, and Christians, there are several other sects, although numerically they are not significant. Two of them are very close to the Jewish faith. The Samaritans until recent times remained pure in blood for 2,500 years. They are the descendants of the Babylonians brought to Samaria in 721 B.C. to replace the population taken into captivity after the fall of the city and the kingdom. They claim Ephraim and Menasseh as their progenitors. Numbering only several hundred souls, because of inbreeding for many centuries, they are the remnants of a dwindling people; lately they have begun to marry Jewish women.

At first the Samaritans felt superior to the Jews, maintaining that they have not changed the original precepts of Judaism, which, they held, Ezra had warped in the fifth century B.C. They do not have much in common with the Arabs, although they speak their language in daily life. They worship in ancient Hebrew, with Aramaic elements.

The religious center of the Samaritans is in Nablus, the biblical Shechem, and their holy site is nearby Mount Gerizim, but some of them have moved recently to Holon, south of Tel Aviv. They hold sacred only the Torah (Pentateuch), with some minor differences from the Hebrew text viewed sacred by the Jews, and the book of Joshua. The Torah is written on lambskin, and the Samaritans believe that Aaron himself inscribed it and that it was brought into the Promised Land by Joshua. They neither acknowledge nor pursue the doctrinal development of Judaism as it emerged in later prophetic or rabbinic literature. Ruled by a high priest, the Samaritans offer sacrifices on Passover in a manner described in the Pentateuch. The entire community residing in Shechem and in Holon leave their homes to camp on top of holy Mount Gerizim. When the full moon rises on the first night of the festival, the high priest intones the haunting prayers of his ancestors as the echoes of remote yesterdays reverberate in ancient accents.

Another group, also originally very close to Judaism, is the Karaites. They accept the Written Law, the entire Old Testament, but reject the Oral Law, which rabbinic Judaism developed in the postbiblical Babylonian period and after. Karaitic interpretation of the scriptures is literal. Some of their observances are more rigid than those of the ultra-Orthodox Neturei Karta of Mea Shearim. For instance, they forbid all Sabbath illumination, whereas even strict Jewish orthodoxy allows light if it is turned on before the Sabbath begins Friday at sunset. Nor do the Karaites celebrate Hanukkah, because it is not mentioned in the Old Testament.

There were several unsuccessful attempts to bring the Karaites into current Judaism. Of about 12,000 of this sect now living in Israel, many came from Egypt. They are concentrated in and around Ramleh and maintain nine synagogues with their own spiritual leaders.

Haifa is the religious and administrative center of the Bahai. This is a comparatively new faith developed from the teaching of Bahaullah (Glory of God) and resting on the earlier foundations laid by the Bab (the Gate), who announced his mission in Persia in 1844. Bahaullah was denounced by both political and clerical authorities in his native land, so toward the end of his days he came to Palestine and died there in 1892. The Bahais stress the unity of God and the need to incorporate the essential truths of all faiths into everyday life, recognizing the changing circumstances of each generation. There are several hundred Bahais in Israel, with the principal shrines in Haifa and in Acre (the burial place of Bahaullah). The golden cupola of the Bahai Temple in Haifa dominates the city's landscape. A magnificent and fragrant Persian garden surrounds the edifice.

Thus Israel is uniquely apart from, and at the same time a focus of, both West and East. It is a land of God-intoxicated people and inspired secularists seeking social solutions. It is a place where nearly everyone is free to find emotionally what he wants and to validate his findings in his own self.

As now conceived by most Jews inside and outside Israel, the Jewish state is not merely a political entity but also a spiritual and cultural center of Judaism. Thus Israel's Jewry, as has been stressed by members of the academic community, faces a difficult challenge. It must learn—and it is learning—the consummate art of being a responsible majority, of so interpreting the idea of a Jewish State that it acknowledges that the participation of Israel's non-Jewish citizens is also significant in the moral flowering of the country.

7 The Substance of the State

Israel is a noisy democracy. Its citizens are easily seduced by whiffs of politics. It is not unusual, as the saying goes, to find in that country two Jews with three opinions. But when the dust is settled, there emerges a rare cooperative art in self-government and astonishing national discipline.

The evolution of a viable Jewish statehood is a fascinating process for political behaviorists. The Jewish pre-independence period of 1882–1948 saw a unique combination of ideological musings, abiding faith in a religiocultural legacy, controlled irreverence for institutions, and sacrificial pioneering. Throughout this era political anxiety etched the profile of the Yishuv as the relevant and the possible became more and more complicated.

The early political casting was done mostly in an East European matrix, with Western tools and values. It was only after 1948 that the Afro-Asian immigrants and the native-born Israelis began pushing against the walls of the old mold and demanding changes in the East European contours of the body politic.

Ottoman and British administrative ineptitude plus the cumulative problems of the Jews in the Diaspora compelled the starry-eyed idealists of the Second and Third Aliyoth to pragmatize their

79

utopias into viable life-patterns and to fashion political tools, which at times did some violence to their pristine principles. Thus, long before 1948 the Yishuv was a going political concern, "a state in the making."

As early as November, 1917, right after the issuance of the Balfour Declaration, a provisional council for the Palestine Jewish community was formed by Bezalel Yafeh. In 1920, when the British military occupation of Palestine gave way to a civil administration, the organizational framework of the Yishuv was secured by the election of an Asefat Hanivharim (Representative Assembly), whose 314 delegates met for the first time in October of that year. A Vaad Leumi (National Council) of thirty-six members was selected to run the Yishuv's internal affairs and to represent it in external matters. A still smaller group of thirteen was entrusted with Cabinet-like functions. The status of this quasi-government was not recognized formally by the British administration until eight years later.

In 1928 the Yishuv, as Knesset Israel (the Congregation of Israel, or the Assembly of Israel), attained an officially sanctioned position. All Jews over twenty years of age who had resided three months or longer in Palestine could cast a secret ballot for the Asefat Hanivharim, which was chosen according to proportional representation. Within the framework of Knesset Israel were also local communal entities, kehillot, wherever there were at least thirty permanent Jewish residents. In cooperation with these kehillot and in pursuance of its organic power formalized in 1928, Knesset Israel, through the Asefat Hanivharim, Vaad Leumi, and Cabinet-like executive committee of thirteen members, heading various departments, acted in the Jewish community in matters of health, education, social work, citizenship, immigration, and defense. Supreme religious authority was vested in the Council of the Chief Rabbinate of Knesset Israel. While at first taxation was voluntary, by virtue of its formal status from 1928 to 1948 Knesset Israel acquired some taxing authority enforceable in the civil courts.

In addition to the Yishuv's quasi-governmental institutions, there was another organization relating to the Jews outside Palestine. When the Council of the League of Nations approved the British mandate for Palestine in June, 1922, it provided for "an appropriate Jewish agency . . . for the purpose of advising and cooperating with the Administration of Palestine in such economic, social and other matters as may affect the establishment of a Jewish National Home and the interests of the Jewish population in Palestine, and, subject always to the control of the Administration, to assist and take part in the development of the country." Thus the World Zionist Organization served as that agency in advising and cooperating with the mandate authorities on immigration, agricultural settlement, education, and other matters to implement the idea of a "national home."

Dr. Chaim Weizmann, president of the World Zionist Organization, seeking to involve as well the non-Zionist communal authorities throughout the world in the task of Jewish self-determination, initiated in 1929 an expanded Jewish Agency, which offered equal representation for Zionists and non-Zionists. This new organ served as a liaison between world Jewry and the Yishuv, and also between world Jewry and the mandate authorities. As time went on, the Palestinian Jews, represented in the Agency along with Jews from other countries, virtually took over the political leadership of the Agency and staffed its technical and clerical positions; by 1948, when Israel declared its independence, the chairman of the Jewish Agency, David Ben-Gurion, became Prime Minister of the state, Moshe Shertok (later Hebraizing his name to Sharett), the political secretary, took over as Foreign Minister, and so on down the line—with a few rare exceptions where Israeli nonmembers of the Agency were given relatively minor posts in the Cabinet. The technical and clerical staff of the organization provided the basis for the Israeli civil service.

The Jewish Agency did not disappear with the establishment of the state, although it could no longer speak for the "interests of the Jewish population" in that country, which now had its own sovereign existence. The Agency continued as an international nongovernmental body and functioned as coordinator of all Jewish overseas efforts for Israel—particularly in matters of stimulating Aliyah (although the settlement and integration of immigrants since 1967 has become more and more a governmental function, with a special Cabinet ministry), of fostering Jewish education and culture in the Diaspora, and of guidance for investment in Israel. In the summer of 1971, the Agency was reorganized and enlarged to include additional non-Zionists.

The British mandate terminated at midnight, Friday, May 14— a calculated or bumbling last act of an embarrassed and embittered British administration. The Jewish Sabbath starts on Friday evening at sundown. Later in the afternoon of that Friday, some 600 hurriedly invited persons gathered to hear the People's Council, under the galvanizing leadership of Ben-Gurion, declare the independence of the new state whose name the invited guests did not even know (Judea was the best guess). Then Ben-Gurion's voice, in clear and forceful tones, sent a thrill through the anxious audience: "Accordingly, we, the members of the People's Council representing the Jewish people in Palestine and the Zionist movement in the world, met together in solemn assembly by virtue of the natural and historic right of the Jewish people and the resolution of the General Assembly of the United Nations, hereby proclaim the establishment of the Jewish state in Palestine, to be called Israel."

Soon after the last signature was affixed to the document and the last words of the *Sheheheyanu,* the age-old blessing of the Almighty for "having kept us in life, sustaining us and enabling us to reach this season," the Sabbath candles were lit in Tel Aviv's homes, but Messianic dreams were soon to be translated into statistics, charts, and graphs and acted out in a cruel struggle for survival.

The November 29, 1947, partition resolutions of the United Nations provided that each of the two states carved out of Palestine establish a provisional council to maintain elementary law and order within their respective boundaries. The Yishuv set up a People's Council in March, 1948, in preparation for independence. Thus, when the state was proclaimed, the People's Council assumed the authority of acting as the Provisional State Council of Israel and its People's Administration was empowered to proceed as a provisional government.

Broadly speaking, the Provisional Government took over the departments of the Executive of the Vaad Leumi and the Jewish Agency, and collated or expanded them into thirteen ministries. The forty or fifty departments and bureaus of the British administration were allocated among the new ministries.

The democratic impulses of the state were in evidence at its very incipience. In the face of a war of annihilation, the Provisional State Council and the Provisional Government could have very well preempted prerogatives and could have served on an emergency basis for an indefinite period. Instead, they voted themselves out of existence upon the election of a broadly based Constituent Assembly and the election of a new Cabinet.

It was a risky business to launch a political campaign with twenty-one political parties vying for public favor! This was "democracy with a vengeance" in a country numbering only about 1 million people. However, it was a risk well worth taking. The elections to the 120-member Constituent Assembly were held on January 25, 1949, eight months after the declaration of independence. All males and females over the age of eighteen were granted the right to vote, and those over the age of twenty-one were eligible for election under the system of proportional representation. Twelve out of twenty-one parties obtained one or more seats. Three of the elected were Arabs.

The first major problem to confront the Constituent Assembly was the definition of Israeli democracy. It soon became evident that in the new state it was easier to practice democracy than to capture it in the printed word. There ensued an intense intellectual struggle splitting the parliamentarians into two camps: those who advocated a written constitution and those who were against reducing democracy to a single "suffocating" document.

The constitutionalists cited the United Nations partition resolution of November 29, 1947, which said: "The Constituent Assembly of each state shall draft a constitution for its state." Moreover, they argued, the idea of a "constitution by evolution" through a series of "fundamental laws" was not the same as a written constitution. Fundamental laws, they insisted, may be changed or rescinded by a simple majority, whereas it usually takes a two-thirds or three-fourths majority to amend a constitutional provision. It would be megafolly and sheer irresponsibility, stormed the constitutionalists —mostly legalists and academicians—to leave the freedoms of the people to the mercies of a simple majority which could be obtained easily by an arbitrary government. As to the argument that constitutions were restrictive and suffocating, Professor Benjamin Akzin of the Hebrew University pointed out that the cumulative experience of other states in modern times could be used to avoid the shortcomings, the "throttling" and "impeding" clauses of the organic document.

The forces opposed to a written constitution were led by David Ben-Gurion. He felt that the country should not be bound by a document, a "holy writ," so long as it awaited millions and millions of newcomers who should have a voice in determining their future. In addition, he thought that under wartime conditions it would be impossible to deal justly with the Arab citizens of Israel. Also, a written constitution would have to either declare separation of "synagogue" from state, thus snatching power from the religious authorities who maintained the Jewish heritage throughout the long years of the Diaspora, or decree Judaism the state religion, which would give the rabbinic authorities and their adherents a privileged position, implying disadvantages for secularists, nonconformists, and non-Jews.

In the end it was Ben-Gurion's point of view that prevailed. The Constituent Assembly, by virtue of the fact that it was freely elected and was fully representative of the people, became the First Knesset. In 1950 the new legislative body resolved that whenever customs and legal processes asserted themselves through general public acceptance, and whenever time and the occasion required, these would be enacted as fundamental laws and would be considered sections of the constitution-to-be—basic-law snapshots to be put together in a constitutional album. Thus far, four such organic measures have been considered and passed by the parliament. The first deals with the makeup and functions of the Knesset (1958); the second with Israeli lands (1960); the third with the powers, prerogatives, and limitations of the Presidency (1964); and the fourth with the functions of the government (1968). Still another, the Fundamental Law of Human Rights, is in preparation at this writing.

In addition, the Knesset had passed significant bills that do not have the designation "fundamental laws" but have the elements of permanence and "constitutionality" and that in time, no doubt, will be incorporated in either their present or a modified form into a constitution. Among such measures are the State Comptroller Law, the Law of Return, the Equal Rights of Women Law, the Nationality Law, the Judges Law, and the Election Law of 1969.

The two most elementary rights of a citizen in a democracy are free speech and the right to vote. The Israelis exercise these, especially the former, with boundless energy—within the confines of very broad regulations such as forbidding the blaring of loudspeakers on vehicles moving through city streets, although amplifiers are allowed at public meetings. Use of films, radio, and TV is restricted for a specified period before election day. Each party is entitled to "equal time" plus a fixed number of additional minutes for each seat it held in the outgoing Knesset. "Nursing" constituents, that is, dispersing free gifts, food or drink, and sideshows and other entertainment to lure audiences to campaign meetings, is also barred.

The Law of Return, which confers citizenship with its rights and obligations to every Jew as soon as he clears customs and is properly entered into the Population Register, has in many cases exuberant effects on election day. The Electoral Register is brought up to date annually and official notification of one's inclusion in this directory is given each new citizen along with information about polling stations. Copies of the registers are placed in post offices and in other public buildings. Thus new citizens who seemingly only yesterday were politically destitute, living in medieval societies or under the oppressive rule of a modern dictatorship, find themselves exercising the other most cherished prerogative of democracy: assent, dissent, or neither—the last least likely in Israel.

Jews acquiring Israeli citizenship need not renounce their previous nationality. It is possible, therefore, for Israeli Jews to maintain dual citizenship. This was deemed desirable because of the task of ingathering and integration. Thus newcomers would not be coerced into adjustment and would be at liberty to leave the country when they wished. It was also felt that immigrants from the "lands of prosperity and freedom" would be less reluctant to give Israel a try.

The Law of Return was a unique experiment in granting a legal right to every persecuted (or free) Jew to return to his "homeland" —except when the immigrant was considered to be acting against the Jewish people or was likely to endanger the health, welfare, and the safety of the land. However, its major purpose was to provide a solution to the specific problem of the stateless Jew.

As far as non-Jews are concerned, naturalization is a process similar to that in most other countries. The applicant must be eighteen or older and entitled to reside permanently in Israel. He or she also must be a resident of the country at the time of application, having lived in Israel at least three years preceding the citizenship request. The applicant must have some knowledge of Hebrew and must renounce former nationality or prove that he will cease to be a foreign subject upon becoming a citizen of Israel, and that he will make the country his legal domicile.

The Knesset, however, attached several exemptions to the Nationality Law as far as non-Jews were concerned. The broadest of these is the authority granted the Minister of the Interior, who has legal jurisdiction in the implementation of the legal provisions, to excuse an applicant for naturalization from any one or more regulations except the condition of being entitled to reside permanently in Israel and making the country his fixed domicile.

Like the elections to the Constituent Assembly, the elections to the Knesset are also universal, nationwide, direct, equal, secret, and

Theodor Herzl, founder
of political Zionism.

David Ben-Gurion, archi-
tect of the state of Israel
and its first Prime Minister.

The Qumran caves, on the shore of the Dead Sea, where 2,000-year-old Hebrew scrolls were found in 1947.

Photo: Israel Office of Information

The Mount of Beatitudes, overlooking the Sea of Galilee, where the Sermon on the Mount was preached.

Photo: Israel Office of Information

Aharon David Gordon,
Labor-Zionist ideologist
and spiritual father of
the kibbutz movement.

Deganiah, the first kibbutz.

An Arid Zone Research Center in the Negev.

Photo: Israel Office of Information

Samaritans praying at their synagogue in Holon.

*Photo: Israel Office
of Information*

Rejoicing at the Western (Wailing) Wall.

Photo: Israel Office of Information

A Bedouin market place in Beersheba.   *Photo: Israel Office of Information*

The new Mosque of Peace in Nazareth.   *Photo: Israel Office of Information*

A family in the Florentin Quarter, Tel Aviv, using antique cups as a Hannukiah.   *Photo: Israel Office of Information*

An instructress talking to a recent arrival from an Atlas Mountain village in Morocco. *Photo: Israel Office of Information*

New immigrants learning Hebrew in an ulpan. *Photo: Israel Office of Information*

The Knesset building—home of Israel's parliament. *Photo: Israel Office of Information*

Yad Vashem, memorial to the 6 million Jews killed by the Nazis. *Photo: Israel Office of Information*

proportional. Thus, all citizens over the age of eighteen can cast a ballot (the usual limitations prevail: insanity, and so forth). Each citizen has only one vote; the entire country is regarded as one electoral region; each voter casts his ballot for the party of his choice and its candidates, with no "electors" or other intermediaries; polling booths offer privacy for sealing the ballot in an envelope, which is then dropped in full view of official observers into a ballot box; and each party list that secures the minimum of 1 per cent of the total vote is represented in the Knesset in accordance with its proportion of the vote.

There is no ticket-splitting in Israel. The voter can cast his ballot for one party only, and each party makes up its own slate of candidates in the order in which they will be seated. The larger ones usually present a roll of 120 candidates (the full Knesset membership); the smaller ones content themselves with shorter lists. If a party gets 25 per cent of the vote, the first thirty on its slate are elected (25 per cent of the Knesset membership). If it gets 10 per cent, the first twelve are seated.

Any citizen of Israel twenty-one years old or older may become a candidate for Knesset, except holders of these offices: President, Chief Rabbi, State Comptroller, judge, government-salaried religious functionaries (rabbis, ministers, qadis, and so forth), army personnel, and senior civil servants, unless they have resigned from their posts at least 100 days before election time.

The First Knesset met initially in Tel Aviv in a converted cinema house, but on December 11, 1949, it took a historic and somewhat defiant decision to move to Jerusalem—as the United Nations was contemplating the internationalization of the city. A great many diplomatic missions—among them the American, Russian, British, and French—remained in Tel Aviv, while a slowly growing number of other states have established their legations in Jerusalem.

Even in the old-new capital, the Knesset's first dwelling place was a converted block of private homes, but in 1966 an attractive building was erected on an elevation commanding a broad view of Jerusalem. The edifice was put up with funds bequeathed by James

A. de Rothschild, a son of Baron Edmond Rothschild, who contributed so much to the building of Jewish Palestine in the nineteenth and early twentieth centuries.

The term of a Knesset is four years, but it may vote on new elections before its time is up. It remains in being until a successor parliament is chosen. The unicameral Knesset has the sole power to make or to amend laws. There is no Presidential veto of parliamentary legislation, nor can the Israeli courts, even at the highest instance, declare a law "unconstitutional" or nullify it, as, for example, the Supreme Court in the United States can.

When a bill is introduced in the legislature, it is discussed "in principle" by the whole House in plenary session as a "first reading." If approved by a majority, it is passed on to one of the committees, where it is considered in detail, amended, or changed if deemed necessary, and then returned to the whole House, again in plenary session, for a second reading. An amendment rejected by the committee may be reintroduced by its sponsor at the second reading and tested by a vote of the full Knesset. When all amendments are considered and voted on, the bill as a whole in its final form, including any changes, is put to a vote, as a third reading. If it gains approval it becomes law upon the signature of the President of the State and the appropriate minister or ministers.

Most bills are initiated by the government, but private bills, that is, legislation introduced by any member of the parliament, or committee bills, proposed by any one of the parliamentary committees, are also common.

The consent of the Knesset is needed for the induction of a new government, which must resign upon losing the "trust" of that body; that is, a new government must be formed as soon as the legislature passes a no-confidence vote. Such a vote may be demanded at any time by any of the parties and takes precedence over all other items on the agenda. When a government falls it continues as a caretaker until a new government is put together.

It is difficult to overstate the significant role that the Knesset committees play in the parliamentary life of the country. There are standing committees dealing with legislation, constitution, finance, labor, foreign affairs, security, House affairs, home affairs, economic affairs, education and culture, and public services. These and other committees also serve as forums for contact between the legislature and other communal bodies. Subcommittees, in some instances, deal with public grievances. The office of ombudsman was recently established and attached to parliamentary committees.

Interpellations, questioning the government by any member of the Knesset, may be done by submitting, through the office of the Speaker of the House, a query in writing to the relevant minister. The latter must reply orally within two weeks during a special period set aside for this purpose at the beginning of every parliamentary meeting. This is known as "quiz-time." A brief supplemental oral question is allotted during that time to the original inquirer. It is usually employed to censure the minister or the government, or to request withheld information to which, in the view of the inquirer, the public is entitled.

An additional way to keep the government responsive is for a member of parliament, believing that in the public interest a particular matter ought to be taken up in open debate, to offer a "motion for the agenda." The minister within whose jurisdiction the matter lies makes his reply, whereupon the Knesset votes on one of three possible actions: conduct a debate, refer the matter to committee, or drop it completely.

Another important function of the Knesset is to approve the annual budget. It also advises the President on appointments to public office.

The parliamentary debates in Israel are often colorful and vigorous. At times they are witty, as when a member of the legislature complained in mock bitterness after the defeat of a bill he sponsored: "For two thousand years we prayed for a state—and it had to happen to me!"

The language of the proceedings is Hebrew, with simultaneous Arabic translation. Arab members of the Knesset may address the House in Arabic, which is simultaneously rendered into Hebrew.

The Knesset elects a Speaker and a number of Deputy Speakers from among its own members. They make up the Presidium of the Knesset. The duties of the Speaker are similar to those in the House of Commons in Great Britain or the House of Representatives in the United States—mainly to preside over the session and maintain parliamentary procedure. In the absence of the President of the State, as, for example, when he is out of the country, the Speaker takes over as Acting President.

Members of the parliament enjoy immunities and privileges that may be lifted only by the Knesset itself. They are protected against libel, slander, and other lawsuits and arrest (unless they are in the process of committing acts of violence, disturbing the peace, or committing treason).

One of the duties of the Knesset is to choose the President of the State, whose office is highly respected but mostly ceremonial. It was during the transitional period before the election of the constituent assembly that the character of the Presidential functions was determined. In fact, there was an intense difference of opinion between the prestigious and world-renowned president of the World Zionist Organization, Dr. Chaim Weizmann, who was picked as the Provisional President of Israel, and the iron-willed "short man who became a giant," David Ben-Gurion. The former proposed the strong American Presidential system, in which the head of state is also the chief executive.

Ben-Gurion advocated the Italian or pre–de Gaulle French system, in which the head of state is only "decorative," as Weizmann called it. Weizmann lost because, like another President, Woodrow Wilson, he was much more popular outside his country than at home. To the Israelis, Weizmann's mildly pro-British sympathies before the establishment of the state were not a Presidential asset. Yet they felt deeply gratified that he, one of the century's most eminent chemists and a statesman whose personal conduct had enriched the moral and scientific treasury of his age, had accepted the highest honor their country had to offer. One of Weizmann's close friends put the President's relationship to Israel in the words of a

Talmudic scholar: "Mount Sinai is lofty only because Moses stood at its top."

Weizmann's personal disappointment in the Israeli Government, which saw in his Presidency an exalted symbol, fumed up from time to time in puffs of indignation. When the American President Harry Truman asked his Israeli counterpart why the latter did not use his powers in bringing about a solution to the Arab refugee problem, Weizmann replied: "I am only a constitutional President, and it is outside my province. My handkerchief is the only thing I can stick my nose into. In everything else it's Ben-Gurion's nose."

The second and third Presidents of Israel were immensely popular in the country but hardly known outside it. Itzhak Ben-Zvi was the chairman of the pre-state Vaad Leumi, the National Council. His naïveté, his love of people, and especially his affection for the Orientals, whom he invited to his unpretentious quarters, contributed a great deal to the smoothing over of early difficulties between the two Israels, the Easterners and the Westerners. To this day, tales abound about the concern of Ben-Zvi, who died in 1963, for the underprivileged. One of the tales has it that when Ben-Zvi became President he was given a sentry to guard the entrance to his home. One cold and rainy night, Ben-Zvi remembered the soldier outside. The President came out and asked the guard to come in and have a glass of tea with him. The sentry replied politely: "Thank you, Mr. President, I am greatly honored, but I cannot leave my post without a replacement." To which Ben-Zvi answered: "I understand. Orders are orders. Why don't you then go inside for a while and I'll stand guard for you?"

The third President of Israel, Zalman Shazar, also was a non-controversial figure. He did much to unify the various labor factions before and after the establishment of the state. Like so many of the elder statesmen in the country, he too was a synthesis of Jewish traditional smalltown upbringing and of secular European culture. A gifted orator and a master of Hebrew style, his speech and writing carried biblical accents. Like Ben-Zvi, a non-Marxist socialist, Shazar's ideology was rooted much more in Isaiah and

Amos than in Marx or Kautsky. Universally beloved, he appealed to
the rank and file of labor and was esteemed by Orthodox Jews in
and out of Israel and by Yiddish secularists and socialists in the
United States. The second and third Presidents have done perhaps
more than anyone else to bring together the "scattered tribes of
Israel."

Above party squabbles and machinations, the President of the
country is chosen for a five-year period and may be re-elected to
another term. His principal duty is to consult the representatives
of the various parties before calling on a leader to form a new government. His other functions are appointing Israeli judges and
diplomats (on the recommendation of the Knesset), accepting the
accreditation of foreign diplomats, countersigning all laws passed
by the Knesset (except those concerning Presidential powers), com-
muting sentences, and pardoning prisoners.

The forming of a new government in Israel begins with the
summoning by the President of the leaders of the various parties
represented in the parliament and learning their views as to whom
they would like to see as Prime Minister and who, in their opinion,
would succeed in setting up a Cabinet capable of gaining the initial
confidence of the Knesset and of keeping it through the foreseeable
future. The Presidential choice is not easy to make. No party, thus
far, has been able to get a majority of the seats in the Knesset to
empower it, at least at first, to control the affairs of the state. Usually
it is the leader of the plurality party (with most but not the majority of seats) who is asked by the President to put together a coalition Cabinet.

The leader, or Prime Minister designate, then begins negotiations
with the heads of other political parties. If he is successful in per-
suading them to join his government, he can secure a majority of
votes in the Knesset and insure for his coalition Cabinet a vote of
confidence.

The number of ministries in a Cabinet varies according to political and personal exigencies. The first Cabinet had thirteen posts,
a recent one comprised twenty-four. Most ministers, but not all,

must be members of the Knesset. The Cabinet is collectively responsible to the legislature. It continues in power until its resignation, the resignation of the Prime Minister, a vote of no confidence in the parliament, or the election of a new Knesset. In any of these cases the Cabinet continues as "caretaker" until the new government is inaugurated. Ministers may appoint deputy ministers after notifying and receiving the tacit if not the formal approval of the parliament.

The chief executive power is vested in the Cabinet. The individual members are in charge of their respective departments. Under the guidance and direction of the Prime Minister, the Cabinet formulates the policies of the government, and after they receive the broad approval of the Knesset they are effectuated by the government. If there is dissatisfaction in the Knesset with the implementation of a plan or a program by any of the ministers, there may be a call for a no-confidence vote. If the motion passes, the entire Cabinet resigns. If a Cabinet member is not in agreement with the Prime Minister or with his colleagues on a major policy to be tested in the parliament in a confidence vote, and if he is inclined to vote against it or abstain from voting, he must resign before the Knesset takes action. (In some rare instances, coalition partners have been allowed by the Cabinet to abstain.)

This principle of collective responsibility in Israeli coalition Cabinets has had its difficult moments. Yet somehow, perhaps because of the constant threat to the very existence of the state, the government has maintained remarkable stability through the years.

One of the formal but key appointments by the President is to the office of State Comptroller. The President makes his designation only upon the recommendation of the Knesset. It is the State Comptroller who keeps vigil over the political well being and economic efficiency of all political agencies in the state, national and local. Even enterprises that are mostly private but in which the state has a share are susceptible to his review. Thus the entire financial structure of the state is subject to his scrutiny. His office has the power to conduct periodic and spot checks to determine proper expenditure of public monies. Also, his office publishes an Annual Report, with balance sheets of state assets and liabilities, which, of course, get tremendous play in the public communications media. Appointed for a five-year period, the Comptroller General may be reappointed at the expiration of his term. Once in office, he is responsible only to the Knesset and is entirely independent of the government and its administrative agencies.

Even Jews, raised on Talmudic disputations and nurtured in the casuistics of later commentaries and law codes, find the legal system in Israel a real challenge. The cloak of justice is a crazy quilt, a patchwork begun when iconoclastic Abraham brought his monotheism from Ur of the Chaldeans unto idol-worshiping Canaan along with, perhaps, some vestiges of the Babylonian Hammurabi Code.

It will be remembered from previous chapters that Jewish religious experience was recorded in the Written Law (the Bible) and the Oral Law (the Talmud), and later, in the sixteenth century, it was codified in the Shulhan Arukh, adhered to mainly by Orthodox Jews in the Holy Land and elsewhere.

The Arab takeover of Palestine in the seventh century stitched new and colorful muslin and damask onto the legal patchwork of the land. The crusaders brought with them their own criss-cross material. The Ottoman conquest superimposed Turkish tapestry over much of the crazy quilt, with French, Italian, and Greek frills. The English imposed their statutory woof and common-law warp in 1922, when they arrived as mandatory power in Palestine.

Thus, when the State of Israel was created in 1948, the legal system was a multi-hued spread, in part top-heavy with several layers of ill-fitting patches, and in part torn and not even mendable.

Personal status law (marriage, divorce, wills, and so on) was reserved for the religious courts, Muslim, Jewish, and Christian; land law and civil law, for the most part, were based on Ottoman practice; criminal law was adjusted to the English system.

The lawmaking institutions in the country, therefore, had a serious problem on their hands. Dressing little Israel in a new cloak of justice made out of material that was partly durable, having withstood the test of time, and partly flimsy, shabby, and faded seemed a hopeless task. In addition, for two thousand years, Jews in the Diaspora tried, for persuasive empirical reasons, to avoid government courts whenever possible. They had their own Batei Din (houses of justice) or appeared with their complaints before their rabbis. It took some mental adjusting for the Jews of the Ukraine, Kurdistan, or Morocco to trust the courts or to appeal to a policeman. On the other hand, there was an element in the Jewish community that took the Israeli law tribunals and enforcement officers rather lightly: Would a Jewish policeman in a Jewish state arrest a fellow Jew? Would a Jewish judge in a Jewish state send a fellow Jew to prison?

Despite the many difficulties, the courts in Israel have been able to work with the ancient fabric of justice and at the same time to assert that orderly change in judicial process, as well as in institutions, must not and cannot be resisted. Thus code law joins with case law and common law to make up the new pattern of the country's legal system.

The first step taken in the new state was to immunize the courts from political influence and to ensure their independence. "Only the law and the judge's conscience bind the judge in Israel." There is no interference in the exercise of his judicial functions. To guarantee the complete freedom of the court, judges and magistrates are appointed by the President on the recommendation of an independent nominations committee, composed of the minister of justice, who is chairman, another Cabinet member, two members of the Knesset, the president and two justices of the Supreme Court, and two practicing attorneys elected by the Association of Advocates. The appointments are for life, or until retirement at age seventy or earlier for reasons of health or malfeasance.

Judges of the various religious courts—Jewish, Muslim, Christian, Druze—are appointed by the respective denominations, and their tenure of office is similar to that of civil judges.

To the uninitiated, the court system in Israel is bewildering.

There are, as noted, the various civil and tribal courts and multifarious administrative tribunals. Among the latter are Tenancy Tribunals, National Insurance Tribunals, Tax Tribunals, and the like.

At the top of the judiciary is the Supreme Court, sitting in Jerusalem. It is composed of ten members—a president, a deputy president, and eight justices. Cases are heard by three or, on rare occasions, five members. This body is both appellate and a court of first instance. In its primary capacity it hears appeals, in a panel of three, against district court judges. Its decisions are final, unless at the discretion of the president a case is directed to be reheard by a panel of five judges. As a court of first instance it acts as a court of high justice, dealing with matters outside the jurisdiction of other tribunals. Thus it may issue orders to officials for the release of prisoners it deems unlawfully detained (writs of habeas corpus), to public authorities whose action or inaction has impeded law, or to other tribunals to confine themselves within their jurisdictions. Any citizen who believes that an official, national or local, has misused or exceeded his legal authority may apply directly to the Supreme Court for redress. The Supreme Court also exercises supervisory powers over denominational tribunals.

Beneath the Supreme Court are four district courts—in Jerusalem, Tel Aviv, Haifa, and Beersheba. The Haifa court also acts as Admiralty Court. Actions not triable by magistrates come within the jurisdiction of the district courts, except for cases of personal status, which may come before the religious courts. As a rule, a trial is presided over by one judge, unless it involves a crime punishable by imprisonment of ten years or more, in which case three judges sit on the bench. There is no jury system in Israel, and it is for the judge or judges to decide all questions of fact or law. The country has no capital punishment except in cases of treason in wartime and collaboration with the Nazis. When a capital case is tried, a Supreme Court justice presides over the district court. The district court also may hear appeals from administrative tribunals or quasi-judicial bodies.

The magistrate courts sit in the major cities and towns of the land and deal with misdemeanors. Their criminal and civil jurisdiction is limited to offenses punishable by no more than three years' imprisonment or to claims not exceeding 3,000 Israeli lire (a lira is roughly equivalent to twenty-four American cents).

There is a maze of municipal courts that have jurisdiction in matters of town planning, public health, factory law, and the like. The maximum sentence that may be imposed by these courts is fifteen days of imprisonment and a fine of up to 750 lire. Outside the largest cities, most municipal judges are laymen appointed by the Minister of Justice and serve without pay. Juvenile courts, labor courts, and traffic courts have limited jurisdiction within very narrowly defined areas.

As for the religious courts, discussed earlier, each of the major denominations has its tribunals of first instance and appeal. These concern themselves with questions of personal status, such as marriage, divorce, alimony, wills, probate, custody of children, adoption, and paternity. They may, if all parties agree, also hear civil suits. Among the recognized religious communities are the Jewish, the Muslim, the Druze, a variety of Catholic, the Protestant, the Greek Orthodox, the Melkite, and the Maronite.

The tribal courts were established by the British and continued by the Israelis to accommodate the special needs of the Bedouins. They settle internal disputes according to their own customs and common sense.

Local government in Israel has retained many of the features of the British-mandated Palestine. To satisfy the nationalist strivings of both Arabs and Jews, the English reluctantly but progressively extended some of the powers of the municipalities. Greater autonomy was granted to urban centers under the Israeli regime, but local government did not play a significant part in the politics of the land because proportional representation tends to focus attention on national rather than parochial problems and because the early settlers who later emerged as the leaders of the country were bent upon "normalizing" Jewish life, negating urbanization and glorifying "self-realization through agricultural labor." (An exception was Tel Aviv, the "all-Jewish city," when arduous attempts were made to render it as autonomous as possible under the British rule.) Moreover, too much local autonomy, it was thought by Jewish leaders, would fragment the national effort, the "united will of the people," particularly in matters of defense. In addition, since municipal elections were also based on proportional representation, the national parties merely localized their campaigns, which were still directed by their central headquarters. Thus on the municipal level administration was merely a miniature of the national government—coalitions among two, three, or more parties.

Elected every four years, local government authorities handled such matters as education, sanitation, social welfare, public parks, and tax rates. The larger urban centers enjoy the status of municipalities. There were about 30 of them in 1971, two of which were Arab. Smaller towns, about 110 in number, including some 50 Arab and Druze, were ranked as Local Councils. Besides these, there were 50 Regional Councils encompassing approximately 700 villages. Various settlements could band together to deal with such problems as secondary education, agricultural projects, sewage, and so forth.

All local units are under the supervision of the Ministry of the Interior, especially in matters of budgeting and expenditure. The Comptroller General also has a right to check the fiscal and administrative procedures of all local authorities.

Eastern Jews, for obvious reasons, find it easier to be elected to municipalities and Local and Regional Councils, especially in the Negev, than to national offices. The national parties also encourage them to run for local posts, to demonstrate their "even-handedness" and the political opportunities they afford to their Oriental brothers. While there was some political solecism in this gesture, it nonetheless provided the inexperienced and politically unsophisticated citizens a good schooling in the art of government, so that in time they were able to assume more important roles on the national level, or at least to make themselves heard.

8 Political Parties

The late Prime Minister of Israel, Levi Eshkol, is reputed to have said that if Moses had to work with political parties, the Israelites would still be in Egypt. Yet ever since the creation of the state, Israelis have been among the stablest voters in the world. Even the tremendous influx of Oriental immigration in the 1950's and the drums of war in the 1960's did not change the basic balance of power among the multitudinous parties in this small land. In the view of political analysts and public opinion experts, this is so because there are in the country several distinct core groups with "floating ideologies," which maintain "separate selves," although they may combine temporarily with other entities for some specific goals. In the United States the aim of the political party is to gain votes and to win control over the government. In Israel the purpose of the party is not only to gain votes but also to gain voters or followers; not only to be part of the government but also to provide it with an ideological pattern, a philosophic orientation. Temporary economic setbacks or successes, therefore, do not have the same impact on the political behavior of the Israeli as they do on the American voter or, for that matter, on the British or the Australian voter.

The core groups have historical antecedents. The various shadings of socialism go back to the nineteenth century and the beginning of

the twentieth, primarily to the Second Aliyah and the Third Aliyah.
Jews had been in the forefront of the revolutionary movements in
Russia, Hungary, and Germany and were also prominent in the
leadership of the socialist parties in Western Europe, hoping that
the universal emancipation and freedom they sought would auto-
matically apply to Jews. Moses Hess, Ber Borochov and A. D. Gordon were among the first to realize that the myth was in trouble.
Later the Jewish socialists Berl Katzenelson and Nachman Syrkin
discovered that even when the revolution succeeded and where
socialism took root, the "Jewish problem" was not solved. It was
therefore natural for Jewish idealists to turn to the land that
sprouted the social justice of Isaiah and of Amos. Once in Palestine,
they advocated the "conquest of labor" (kibbush avodah), the "religion of labor" (dat avodah), and the "normalization of Jewish
life"—the doing away with expropriation and exploitation on the
one hand, and the fostering of cooperative and collective projects,
on the other.

The first labor party in Palestine, Hapoel Hatzair, was organized
in 1905. It advocated personal settlement on the soil and "personal
realization through labor." Like the Fabians in England, it rejected
the concept of class struggle. It also declined to join the international workers' movements. Members of Hapoel Hatzair founded
the first kibbutz and the first moshav ovdim. In 1907 it inaugurated
an ideological journal, giving it the name of the party, *Hapoel
Hatzair* (the young worker).

In 1919 another party, somewhat more radical in socialist orienta-
tion was founded—Ahdut Avodah (not to be confused with a
later party, LeAhdut Avodah, but popularly called also Ahdut
Avodah). The two workers' groups had combined in 1930 into
Mifleget Poalim Eretz Yisraelit (The Labor Party of Eretz Israel)
—Mapai.

Mapai emerged as the strongest single political entity before and
after the establishment of the state. It became even more potent
when it virtually absorbed two other labor groups in 1968 to become
Mifleget Avodah Yisraelit (Israel Labor Party) or, for short, Avo-

dah. Nevertheless, despite its added strength, it could not quite attain majority status in the multiparty state.

In its phrased ideology of 1930, Mapai declared:

Jewish labor is united by these historic aims: devotion to the rebirth of the Jewish nation in Palestine as a free laboring people, rooted in all branches of the agricultural and industrial economy; dedication to the development of the Hebrew language and culture; membership in the working class of the world in its struggle for the abolition of class oppression and denial of social rights in any and every form; the aspiration to transfer natural wealth and the means of production to the control of all workers; the building of a society based on labor, equality, and liberty.

Soon after its formation, Mapai joined the Second Socialist International, to which the British Labour Party and similar national organizations belong.

Mapai's major tenets did not change much through the years. The socialist but non-Marxist platform, because it refused to promise "absolutes," appealed to many people. Led by such personalities as Berl Katzenelson, David Ben-Gurion, Levi Eshkol, Itzhak Ben-Zvi, Zalman Shazar, Golda Meir, and Abba Eban, it did not indulge in moralizing on the evils of capitalism, nor did it deplore "primitive Marxism." It was open to new ideas but did not abandon old ones without a struggle.

While in fact running the powerful Histadrut, the General Federation of Labor—a nonpolitical, all-embracing trade union organization—Mapai did not discourage the private sector in the country, working on the Ber Borochov principle that Jewish capital must be funneled into Israel to create a demand for Jewish proletariat as a process in occupational redistribution and economic normalization of the Jewish people. It supported what its leaders considered "very constructive initiative, public or private." In foreign affairs it attempted a policy of "no identification" with the Western bloc or Eastern bloc, but in outlook, orientation, and support it leaned more and more to the West.

As the prime and dominant element in every coalition government Israel has ever had, Mapai took accumulatory pride in, and credit for, the achievements of the new state. As an opposition leader remarked sardonically, "In the beginning God created the heavens, the earth, and Mapai. Then Mapai did the rest." In the eyes of the new immigrants, it was Mapai who brought them to Israel, who provided them with shelter, who fed them. Thus even the unsophisticated, socially unaware, and mostly devout Orthodox newcomers voted for the socialist Mapai. The party eventually became the Establishment, with all that the term implies—bureaucracy, red tape, an "old guard." Mapai's representation in the Knesset from 1948 until its union with the labor groups in 1968 ranged between 42 and 47 out of the 120 seats.

LeAhdut Avodah or Ahdut Avodah (For Unity of Labor) was a reincarnation of sorts of its 1919 namesake. It broke away from Mapai in 1944 to join more leftist laborites and to form in 1946 the Marxist Mapam. In 1954, however, it split with Mapam to maintain a separate existence until it completely merged with Mapai and another group to form Mifleget Avodah Yisraelit, or Avodah party. Why this tortuous road? Mapai's socialism was too vague, too innocuous for leaders like Itzhak Tabenkin (the party's octogenarian theoretician who died in the summer of 1971), Yigal Allon (military commander and future Deputy Prime Minister), Israel Galili (underground commander and later member of several Cabinets), Itzhak Ben-Aharon (in time to become secretary of the Histadrut). They felt the need to uphold the "fragile dignity of the socialist state." Intellectually mobile, Tabenkin and his comrades had a commitment to socialism *per se*. They were struggling with the problem of not only how to make a man fit into present society, but also how to make him outgrow it, nurtured by the Jewish heritage and universal socialist values. Mapam's inflexible Marxism and its support of the Soviet Union despite that country's anti-Zionism and anti-Semitism impelled the less doctrinaire Tabenkin, Allon, Galili, and Ben-Aharon to split with their comrades in 1954 and to form Ahdut Avodah.

The new party's aims included a more pioneering Zionism, wide-spread agricultural settlement, a foreign policy of nonidentification with either East or West, and an activist defense posture vis-à-vis the Arab neighbors. Mainly due to the efforts of Ben-Aharon, then referred to as the "conscience" of the labor movement and as the guardian of the political hygiene of the country, who pointed out that the ideological gap between Mapai and Ahdut Avodah was more theoretical than factual, and due also to the receptiveness of the then Mapai Prime Minister, Levi Eshkol, the two parties formed an "alignment" for the Knesset elections in 1965. As the threat to Israeli society increased in 1968, the two parties were joined by a third splinter group to become the Avodah party. During its life-time, Ahdut Avodah elected seven to ten deputies to the Knesset.

Mapam is struggling to maintain its Marxist heritage despite many disappointments regarding the Soviet Union, Mainland China, Czechoslovakia, and other Communist countries. "The joy of being a Marxist is gone," moaned one of the party leaders. Founded in 1948 by the merger of Ahdut Avodah with the leftist Hashomer Hatzair, Mapam, led by Meir Yaari, was initially a strong advocate of closer relations with Moscow but became progressively disap-pointed in the Kremlin's attitude toward Israel and with the treat-ment of the Jews in Russia. The trumped-up charges of spying against Mordekhai Oren, a Mapam leader, during his stay in Czechoslovakia, and his long-term imprisonment in the 1950's (al-though he was later "cleared" and released) embarrassed the party no end.

Kibbutz-oriented, Mapam now stresses more militant domestic socialism and closer cooperation with, and a more generous policy toward, the Arabs. It is especially concerned with Jewish-Arab work-ing-class solidarity. Thus Mapam's representatives in the Knesset in-cluded Arabs (the Communists, as well as Avodah-affiliated Arab parties, also have Arab deputies). In foreign affairs, Mapam now favors a sort of neutrality between East and West for the entire Mid-dle East region.

As the government in Jerusalem continued to relax its security measures against the Israeli Arabs, granting them all civil rights except compulsory service in the army, and as Moscow failed to stir in a significant way from its refusal to accept permanent peace in the Middle East, the differences between Mapam and Mapai (in its new transformation as the enlarged Avodah party) became less important. They reached a point in 1969 when Mapam joined Avodah in a new "election front" (Maarakh). It had also become a post-election member in the national coalition government. Up to that time it obtained an average of nine seats in the various elections to the parliament.

It was the relentless activist, the scouring moralizer, the premier advocate of a two- or three-party system in Israel, David Ben-Gurion (nearing eighty at the time), who caused a critical rift in the ranks of the proletariat and in the political life of the country in 1965.

Ben-Gurion was born in Plonsk, Poland (then part of Russia), in 1886 and settled in Palestine in 1906. Upon arriving in the new land he worked in various agricultural settlements and set out, with the help of others, to organize a Jewish labor movement, serving later (1921–35) as the chief executive officer of the newly formed, powerful Histadrut. Earlier, feeling the need for more systematic education, Ben-Gurion spent two years (1912–14) studying law in Constantinople. When he came back to Palestine he was expelled by the Turks, who then governed the area, because of his Russian origins and socialist-Zionist activities. From 1915 to 1918 he lived in the United States, where he was active in organizing the Jewish Legion (under British Command), returning to Palestine as a soldier. His dynamic personality eventually brought Ben-Gurion the chairmanship of the Jewish Agency for Palestine (1935–48). In 1942 he formulated the Biltmore Program for the establishment of Palestine as "a Jewish Commonwealth integrated in the structure of the new democratic world."

Ben-Gurion's forceful leadership was largely instrumental in Israel's declaration of independence in 1948. He served as his country's first Prime Minister and Minister of Defense until 1953. For political reasons, sensing a need for the country to "be on its own" or, as others would have it, for "testing the state as to its ability to be on its own," and for personal considerations, Ben-Gurion retired to Sdeh Boker in the Negev to meditate and to study Greek and Buddhist thought. In 1954 a hideous "security operation" in which Israeli agents disguised as Egyptians were sent to blow up the U.S. Information Agency Library in Cairo misfired. The agents were captured and hanged by the Egyptian authorities. Pinhas Lavon, a rising and powerful politician, was Minister of Defense at the time. He claimed that a senior officer, without Lavon's knowledge, had given the orders for the "project." Ben-Gurion was among those who questioned Lavon's innocence, even after he was cleared by a Cabinet committee.

The Lavon Affair and other security considerations brought Ben-Gurion back as Minister of Defense in 1955 and again as Prime-Minister from 1956 to 1963. By the sheer force of his personality and by his insistence that Israel must not be "like unto the other nations" and condone "nefarious international acts," he forced Lavon out of further effective political activity. But Ben-Gurion also developed other deep ideological and personal differences with his colleagues in the government and in Mapai. He insisted on electoral reform, aiming at a constituency system; a shifting of emphasis from East European to West European democratic processes; a diminution in the number of political parties; universal and free secondary education; and the removal from Mapai and the Histadrut of the Old Guard, who, he felt, could not administer a young democracy in the second half of the twentieth century.

Supporting Ben-Gurion was a younger man of great promise, Shimon Peres, who was the former Prime Minister's right hand in the government, especially in matters of defense. Less demonstrative, but nonetheless also a supporter of Ben-Gurion, was Moshe Dayan, former chief of staff and later Minister of Defense. These two also insisted on economic modernization and "self-reliance" in matters of security.

When the Old Guard, under the leadership of Levi Eshkol and Golda Meir, resisted the former leader, Ben-Gurion and his followers formed a new party, Rafi. In spite of the popularity, admiration, and reverence he commanded, Ben-Gurion failed in his political effort. The 1965 Knesset election gained Rafi only ten seats. Piqued, Ben Gurion returned to his kibbutz, Sdeh Boker, in the Negev.

Rafi continued its political activity for a while under the spiritual guidance of Ben-Gurion and the day-to-day leadership of Peres and Dayan. Neither the brilliance of Peres nor the charisma of Dayan could lift the fortunes of the party. After the 1967 Six-Day War, the younger leaders—but not Ben-Gurion—returned to Mapai, which aligned itself with Ahdut Avodah to create the Avodah party. Within the framework of the new political constellation, the struggle between the two major and comparatively young aspirants to the premiership continued. Moshe Dayan was supported by the former Rafi members and other restive elements. Yigal Allon was favored by the former Ahdut Avodah members and the Mapai Old Guard. To avoid damaging conflict between the two after the death of Levi Eshkol, a compromise was struck with the selection of Golda Meir as Prime Minister in March, 1969.

Although a socialist, Meir was a sceptered lady. Born in Russia in 1898 and brought to the United States in 1906, she came to Palestine in 1921 and settled in a cooperative as an agricultural worker. In 1948 Meir was appointed first Israeli Ambassador to the Soviet Union. Later she served as Minister of Labor and as Minister of Foreign Affairs. In 1966 Meir was induced to accept the task of secretary general of the faltering Mapai. During her stewardship of the party she probably wielded more influence than anyone else in the country. When she became Prime Minister in 1969, despite formidable opposition from Ben-Gurion, Moshe Dayan, and Shimon Peres, she had captured the imagination of many of her countrymen, mainly because of her firm stand of not accepting what she called the Arab position of *quid pro nil*. She was also inching toward electoral reforms and moving away from the strict party "curia." In addition, she succeeded in establishing a more cordial relationship with Moshe Dayan, whom she retained in her Cabinet, and Shimon Peres, whom she included in the national coalition government of

1969, without at the same time alienating Yigal Allon, who remained Deputy Prime Minister.

The Avodah party, under the leadership of Meir, thus united three labor groups into one political entity with a total of fifty-five seats in the Knesset (Mapai-Ahdut Avodah, forty-five, and Rafi, ten). When the 1969 parliamentary elections approached, Avodah worked out an "alignment" (Maarakh), not a fusion, with Mapam, which had eight seats in parliament. Thus all the "secular" socialist parties had a total of sixty-three seats—a foreseeable majority in the 120-member Knesset. But the foreseeable did not eventuate. The alignment picked up only fifty-six representatives in the October, 1969, elections—five short of a majority and seven fewer seats than in the previous Knesset. The reason? Most political observers felt it was the desire on the part of the electorate not to change the basic balance of power; not to be at the mercy of a majority party; to preserve maneuverability; and in times of national emergency to have a national coalition government rather than a one-party regime. The tradition of political stability, despite alliances, alignments, and agreements, which had marked Israel since its birth, was therefore maintained.

The Communist "core group" also goes back to 1919. Functioning under a variety of names (Mopsim, Poalei Zion Smole, the Palestine Communist party), it finally crystalized its identity as Maki, Miflagah Kommunistit Yisraelit, in 1948. Its orientation was Marxist-Leninist, and its allegiance was to Moscow. Before the establishment of the state it resisted the notion of Jewish independence in Palestine, viewing Zionism as an instrument of British imperialism. Maki aimed at the "liberation of the Arab masses from both." But in 1948 it accepted the inevitable, especially because the Soviet Union at that time supported the idea of Jewish self-determination. Meir Wilner, one of its leaders, signed the Declaration of Independence. When the Kremlin turned anti-Israel, so did Maki.

For a while Maki followed the Moscow line blindly. The story was told of a Communist member of the Knesset who got up in the House to make a scathing speech against the Israeli Government, the "lackey of Western imperialism," the "oppressor of Arab liberal forces." While talking, he pulled out an umbrella and opened it. Startled, the Speaker of the House asked the Maki leader, "Why did you do that?" The indignant deputy snorted: "It is raining in Moscow!" This apocryphal tale made the rounds on the eve of parliamentary elections, and it cost the Communists many votes. Their following in Israel was small anyway. In its early days, most of the party's membership was Jewish. After 1948 it attracted many more Arabs than Jews, not because the Arabs were won over by Communist ideology but because it gave dissident individuals an opportunity to express their nationalist Arab feelings and to protest against a multitude of real or fancied grievances.

In the early 1960's the party was fragmented along ideological (Peking versus Moscow) as well as ethnic lines. The Six-Day War of 1967 finally brought about a split in the organization and a legal struggle over the name of the party. In January, 1969, the courts ruled that the group headed by Dr. Moshe Sneh, who died in 1972, and Shmuel Mikunis had the right to the original name. The rival faction, with most of the Arab and some of the Jewish following, had assumed the name of Rakah (Reshimah Kommunistit Hadasha), under the leadership of Tawfiq Toubi (Arab) and Meir Wilner (Jewish).

Maki's Marxist diction was somewhat blurred because its ideological landscape—not its principles—had shifted away from Moscow as a result of the Kremlin's adamant stand in the Arab-Israeli struggle, the Czechoslovak occupation, and the hardening of the U.S.S.R.'s doctrinal arteries. It advocated domestically a soft-line Marxist-Leninist economy, and in foreign affairs it wanted more Israeli initiative toward a durable and just Arab-Jewish peace, without the intercession of either Moscow or Washington.

Rakah visited its wrath on capitalism in Israel and fulminated against the evils of bourgeois institutions and the "pseudo-socialist" government, which, Rakah alleged, brought about an imperialist-colonial confrontation with the Arab countries, especially Egypt and Syria, which Rakah felt were on the road to revolutionary socio-economics.

Although both Maki's and Rakah's claims often sounded like tired international Communist phraseology, they were meaningful in Israel and elsewhere because they were freely uttered in their country and abroad. They provided, especially for the Arabs of Israel, an opportunity to break out of their parochialism and to make contact with the outside world. For instance, the most anti-Israel speeches delivered in the Moscow Centennial Lenin celebrations in 1970 and at the Twenty-fourth Communist Party Congress in March, 1971, were made by the Rakah representatives. They were even more extreme than those of the Egyptian delegates.

Neither of the two Communist groups was involved in security-sensitive committees of the Knesset, although Dr. Moshe Sneh, in his earlier days as a member of Mapam and of the General (Liberal) Zionists, was for a while "chief of staff" of the prestate underground Haganah, the defense army. In the 1969 elections, Maki won only one seat and Rakah three seats—two Arabs, one Jew.

Another "core group" was the centrist "private sector" element, which appeared in Palestine during the Third Aliyah (1918–23) but increased in numbers during the Fourth and Fifth Aliyahs. Two factors contributed to the growth of private enterprise in the country. One was the worldwide economic crises of the 1920's, which brought to Palestine entrepreneurs from Poland, Great Britain, the United States, and even South Africa. The other was the rise of Hitler and the flocking of German Jews to Palestine in the 1930's. The country during those years enjoyed a mild economic prosperity, and many of the Nazis' victims chose not to "remain among the tombstones of Europe" but instead to cast their lot with the "Jewish state in the making." It was a selective immigration, especially in the late 1920's and early 1930's, since, courtesy of the British, the gates were open almost exclusively to "capitalists"—anyone with $5,000 or over could enter the country.

Industry and trade grew rapidly in Palestine to the point where they became "distasteful" to the agricultural workers, especially the moshav (cooperative) and kibbutz (collective) elements. As the number of private entrepreneurs increased, they began seeking political power. Two groups emerged. One, appealing to the upper middle class, called itself Zionim Klaliyim, General Zionists. The other, a smaller group, was formed mainly by Central European intellectuals who could not quite identify with socialism yet were fearful of "big business" and possible capitalist exploitation. It chose the name Progressive. In 1961 the two groups coalesced into the Liberal party, but some of the Progressives were unhappy with the fusion and later split away to regain their original existence under a new name, Independent Liberals.

The Liberal party's objectives were expressed in its various election platforms as championing national interests above partisan motives and class needs, encouragement of private and public enterprise as major contributors to the development of Palestine's (later Israel's) maximum absorption capacity, unification of the various parochial and partisan schools (religious, labor, and general) into one national education system. In the late 1960's it added these goals: electoral reform, "depoliticization" of the civil service, national health insurance, and a written constitution.

The Liberal party's political fortunes fluctuated. In 1951, as General Zionists, it elected twenty-three Knesset members and was talking glowingly of forming an "alternative" to Mapai. But, centrist in its orientation, it suffered the fate of centrist movements in many other lands. It failed to develop the kind of imagination, enthusiasm, and devotion that leftists and rightists elicit. It missed creating an image of "pioneers," "militants," "utopians," or "nationalists." It did not come up with "absolutes," "irreducibles," and "nonnegotiables." In fact, in order to salvage some of its sinking fortunes, the Liberal party in 1965 formed an alignment with the rightist, ultra-nationalist Herut to counter the labor alignment of the same year.

Herut had its nascence in the Revisionist movement, founded in 1925 by Vladimir Jabotinsky—a fiery speaker, incandescent writer, and charismatic personality. The Revisionists demanded more militant Zionist dealings with the British and more "class collaboration" in the Yishuv. Before independence, the party advocated the inclusion of "both sides of the Jordan" in the future Jewish state. The Revisionists were the spiritual fathers of the Irgun Zvai Leumi and the Stern Group, the two verbally most martial and functionally most activist underground groups in the resistance to, leading to the breakdown of, British rule in Palestine.

Jabotinsky died in 1940, before the state was established. In 1948, the commander of the Irgun, Menahem Begin, reluctantly acquiesced, after a near-disastrous clash with Ben-Gurion, in the dissolution of his underground organization and formed the Herut (Freedom) party. Much like Jabotinsky, but lacking the magic of distance and the halo of historicity, Begin was a great orator and sharp polemicist whose style had momentum and color, especially in Hebrew. Herut under his leadership became a responsible parliamentary opposition party to the Mapai-dominated coalition governments. To offer more coherent competition to labor, Begin helped form a political front in 1965 of the centrist Liberal party and his own movement and called it Gahal (charcoal, but also the acronym of Gush Herut Liberalim). The new formation did not do well in the 1965 Knesset vote but achieved greater success in the 1969 elections, gaining twenty-six seats, compared with twenty-two in 1965. Still, Gahal did not pose a threat to the combined workers' parliamentary contingent.

Considering the labor governments too "socialistic" and their foreign policy too moderate and conciliatory, Gahal (as a bloc, with Begin as its leader) nevertheless cooperated fully with its political antagonists at all times when the state was threatened by its Arab neighbors. In 1967, on the eve of the Six-Day War, Begin and others in the country pressured Levi Eshkol, then holding the offices of Prime Minister and Minister of Defense, to relinquish the latter post in favor of Moshe Dayan, a political opponent of Begin and the charismatic hero of the 1956 Sinai campaign. The Defense Ministry inevitably would boost Dayan's chances for eventual premiership and certainly would affect Gahal's political stance adversely. But Begin felt that Dayan was the "man of the hour," and he put aside partisan consideration. Moreover, he and another member of Gahal, representing the Liberals, joined a national coalition government in relatively unimportant Cabinet roles under the premiership of Eshkol, with Dayan at the defense helm. In the early 1970's, Begin and five other Gahal members continued to serve in an enlarged coalition, under Avodah Prime Minister Golda Meir, but they quit the government when it indicated it would give up substantial occupied areas for a peace settlement.

Like Mapai and Mapam, the leadership of Herut and the Liberals suffered from a lack of new ideas and new talent, partly because of the hanging-on of the Old Guard. These faults were not accidental: They were moored in East European political tradition.

Still another core group, with floating ideologies sometimes coalescing and sometimes drifting apart, was the religious element. Many of the pious Jews who accepted Zionism had hopes of Jewish religious restoration in the Holy Land. In 1902 the Mizrahi (abbreviation for Merkaz Ruhani, or Spiritual Center) was initiated within the Zionist movement, striving specifically for a homeland in the spirit of the Torah and in observance of the rabbinic laws.

Mizrahi did not envelop all the religious Jews. Many devout as well as nonpious Jews felt that religious political parties were anomalous in the twentieth century, that people of "good faith" should work within the state's secular framework and imbue the institutions with the lofty ideals of Judaism, holiday observance, social justice, and ethical behavior. There were also some ultra-orthodox Jews who distrusted Mizrahi and its involvement in every coalition government since the inception of the state. They argued that moderate Mizrahi made dangerous concessions to heretical ideas, as, for instance, in the matter of "who is a Jew?"

In reply to their opponents, Mizrahi leaders said that one of the most effective ways of stopping current estrangement from institutionalized religion and curbing antireligious legislation was by having parliamentary representation committed to tradition, a group to speak up for or against lawmaking that affected tradition, and to work out compromises on matters that do not touch the very essence of Judaism.

In mundane political affairs the Mizrahi membership had greater affinity with Gahal than with labor, but a sister organization, Hapoel

Hamizrahi (the Mizrahi Worker), was closer to proletarian ideals. It stood for the politicoeconomic principles of socialism within the framework of orthodox Jewry. It spoke of more flexibility in religious ritual and of incorporating relevant contemporary expressions in its youth movement and collective settlements. It also explored the idea of spiritual propinquity with the nonreligious elements in the labor movement. Freedom of conscience was one of its main appeals.

To strengthen the religious front in Israel, Mizrahi and Hapoel Hamizrahi had come together in a political formation for parliamentary elections—Mafdal (Miflagah Datit Leumit, or National Religious party). Mafdal was a "swing" element in the Knesset, in that it held the balance of power between the labor and Gahal blocs. It had participated in all the coalition governments, although it usually elected only ten to twelve members to the Knesset. Because of its strategic position, it was able to exact concessions regarding Sabbath observance, dietary laws, and the like. Mafdal also derived much power from its affiliation with strong religious bodies outside the country, especially in the United States.

Agudath Israel (Union of Israel, but "Israel" in the sense of peoplehood, not statehood) was the ultra-orthodox party. When it was founded in 1912, it was opposed to the idea of a Jewish state, choosing to wait for divine revelation rather than to engage in political activism. Deteriorating economic conditions in the 1920's and 1930's in Poland, where the main strength of the party lay, and the advent of the Nazi regime resulted in an erosion in Agudath Israel's membership. Those who survived and escaped to Palestine soon began gravitating to parties that had espoused, in addition to the study of Torah and the fulfillment of its commandments, a new social consciousness, while some younger Agudath Israel members even joined "heretical" Zionist and socialist groups. To avert the menace to its very existence, the party began organizing its own *halutz* pioneering movement and to establish its own agricultural settlements of both the kibbutz and the moshav types. But even in Palestine, Agudath Israel did not participate fully and cooperatively with the Zionists. When the Yishuv, the Jewish community in Palestine, felt the need in 1928–29 to consolidate all its factions under one organizational roof, Agudath Israel rejected participation in the new and formalized Jewish body because of its bitter opposition to women's suffrage and because it considered Jews primarily a religious and not a national entity. However, World War II, which completely destroyed its power base in Poland, forced the party to accept the founding of the State of Israel and to share in political life to the extent of serving in the Cabinet of the first coalition government.

Agudath Israel's insistence on a virtually theocratic regime, on the incorporation of rabbinic law in the Knesset legislation, on strong kashruth (dietary) regulation, on strict Sabbath and holiday observance in all phases of public life, and on separate and independent systems of education for its elementary schools and *yeshivot* (Talmudic academies) made its participation in the government a problem for the party's Cabinet ministers, as well as for their coalition colleagues. Agudath Israel, therefore, stepped out and moved into the opposition.

Like the moderate Mizrahi, Agudath Israel received much of its support outside Israel, especially in New York, where most of a group called Moetzet Gedolei Hatorah (Council of Great Torah Authorities) resided. This relatively small and totally unofficial body provided the spiritual guidance for the party. Also like the Mizrahi movement, it was split into two factions—Agudath Israel itself, and its offshoot, Poalei Agudath Israel (Workers of Agudath Israel), an ultra-orthodox group with socialist tendencies, most of whose members had collective settlements or were found among the younger elements in the Talmudic academies. But unlike the Mizrahi factions, the two have failed, despite earlier experimentation, to combine into a political alignment for parliamentary elections. In the 1969 Knesset, Agudath Israel attained four seats and Poalei Agudath Israel only two.

The major political divisions in Israel have now been introduced, but there were literally scores of other parties—leftovers from earlier days and new parties with unasserted principles, chasing elusive ideologies. Some of them have even succeeded in electing one or two members to the Knesset. Among the many stillborn parties are the Jewish ethnic lists, usually formed by opportunists attempting to exploit the malaise of the Oriental Jews and to cultivate it. To the credit of the young democracy, and especially of its citizens with antecedents in North Africa, Yemen, and other Arab countries, these lists have inevitably collapsed at the polls. In the 1969 elections only 2,116 voted for the Young Israel (Sephardic) party; it failed to elect, of course, even one Knesset member.

Other fringe groups and extremists who did not even win one seat in Knesset elections were the Land of Israel list, headed by onetime Stern Group commander Dr. Israel Eldad, who insisted that Israel not yield one inch of its 1967 occupied territory, that it establish its sovereignty over "the historic land of Israel," and that it "coax" emigration of the Arabs in that area to neighboring countries. The other extreme, the Peace List (referred to as the Professors' List) was made up of intellectuals, many of them members of older and defunct movements such as Brit Shalom and Ihud, which thought of Palestine as a "cultural center"; they followed the teachings of the Jewish philosopher Ahad Haam, who wrote as early as 1897 that "our ancient people, which was once a beacon to the world, must not think in terms of narrow nationalism, but must bring about a renaissance of Jewish ethics as well as universal values." The Peace List, paradoxically, also attracted a former commander of the Sternists, Nathan Yellin-Mor. Its platform advocated the return of every inch of the 1967 occupied territory and even more, if necessary, for the sake of peace and the possible creation of a binational state. Neither the extreme hawks nor the extreme doves won a single seat in the 1969 Knesset contest.

In the discussion of the core groups and the major party constellations, no reference was made to their attitudes toward the 1967 occupied areas. The reason was simply that most of these formations, except Rakah and some of the fringe rightists, took no firm stand on the matter. Practically every party had its hawks and doves—there were no major party lines in the issue.

Several minority lists managed to elect one or more Knesset members and must be included in any description of Israeli political realities. One of them was the Hamerkaz Hahofshi (Free Center), a right-wing, ultra-nationalist splinter from Gahal, led by Shmuel Tamir. Tamir asserted that no political party should be allowed to maintain private enterprises in industry or in agriculture, which make many voters economically dependent on the sponsor-party. The barbs were aimed at labor and its close association with the Histadrut, and to a lesser degree at Gahal. In terms of economics, Hamerkaz Hahofshi had the most conservative orientation in Israel. The party won two seats in 1969, a loss of two from the previous Knesset.

A party that made a big splash in the early 1970's was Haolam Hazeh-Koah Hadash (New Force). At its head was Uri Avnery, the *enfant terrible* of Israeli national affairs. Accused by many of being a sycophant, his feuilletonistic verve and journalistic "go" made him a factor in national politics. Deemed a professional collector of injustices, Avnery championed the cause of the Jewish Orientals and of the Arab minority in Israel. His ideological outlook was somewhat ambivalent, with a leftist slant. His central theme was the "Semitic Idea." Since neither Arab nationalism nor Jewish nationalism could under the circumstances prevail in the Middle East, he suggested the "combining of the two nationalisms, an ideal with which nationalists on both sides can identify." His views were different from the binationalism of the leaders of the Peace List in that he felt Israel should abandon, or at least weaken, its identification with Zionism, the Jewish religion, and the Western world to become a part of the Middle East expanse, as a Semitic state in a new regional union or confederation of Arabs and Jews. His party won one seat in the 1965 Knesset and two in the 1969 Knesset. (The two, however, clashed frequently in the 1970's.)

When Moshe Dayan and Shimon Peres, the two brilliant Rafi disciples of David Ben-Gurion, returned to the labor alignment, the Old Man of Sdeh Boker did not budge from his position. In 1969 the eighty-three-year-old architect of the Jewish state continued to pour his wrath on what he deemed the political solecism of the government, the Old Guard, "gray-beard dogmas," and "aimless democracy." Prophet-like, he called for "vision and vitality" for "eternal, not invented, truths." For the 1969 Knesset some of his stanchest followers put up a slate (Reshimah Mamlakhtit—State List) headed by the old warrior. Without money, organization, or campaigns it still won four seats. But in May, 1970, Ben-Gurion announced his retirement from the Knesset and from political activity to private and unaffiliated dissent and to write the history of Israel, with which he in so many ways is synonymous.

In every Knesset election since the inception of the state there have also been separate Arab lists associated with Mapai, and later with Avodah. In the 1969 elections two Arab parties won four seats—two Muslims, one Christian, and one Druze. The reason for separate but affiliated Arab seats was that, in full conscience, the Arabs could not approve a labor platform that was vague, at best, on national Arab aspirations. Another Arab, Abd al Aziz Zuabi, appeared on the list of Mapam, which championed the Arab cause much more vigorously. He, too, was elected and in 1971 became Deputy Minister of Health. In addition, two Arabs of Rakah won parliamentary seats. Thus in the early 1970's there were seven Arabs in the Knesset.

The major political parties in the country, it must be reiterated, are interested not merely in electing members to the parliament but in providing Israel with socio-economic, psychopolitical, and religiomoral bases. Hence, most of them sponsor newspapers, publishing houses, banks, kibbutz and moshav settlements, housing projects, funds for the sick, youth movements, schools, and other undertakings. These help to institutionalize and perpetuate the multiparty complex of the country. Political alignments are one thing, but complete mergers are more difficult objectives to accomplish with so many vested interests working against them.

There is also the unwillingness of the electorate to entrust its fate to one party, even if the latter is a majority segment of the population. Yet it desires a uniform approach to the solution of problems confronting the country. Coalition governments have thus far served the people well, even though the Israeli variety of coalition is usually the strangest collection of bedfellows since the invention of the bed. For instance, the first Israeli Government included members of the ultra-orthodox Agudath Israel, as well as the free-thinkers of Mapam. The national government in the early 1970's also had almost a wall-to-wall coalition, containing labor (excluding the Communists), the middle class (omitting the extreme right, Hamerkaz Hahofshi), and the religious parties (without Agudath Israel).

After two thousand years of statelessness, there was something glamorous and magical in the terms "minister" or "cabinet," especially for the East European Jew. The word "minister" had been fondled in the Yiddish *shtetl* culture—a bright person had *ah kop foon ah Meeneester."* Thus the bargaining and the haggling, the "chase for the chair" (*kissuf lekiseh*) in coalition, negotiations, and the guessing games of the press were quite intriguing as well as politically edifying. The 1969 coalition ended up with a twenty-four-member Cabinet, the largest ever, so that the chairs at the Government Table in the Knesset had to be made smaller to accommodate all the new ministers. Another accommodation was made in the latest government combination in allowing Mapam to accept collective Cabinet responsibility only in matters of security, foreign affairs, and budget. In other affairs, such as electoral reform and relations with Germany, Mapam may choose not to vote with the government.

Even though the system of electing coalition governments has seen Israel through many crises ("We now work for survival and not for socialism," said the late Prime Minister Levi Eshkol), and despite the difficulty in shaking up the institutional *status quo,* Ben-Gurion's constant hammering at electoral reform had elicited echoes not only from labor ranks but also from the membership of smaller parties, who had fears that new "territorial designations" would bring about their extinction.

The system under which Israel has operated is one of proportional representation. It regards the entire country as a single electoral region, promising each list possible membership in the Knesset if it secures a minimum of 1 per cent of the total vote. This method, plus the insistence of the ultra-orthodox Agudath Israel in the 1920's that membership in the organized Jewish community (Knesset Israel) should be individual and voluntary, has encouraged political fragmentation, so that public life has taken on a pluralistic (coalition) rather than a dualistic (two-party) structure.

In the late 1960's and early 1970's there were several plans to diminish party plethora. One of them proposed regional or territorial majority elections, similar to the British system. Various areas in the country would vote for only two parties: Labor and Liberals (the latter to be made up of Gahal, the religious constellations, and all right-of-center factions). Another possibility, not as far-reaching, envisioned a Scandinavian-style method of four representatives for each constituency: Labor, Gahal, religious factions, and a left-wing grouping. A third suggestion was to raise the minimum percentage for Knesset party qualifications from 1 per cent to 5 per cent, as in West Germany. This design would eliminate all dwarf parties or force them to merge with larger groups of similar sociopolitical ideology.

A former Minister of Justice and a leading member of Avodah, Dr. Dov Joseph, heading a special task force, recommended in a June, 1969, report (and his recommendations were taken up by Knesset committees in the early 1970's) that the entire country be divided into thirty regions of approximately equal population, with three elected representatives from each. The remaining thirty Knesset members would be elected in the nationwide proportional representation already prevailing in the country. This compromise plan evoked a great deal of interest, especially among the Oriental Jews and among the inhabitants of the Galilee region, who had been underrepresented in the Knesset.

Any of the various proposals, if carried out, would affect the Old Guard in each political party where it has chosen parliamentary candidates in tight party caucuses or in special and small "apportioning committees," where the general electorate has had virtually no voice.

While substantial changes in national voting designs have been considered seriously in Israel, much nearer implementation were municipal reforms to which the Knesset already has given its approval in principle. These primarily stipulate direct election of mayors and thus provide a psychological breakthrough toward future refashioning of the electoral system.

9 In Search of Security

The Jews of the Old Yishuv in the nineteenth century were concentrated in the four holy cities: Jerusalem, Hebron, Safad, and Tiberias. They lived mainly on Halukkah, funds collected abroad for the sustenance of academies and scholars, and were not acclaimed for their great military prowess.

With the beginning of Bilu and modern Jewish agricultural settlement in Palestine in 1882, defense of the new homesteads against marauders became a necessity. Several sporadic vigilante groups sprang up to meet specific emergencies, but by 1907–8 two more permanent organizations had emerged, Hahoresh and Bar-Giora. The first meeting to coordinate the efforts of the various security units was held in the small, ramshackle one-room residence of Itzhak Ben-Zvi, who later became the second President of Israel. The new organization's aim was to "straighten the slouched shoulders of the Jew." It decided that the safeguarding of Jewish settlements should be the responsibility of Jews rather than hired Arabs. Similarly, they felt that even the hardest agricultural labor in the Jewish settlements should be done by "Hebrew hands" rather than by the Arabs (*kibbush avodah*).

This was the beginning of the vaunted Hashomer (Guardsman). It was perhaps the most romantic period of Jewish pioneering in Israel. Proudly and valiantly galloping on their steeds through the valleys and over the mountains of Galilee, these young products of dehumanizing ghettos represented a new Jewish breed. They also established several new frontier settlements, among them Tel Hai and Kfar Giladi, in which some of them later lost their lives. They were regarded as the forerunners of both the Haganah—eventually to become the Defense Army of Israel—and the Gedud Haavodah, the Labor Brigade, a founding element of the Histadrut.

Among the national heroes of that period was Caucasus-born Joseph Trumpeldor. In 1904, at the outbreak of the Russo-Japanese war, he volunteered for the Tsar's army. He lost his left arm in the siege of Port Arthur, was decorated four times for his bravery, and rose to become the only Jewish officer in the Russian military forces. A series of pogroms against the Jews turned Trumpeldor to Zionism. In 1912 he came to Palestine and used his one arm not only to fire weapons but also to till the soil. During World War I he was exiled by the Turks to Egypt because of his Russian origins.

In the land of the Nile, Trumpeldor, in cooperation with Vladimir Jabotinsky (the founder of the Revisionist movement and the spiritual father of both the militant Irgun and the Herut party), attempted to organize a Jewish fighting unit for service with the British against the Turks in Palestine. London did not relish the idea, but Trumpeldor and Jabotinsky persisted in their pressure and finally were allowed in 1915 to raise a transport unit—the Zion Mule Corps. However, instead of being dispatched to Palestine, it was sent to Gallipoli. From this beginning, though, grew the Jewish Legion, which Trumpeldor was not permitted by the British to join on the same grounds as the Turks had employed to exile Trumpeldor—that he was a onetime Russian officer. At the end of the war Trumpeldor returned to Palestine and found a martyr's death, along with seven comrades, defending the frontier settlement of Tel Hai. As he fell, he uttered these words, which have reverberated ever since among the youth of the land: "Never mind, it is worth dying for our country." His grave to this day is a shrine for many Israelis.

The bravery with which the Zion Mule Corps performed its tasks paved the way for the Jewish Legion. The idea of a Jewish fighting unit occurred almost simultaneously to Trumpeldor in Egypt, Jabotinsky in London, and Ben-Gurion in New York (Ben-Gurion, like Trumpeldor and Jabotinsky, was "invited out" of Palestine by the Turks). The British War Office based most of its objections to a Jewish Legion on the fears of some Englishmen that it would invite reprisals against the population in enemy countries. But when the British began recruiting Russian emigrés in Great Britain, Jabotinsky finally succeeded in overcoming British aversion. In 1917 the initial Jewish fighting battalion, the 38th Royal Fusiliers, commanded by Colonel J. H. Patterson (a non-Jew), was organized. This marked the first time since the revolt of Bar-Kokhba in A.D. 135 that Jews had taken up arms officially as Jews in defense of their historic homeland.

Meanwhile, David Ben-Gurion and Itzhak Ben-Zvi had mobilized young North American Jews into the 39th and 40th battalions (this time under Jewish commanders). They joined their comrades-in-arms in Palestine to help turn the Turks away from the Holy Land —especially from Samaria, Galilee, and parts of Transjordan. By the end of the war, the Jewish Legion had been dispersed, but its legacy remained in lore and valor. Colonel Patterson told of a most un-military-looking, lackadaisical, skinny, pale-faced young Talmudic scholar who, at the sight of Jerusalem, broke ranks and ran forward in a frenzy, presumably to capture the Holy City singlehanded. Other sources, less reliable than Colonel Patterson, describe a notice put up on the 39th Battalion's bulletin board: "Privates will kindly refrain from giving advice to officers."

When Britain took over the administration of Palestine, it naturally assumed the protection of its inhabitants. The frequent outbreaks against the new authority and the clashes between Jews and Arabs prompted Jewish and Arab leaders to request police recruitment from their respective people. It was with much reluctance that the British complied with the demands, and their half-hearted attempts did not satisfy the "natives." In 1936, for instance, the Jews made up about 33 per cent of the total population, but there were only 397 Jewish policemen out of a total of 3,924, or slightly more than 10 per cent. As the 1936–39 clashes became so ominous as to threaten a total breakdown of authority, the British yielded and allowed the enlistment of 2,500 Jewish settlement police.

When Israel was created, it did not follow the pattern adopted by most Western states of putting its law enforcement agents under the Ministry of the Interior or the Ministry of Justice. It established a separate Ministry of Police, which also supervised the prison system. The police force was administered by an inspector general and served the entire country, including the cities; it was divided into three main districts with headquarters in Jerusalem, Tel Aviv, and Nazareth and into many subdistricts, stations, and posts.

In 1972 there were close to 13,000 law enforcement agents, including about 1,200 policemen from the Arab and Druze communities. The prison system was geared to rehabilitation rather than punishment *per se*. Hence prisoners were examined respectively by the staffs of the observation, classification, and research divisions, who made much use of psychiatrists, psychologists, social workers, physicians, and the like. Offenders were categorized and then sent to seven main prisons in accordance with the tests administered by the professional personnel. Vocational guidance and education were available to those desiring it, especially young offenders.

The Defense Army of Israel (Zva Haganah LeYisrael, or Zahal) is different in many ways from other military establishments. An American correspondent reported in 1968 that there were three super-secrets in Israel: the annual increase in population, the amount of money given the country each year by American Jews, and the nation's defense details. Nevertheless, Israel's security force has remained essentially a citizen army, as its antecedents indicate.

The Tel Hai attack in March, 1920, during which Trumpeldor fell; the Passover outbreaks that followed several weeks later; and the bloody riots in Tel Aviv–Jaffa the same year convinced many Jewish leaders that an organization other than Hashomer—somewhat less glamorous than the French Foreign Legion and a great deal more inclusive—was needed for the security of the growing

Yishuv, especially in the urban centers. Thus the Haganah (Defense) emerged, at first as a loose confederation of independent, illegal units. Hashomer, the Zion Mule Corps, and the Jewish Legion provided the primary sources of recruitment for the underground groups. Eliahu Golomb, Dov Hoz, and Yaakov Dori (who became the first chief-of-staff of the Defense Army of Israel in 1948) were the unofficial coordinators of the tenuous network of subterranean defense cells.

Golomb more than anyone else nurtured the incipient military establishment in the 1920's when it had no central guidance and no permanent links among the many separate groups. It was Golomb who prevailed upon Ben-Gurion and Ben-Zvi to bring these units, sponsored by various parties or settlements, together under a security committee of the Vaad Leumi. Thus in 1929 the Haganah, more solidly established, became formally the "illegal" army of the embryonic state. The institutionalized Yishuv, however, in the face of what its leaders deemed British and Arab harassment, followed a policy of *havlagah*—self-restraint and no retribution. It was not easy to muzzle young hotbloods who were raring for action and revenge. It was during this period that the exemplary discipline of the future Jewish army was forged.

Because of the unsettled conditions in the country in the 1930's, the British imposed strict bans on weapons for Palestinians. Thus the Haganah from the beginning had to secure from abroad illicit equipment, mostly light arms, and it had to train under cover, without air or naval forces. Through the foresight of Ben-Gurion, Golomb, Hoz, and eventually Peres, in the late 1930's and early 1940's secret procurement centers were established in Europe and America. In due time, employing ingenious ruses, they began clandestine shipment of heavy equipment parts and components to Palestine. Even more improbably, the parts were assembled under the very noses of the British into the first tanks, planes, and other military weaponry of the Haganah.

Most of the mandate authorities in Palestine followed Lord Palmerston's famous dictum: "England has no eternal friends and no eternal enemies. It has eternal interests." Several Britons, however, had befriended the Arabs, while others assisted the Jews. One of the latter was Major Orde Charles Wingate, who in later years demonstrated his skill as a general in Africa and in Burma. A keen student of the Bible, deeply idealistic and drawn mystically to Jewish national resurrection in Palestine, Wingate, arriving in the Holy Land in 1936, discovered in the kibbutz youth magnificent human material for effecting his dreams.

When Arab outbursts grew excessive, augmented by infiltration from Syria, Lebanon, and Transjordan, and the British could not or would not cope with the problem, Wingate asked permission of the mandate authorities to organize and train Jewish defense units. His request was turned down. At first even Jewish leaders did not quite trust this intense, fervid Englishman, as Ben-Gurion and Golomb themselves later testified, but in the end they were overwhelmed by his personality and zeal. In 1937, a new commanding general, Archibald Wavell, arrived in Palestine, and he too was won over by the young major. Wingate then established his headquarters in Ein Harod, a kibbutz at the foot of Mount Gilboa, and proceeded to raise his soon-to-be-famous Night Squads, the astonishingly effective commando groups known for their rapid mobility and surprise tactics. The Night Squads and the Special Field Commandos raised by Itzhak Sadeh, a companion of Trumpeldor, formed the hard core of an invigorated Haganah and furnished many future Israeli military commanders, notably Moshe Dayan and Yigal Allon. The British recalled Wingate in 1938, and he achieved military grandeur elsewhere, but he remained a legend in Israel, where settlements and schools were named for him.

Despite "Wavell's waiver," the Haganah as such remained an illegal organization, but it intensified its activities, such as erecting impromptu overnight settlements, the "stockade and tower" projects. These were construction camps that usually took one day to erect walls and a watchtower, using prefabricated parts, to protect the nucleus of a permanent village. The sites were chosen in accordance with a preconceived strategic defense plan for an entire district. The

Haganah also increased its illicit immigration ventures. When World War II broke out, the Haganah encouraged 30,000 volunteers to enroll in the British Army to fight Nazi Germany. As the military situation in Palestine grew darker, the British authorized in 1941 the formation of Palmah (Plugot Mahatz) commando companies, which performed valiantly on the northern front, along the Syrian and Lebanese borders, against the Vichy French forces. It was in the course of these engagements that Yigal Allon and Moshe Dayan first distinguished themselves as military leaders, Dayan losing an eye in one of them.

As the immediate threat from the enemy subsided, Palmah, then numbering some 2,500 soldiers, was disbanded by the British but went underground to perform special duties for the Haganah. It became an elite corps and wanted to preserve its identity within the Defense Army of Israel even after the state gained its independence. Ben-Gurion, however, insisted that Israel must have a unified army, without preferential treatment of individuals or groups. The iron will of the first Prime Minister of Israel prevailed even against the popular heroes of the War of Liberation. In November, 1948, Palmah, then a force of 5,500 with remarkable esprit de corps, was effectively dispersed, liquidating the dreams of their commanders. All that remained of its days of glory were the Battle Songs of Palmah, still sung fervently by all members of the Israeli military forces.

Ever since the outbreak of World War II, the Jewish Agency had pressed the British authorities for a separate Jewish fighting force, not merely commando units of the Palmah type. In September, 1944, London yielded and a Jewish infantry brigade was raised and went into action (as part of the Eighth Army) in Italy, Austria, Yugoslavia, and later Holland. The presence of organized Jewish fighting forces in Europe had an electrifying effect upon the survivors of the Nazi miasma. With the aid of the Jewish Brigade, many of them began pushing toward southern Italy, hoping eventually to reach Palestine. The British were not too happy with the extracurricular activities of the Brigade, and friction soon developed in the relationship between the English and the Jews. The Brigade was returned to Palestine in 1946 and dissolved, swelling the ranks of the Haganah.

The attitude of the mandate authorities toward the Haganah at that time of necessity was ambiguous. Although they did not recognize the organization, which continued to function underground, they felt that the Haganah as an instrument of the institutionalized Yishuv exerted a restraining influence on the more militant elements in the Jewish community. Many Jews in Palestine did not relish the policy of *havlagah* followed by the organized community in the face of Arab disturbances and British unwillingness or inability to control the situation. Disciples of Jabotinsky in the Revisionist movement, which split from the Zionist Organization headed by Dr. Weizmann in 1935, and members of its youth group, Betar (Brit Trumpeldor, named for the defender of Tel Hai in 1920), decided in 1937 to move out of the Haganah and set up their own outfit, the National Military Organization—Irgun Zvai Leumi (Ezel).

At the outset the Irgun's goal was to resist Arab attacks, but by 1939, when London issued a White Paper restricting Jewish immigration to Palestine, it turned also against the British, sabotaging the mandate administration and attacking its personnel. Both the Vaad Leumi and the Jewish Agency dissociated themselves from the acts of the Irgun. When World War II flared up, the Irgun announced a temporary truce and undertook to help the allies in the struggle against Germany. David Raziel, the first commander of the Irgun, was killed in Iraq on a British mission. He was succeeded in 1943 by Menahem Begin, who later organized the Herut party and helped set up the Knesset coalition with the Labor party after the events of 1967.

In 1944, as the British once again undertook restrictive measures against Jewish immigration to Palestine, the Irgun, ending its truce, resumed the struggle against the English, promoting illegal Aliyah, debilitating government authorities, and attacking Arab villages. The British retaliated by imprisoning and deporting Irgun members to Africa.

To some Jews even the Irgun was not militant enough. Fighters for the Freedom of Israel (Lohamei Herut Yisrael, or Lehi), under the leadership of Abraham Stern, therefore better known as the Stern Group, split off from the Irgun, insisting that the British must be fought regardless of the war effort against Germany. Proceeding on this theory, the Sternists literally terrorized the lives of the English in Palestine.

At the end of the war a kind of division of labor developed between the Irgunists and the Sternists, the former concentrating on demolishing British installations and the latter aiming at British personnel. Among the Sternists' most noted victims was Lord Moyne, the British Minister of State, who was murdered in Cairo. They also made an attempt on the life of the British High Commissioner in Palestine and assassinated the Swedish Count Bernadotte, who came to Israel in 1948 on a U.N. peace mission that envisaged the severance of Jerusalem from the newly created state of Israel. The Sternists numbered only 300, and their excesses shocked the Yishuv. While the Haganah from time to time cooperated with the Irgun in illegal immigration projects and even in wrecking British installations, it neither could nor did condone the atrocities committed by the Sternists. Count Bernadotte's murder occurred during the first months in the life of Israel. The government took prompt action to round up some 200 Sternists and their sympathizers to find and punish the assassins.

When Ben-Gurion assumed the premiership of Israel, his problem with the Irgun was even more difficult than his confrontation with Palmah. Begin, claiming a conspiracy against the future of Israel, refused to dismantle his organization, numbering at the time about 5,000, and to integrate it into the Defense Army of Israel. In June, 1948, an Irgun vessel named *Altalena* (Jabotinsky's pseudonym) arrived at Tel Aviv during a ceasefire with the Arabs. The government of Israel forbade the unloading of the ship's cargo of arms. Begin defied the order, addressing the nation via radio in an impassioned plea. After repeated warnings, at Ben-Gurion's command, the vessel was fired upon and destroyed, and lives were lost.

It was this act, some insist, that really established Ben-Gurion as the *de facto* as well as the *de jure* leader of Israel. The rightist Irgun, like the leftist Palmah, several weeks later was dissolved into the Israeli Army in September, 1948.

Formally the army was established in September, 1949, by the Defense Service Law under the civilian policy-making of a Defense Minister, who was a member of the Cabinet with direct responsibility to the Prime Minister and the Knesset—the locus of ultimate power in the state. Without organized military experience for some eighteen centuries, the Jews have evolved from romantic bands of vigilantes at the turn of the century and from the ragtag underground outfits during the mandate regime into one of the most effective fighting machines the world has known. How did they achieve it? In the words of Golda Meir, the credit was due to "General Ain Braira," or "General No-Choice." Restraining their modesty, Israeli parents also credited their sons, the "normal Jewish geniuses," with the ability to improvise and if necessary to invent solutions to obdurate problems—making tanks and planes perform beyond their intended capacity.

Israel has invested masses of energy and money in its military establishment but has created between the people and the army a bond that has made Zahal in the truest sense a citizen's army. It was mostly a force of minutemen, similar to that of the American colonies in the 1770's, built around a core of about 80,000 long-service officers, noncoms, and the periodic intake of recruits.

Organized on a territorial basis, the mobilization system for the reserve units enables the reservists to be called up and rushed to the front lines within a very short time. In the emergencies of 1956 and 1967, fully equipped formations were combat ready in a matter of hours after a coded radio alert was issued. Its total mobilization strength was put in 1971 at 300,000–350,000 out of about 3 million people. The Zahal was noted for its remarkable discipline and mobility and its readiness to wage war at night. Evident above all, however, was the unique versatility of the combat pilots, especially in the June, 1967, war and the period following that conflict.

Virtually all able men over eighteen and under twenty-nine were conscripted for regular service of up to thirty months. Students in the rabbinic academies could be exempted, although some preferred to serve. A great many women over eighteen and under twenty-six were called up for duty of twenty months (mothers and married females were exempted). Women claiming religious convictions could be absolved of military tasks and assigned other national service chores, such as nursing or teaching. Basic training was practically the same for both boys and girls, but after completing psychological and aptitude tests, as a rule, women were assigned to administrative and noncombatant duties such as those of radio operators, teleprinters, clerks, parachute packers, instrument checkers, vehicle drivers, mechanics, and teachers. Some, however, became active armed defenders of settlements.

After finishing his term in the national service, a man went into the reserve until he was fifty-five, and a childless woman enrolled until she was thirty-four. Up to the age of forty a man had to do thirty-one consecutive days of service annually. A male between forty and fifty-five had to report for fifteen consecutive days of training. A childless woman in the reserve drilled for thirty consecutive days annually. Commissioned and noncommissioned officers in the reserve added seven days of duty.

In 1950, Pioneer and Military Youth (Noar Halutzi Lohem, or Nahal) was founded. This was an organization of young people who wished to serve in the army as units and later continue as a group to establish for themselves or help others establish agricultural settlements on the borders. Usually the members of Nahal received several months of intensive military training and then were assigned to a frontier village, where, still under army discipline for a year, they underwent rigid agricultural tutoring. Eventually they set out on their own to found a new outpost in some desolate region or to supplement and invigorate a struggling settlement, especially of new immigrants.

Another paramilitary project was the Youth Corps (Gedude Noar, or Gadna). These were groups of boys and girls fourteen to eighteen years of age in some 300 high school, extension, and vocational centers, supervised jointly by the Ministry of Defense and the Ministry of Education and Culture. Originally they were set up by the Haganah in 1939 as an underground messenger and signal service. After 1948 the youngsters were trained along scout lines with a heavy dosage of military and agricultural schooling. Gadna comprised land, air, and naval sections. Air Gadna learned to pilot light aircraft, and Naval Gadna navigated small boats. Of the more than 100,000 members in this organization, about 20,000 each year took special training. Also annually more than 1,000 completed courses for Gadna instructors and sport coaches, creating a pool for future military commanders.

While the martial aspects of the Gadna program were in evidence, it was the physical conditioning and the athletic activities that were the important goals of the government—to mold a normal, healthy people of the descendants of the ghetto and cave-dwellers, of the refugees from the crematoria. Both Gadna and Nahal have served as models for many developing countries in Asia, Africa, and Latin America.

Perhaps the most important function of the army next to national defense was its role as an agent of socialization and education. The defense forces absorbed many immigrants who had received inadequate schooling in their countries of origin. Elementary health care, diet advice, and vocational and academic courses were offered by the military. Every recruit was compelled to take such subjects as history, Hebrew language, geography, mathematics, and civics to bring him up to the minimum standard of elementary school education, if he had not reached that level prior to his call-up.

The pedagogic techniques developed by the army were so effective that they were sometimes carried over to the civilian institutions and were emulated in foreign countries. One example cited in a report by a colonel was the battalion that undertook a route march of 200 miles. It was divided into nineteen classes according to educational background. Ten days before the march started the classes studied, with the aid of various multisensory devices, the places through which they would pass; they learned what happened there in biblical and modern times and the development plans for the future of the area. During the actual march they learned new words, songs, customs, and ceremonies. In the evening they gathered around a campfire in a festive spirit binding all soldiers—Orientals and Occidentals—in a bond of common memory and common knowledge, and in a sense of a common past, present, and future.

The religious and recreational needs of the soldiers were fully recognized and provided for with particular emphasis on the "ingathering" theme. The Jewish dietary laws were observed, festivals and holidays were celebrated, and the Sabbath was a day of rest, except in rare emergencies. The chaplains identified themselves completely with the interests, aims, and spirit of the army, to the extent that the chief chaplain had earned his parachute wings along with many soldiers much younger than he.

The reservists, from age twenty-nine to fifty-five, who could be called up at a moment's notice and who manned the tanks and did the ground fighting, returned as soon as the emergencies were over to their kibbutz, university posts, shops, factories, and businesses almost as quickly as they were mobilized, so as to disrupt as little as possible the economic life of the country. The standing army and its officers remained youthful. As soon as a senior commander reached middle age, he stepped aside for younger officers and new ideas, so as not to perpetuate entrenched patterns and interests. That principle held true even in the case of chiefs of staff, no matter how brilliant they were.

Perhaps the most distinguishing mark of the army is that an officer's command is not "Forward, march!" but "Follow me!" Military statisticians have indicated that the casualty rate among Israeli officers, compared with commanders of other armies, has been among the highest.

10 The Struggle for Economic Viability

Israel's economy is a nightmare to the country's university professors and defies the theories of most other experts in the world. It always teeters precariously on the edge of implausibility because it is apocalyptically structured. Blueprint and practice are usually in conflict. Its line of reasoning is something like this: "If we don't have enough money to settle 50,000 people, why not settle 300,000?"

What were and are the economic problems besetting Israel? Skimpy natural resources; water scarcity; mass immigration from poverty-stricken parts of the world; newcomers who are either manually unskilled or culturally undernourished, in some cases both; prolonged "hot" and "cold" war, sapping the energy and draining the capital of the country; an unfavorable trade balance; partial dependence on aid from the Jews of the Diaspora; recent virtual stoppage of German indemnities for Nazi atrocities; a low index of economic attractions for foreign capital (meager natural resources and war); labor governments that, although consistently liberal, are nevertheless a deterrent to large-scale outside investments, because some of Jerusalem's policies smack of welfarism; ambivalent standard of living—too low for Western Jews to induce savings, too high for Eastern Jews who are not attuned to banking practices; a cumbersome bureaucracy; spiraling costs and runaway inflation; a French arms embargo; an Arab boycott.

With all these difficulties, how did Israel become the most economically advanced country in the Middle East? When confronted by American businessmen and industrialists with a similar question, the late Eliezer Kaplan, Israel's first Minister of Finance, typically replied with a story: "Once there were two frogs who fell into a tub of sour milk. One sank and perished immediately. The other began squirming and thrashing about and soon found himself on top of a tub of butter. That's us in Israel."

There are those who insist that if it were not for the war and the boycott of the Arabs, Israel would have remained a small (5,600 square miles) state, dependent on the Arab hinterlands for agricultural products and on foreign protection for its security—a nation of managers, manipulators, and weary bourgeois. Now it still retains many aspects of its early social awareness. It has become nearly self-reliant in most food supplies, has developed diversified commerce and industry, and is on the verge of producing its own jet fighter planes and atomic bombs (if it does not already have one or two crude ones).

While not sitting on top of a tub of butter, Israel has become a viable state—a medium world power, despite relatively small population and area. What economic squirming and thrashing about saved the country from drowning or from a continued suspension in sour milk?

As in any place in antiquity, agriculture was a most important element in the economy of the lands of the Bible. After the loss of independence and the dispersion among the nations of the world, small groups of Jews tenaciously clung to their soil in Palestine. Tradition has it that the Jews of Pekiin, in Upper Galilee, never left their village, continuing to live there from the time of the Second Temple. In the eighteenth century, some fifty Jewish families in the settlement eked out a niggardly living from the land. In 1936, because of Arab disturbances, only fourteen families remained, completely indistinguishable from their Arab neighbors except in religion. Today, naturally, the number of Jews has increased, although they are still a minority in a much larger Arab-Druze population.

The Jews were thus originally an agricultural people, preferring to till the soil rather than engage in trade or industry, so that the first-century Jewish historian Josephus Flavius could write: "We do not take pleasure in merchandizing . . . and having a fruitful land for our dwelling places, we exert ourselves to cultivate it." But in the course of their exile, Jews were forced to take up other occupations. During the Middle Ages they were denied the right to own, purchase, or lease land virtually in all countries of their dispersion. This practice later spread to the Ottoman Empire when it encompassed Palestine; Jews could use land only for religious or charitable purposes.

At the beginning of the nineteenth century various efforts were made to free the Jewish inhabitants of the Holy Land from the stigma of Halukkah, living on overseas handouts. In 1839 a group of Jerusalem Jews asked Sir Moses Montefiore, a noted philanthropist, to purchase a tract of land nearby so that they could establish an agricultural village. Nothing much came of the idea. In 1855, as a result of some changes in the Turkish land laws, several Jews acquired a stretch of real estate on the outskirts of Jerusalem, where much later, in 1894, the settlement Motza was founded. However, in 1870 the Alliance Israélite Universelle, based in Paris and gaining much Jewish recognition for its educational activities, inaugurated the first modern Jewish agricultural school in Palestine—still functioning today—Mikveh Israel.

But 1878 marked the beginning of real and sustained agricultural activity. In that year a stalwart Jerusalemite, Moses Salomon, with the help of two Hungarian coreligionists, established the "mother of colonies," Petah Tikvah. It was followed by other villages started mostly by the Hovevei Zion (Lovers of Zion), who left Russia after the 1881–82 pogroms. By 1900, there were twenty-two Jewish "colonies" or moshavot in Palestine. Most of them went through periods of excruciating trials and were at one time or another on the verge of collapse.

The early settlers were small townspeople from southeastern Europe. Their agricultural experience consisted of casual contact as peddlers with the peasants of the Russian, Polish, or Bessarabian flatlands, who plowed long and straight furrows and cultivated grain. Reaching Palestine, they looked for similar flat and black land. They found small areas of it on the coastal plain near the Yarkon River and in the north along Lake Hule. To their amazement, these areas were not settled by the Arabs, nor was the price of the land prohibitive. The would-be farmers soon discovered why the *fellahin* had overlooked this seemingly rich soil: It was black or brown because it was marshland, and the only thing that would flourish there was malaria.

It was at that time that Baron Edmond de Rothschild, the "Father of the Yishuv," came to the rescue of the inexperienced, woe-beset colonists. He sent over enormous sums of money to cover their deficits and to help them initiate new projects. He also dispatched instructors, agronomists, and administrators to train the settlers in their ventures.

The experts provided by the baron initially were of tremendous help. Modern methods for growing citrus and vines were adopted. Plans for swamp drainage were introduced. The Australian eucalyptus was transplanted to Palestine to soak up the marshes—and the Arabs immediately dubbed it the "Jew-tree." Rothschild's representatives also insisted that Palestinian agriculture be modeled after southern France's farming rather than after the Ukrainian pattern. Vineyards and orchards were thus cultivated instead of grain. In the arid sand dunes and in the redlands of the central plains, deep wells were dug for groundwater, which was brought up in abundant quantity.

All this was a triumph not only of economics but also of the spirit. It proved that the exilic Jew indeed was capable of reverting to his old biblical self, that the despised *luftmentsch* ("floater") was ready to sprout roots in the soil. But then the negative aspects of paternalism, subsidies, and bureaucracy became evident and oppressive to the nouveaux riches, who felt they were being stripped of their dignity, initiative, and independence by the baron's officious technicians.

The "Father of the Yishuv" was not only generous but also wise. Rothschild realized that the Jews had come to Palestine to escape the *chinovniki,* the flunkies of the Tsar, to find freedom and self-esteem in their own homeland. In the year 1900 he turned over the administration of villages in Palestine he had supported to the Jewish Colonization Association (ICA), which was founded by Baron Maurice de Hirsch in 1891 to finance Jewish resettlement mainly in South America (later, after the Russian Revolution, also in Birobidjan, Siberia). Originally the agency regarded colonization of Jews in Palestine as impractical, but by 1900 it began to evince an interest in the Holy Land. Rothschild, in addition to the transfer of his assets in Palestine to the ICA, funded that agency with 15 million francs. In 1923 ICA's activities, with the consent of Baron Rothschild (he died in 1934 at the age of eighty-nine), were taken over by PICA, the Palestine Jewish Colonization Association.

Under the new management, the settlers gained more and more autonomy, achieving eventual independence. The subsidies decreased and experimentation was encouraged, even in cereal farming. As the settlers began to prosper, a serious socio-economic problem arose. To begin with, there was need for additional labor. The farmer and his family could no longer manage the increased acreage and the attendant arduous tasks. Very few Jewish farm workers were available at the time. Because the Arabs provided a plentiful and cheap labor source, a constantly growing number of them were employed by the Jewish farmer. It did not take long for the settlers to become overseers instead of toilers in the fields.

All this coincided with the beginning of the Second Aliyah, marked by the social consciousness and the pristine principles of its pioneers, motivated by the ideal of *dat avodah* (religion of labor), *kibbush avodah* (conquest of labor), and the notions of collectivism and cooperative ventures. Even the more moderate element of the

Second Aliyah looked askance at this new "colonial" class of employers. The Zionist goal of normalizing the occupational composition of the Jewish people was being menaced.

One aspect of individualistic farming was the emphasis put on cash crops. Settlers who had produced enormous quantities of grapes or oranges had to buy their own tomatoes or melons. The preoccupation with such monetary return worked, it appeared, against the national interest of the Yishuv. A bad season for a major crop would sometimes force settlers to claim bankruptcy or leave the village. Moreover, the Arab (because of centuries of conditioning, in addition to his receiving low wages) tended to be more subservient to the Jewish landlords than the new class-conscious arrivals from Europe, when the latter hired themselves out to the farm.

Intense and ugly struggles between the colonists and the *halutzim* (pioneers) ensued. It was the latter, it will be remembered, who conceived the idea of the kevutzah in 1909–10 and later its derivative the kibbutz. All assets of this form of settlement, except personal effects, were owned by the group. Production of goods and supply of consumption articles were collectivized. The members of the kevutzah-kibbutz placed at the disposal of their community all their time and energy, while the settlement provided them with all available needs. Thus internally it was a moneyless society.

From the economic point of view (its sociocultural aspects will be considered in the next chapter), the kibbutz was in absolute contrast to the moshava, the conventional village. It was based on the abandonment of private ownership of land, rejected hired labor, and stressed mixed farming. These tenets to a very large degree determined the forms of Jewish labor settlements and even the national-economic makeup of the Yishuv.

The kibbutz insisted also on the equal dignity and value of all kinds of work. The material status of the laborer was not to be affected by the task performed. Since the purpose of the community was to raise its own food, initially it engaged in vegetable growing, dairy husbandry, and grain cultivation in preference to citrus farming and viticulture. This approach, the kibbutz members believed, assured more permanent roots in the soil.

The kibubtz was not and is not an escapist movement or a monastic life-pattern. On the contrary, at its very genesis it was supported by national organizations, and from the very start it became involved in every aspect of Zionism and the building of a Jewish homeland. In fact, its twin theme was and is personal regeneration in a reconstructed Jewish society. Thus the first kevutzah (a smaller settlement than a kibbutz), Deganiah, was established on Jewish National Fund land. This agency was formed by the Fifth Zionist Congress in 1901 to acquire large tracts of land with small donations from as many Jews as possible anywhere. The Congress specified that the land to be purchased would never be sold or mortgaged and would remain forever the property of the Jewish people. A part of the JNF's program to this day is the afforestation of the barren country. Some 30 million trees have been planted by the agency since its inception.

By settling on JNF soil, the kibbutz reaffirmed the principle that no land acquired by the Fund could ever be alienated from the people as such. Today over 90 per cent of the land in Israel is held by the state and owned by the nation. The kibbutz, or other groups and individuals, may lease land for a renewable forty-nine-year period (the biblical jubilee principle) at a minimal rent. This practice eliminated much land speculation, which could have snuffed out the very life of the embryonic state even before it was born.

The communal form of life was a great attraction to the newcomers of the 1930's. Disappointed in the liberalism, socialism, and communism of Europe, and having left the warm family life of the *shtetl* (small town), they gravitated to the kibbutz. It provided them with an outlet for both their pioneering desires and their nationalist strivings.

A kibbutz got not only a lease on the land at low rates but also initial financial and technical assistance from national institutions such as the Jewish Agency, in the prestate period, and the Ministry of Agriculture and other government sources after 1948. By applying rigorous scientific and behavioral standards and by going into areas where private capital would not venture for economic or safety reasons, the kibbutz was able, at first with some difficulty, to develop resources for self-finance out of profits. The reinvestment level in the communal settlements was very high—in the beginning for patriotic reasons and later also because of governmental pressures from the new state. It thus reached a point in its development where it needed more labor than the membership of the kibbutz itself could muster.

Recent immigrants to Israel were not as socially conscientious as the pioneers of the first part of the twentieth century, so that although membership requirements of the kibbutz were somewhat relaxed, newcomers, even from Western countries, chose the moshav cooperative rather than the kibbutz collective. Certainly the majority of immigrants from the Oriental states would not and could not be attracted to the strange and totally incomprehensible collective way of life.

Bereft of a fresh and constant flow of members, the kibbutz had to face the alternative of hired labor to maximize the utilization of land and tools. Moreover, as wave after wave of refugees inundated the country, resulting in the sordid *maabarot* (transit camps) and mass unemployment, the kibbutz collectives could not remain, even from an ideological point of view, islands of prosperity in a sea of misery, and had to offer jobs to the newcomers, playing the doctrinally uncomfortable role of employers. They also had to shift from another original and fundamental aim of the movement, agricultural pursuits, since in many areas of farm products Israel was fast becoming self-sufficient. By 1965–66 more than half of the kibbutz income was derived from industrial enterprises, and such income continued to increase in ratio in the ensuing years.

These developments presented an acute problem for the kibbutz and caused serious rifts in the movement, even before the establishment of the state. As the number of collectives increased, ideological differences cropped up. The Kibbutz Artzi, with about seventy-five settlements and a population of nearly 35,000 was founded in 1927 and is affiliated with the Marxist Mapam. Hakibbutz Hameuhad, with some sixty collectives and 25,000 people, also was organized in 1927 and is associated with the milder Ahdut Avodah, now part of the Avodah party. Ihud Hakevutzot Vehakibbutzim came into being in 1951 and has about eighty collectives with a total population of approximately 35,000. Additionally, there are smaller groupings like Hakibbutz Hadati, a religious kibbutz association, sponsored by Hapoel Hamizrahi. Membership in the individual kibbutz runs from 25–50 (in which case it is usually called kevutzah) to 2,000–2,500). The total number of collectives is about 250, and the total membership is near 90,000.

To "stop for breath" and solve in part the crucial doctrinal and philosophical dilemmas of "Gordonism" in an industrial society, some collectives, separately and in groups, have entered into a partnership with cooperatives of city workers, so that wages are paid to groups rather than to individuals. Also a number of them have banded together and established a special company to work the land owned by these collectives, which is beyond the ability of the respective membership to cultivate alone—a distribution of ideological guilt. The doctrinally tainted profits of the company are plowed into further land development instead of accruing to the participating kibbutz. In addition to farming areas adjacent to their homes, members of the company have undertaken to till large stretches of the arid Negev, with the almost inevitable success marking kibbutz projects.

While the kibbutz is still a far cry from the private ownership, the specialization and the "exploitation" (in socialist terminology) that marked the moshava at the turn of the century, the ideological problem of the collective remains, even when it is wrapped in patriotic cloth. One- or two-crop specialization instead of diversification (although most of the collectives continue to raise the essentials for their own subsistence) is at present the norm rather than the exception. The kibbutz now runs a variety of industries, producing furniture (the plywood plant in Afikim was in 1971 the largest and most modern furniture producers in the Middle East), toys, plastics, electronic equipment, kitchen utensils, agriculture machinery, and fishing vessels, as well as hotels and restaurants. The standard of living of a "kibbutznik" in many cases is higher than that of the independent Israeli agricultural or industrial worker. In the Kibbutz Shephaim it was decided at a general meeting in the summer of 1971 to allot each member a television set. The kibbutz will have, though, one central "collective" antenna.

The moshav had less of an ideological challenge than the kibbutz, because the Gordonian legacy was not as essential to its socio-economic scheme and because it did not feel the heavy obligation of propitiating Marx or his credal offspring.

The moshav is of two types. The moshav ovdim is based on the family unit and on cooperative rather than collective effort. All its produce is marketed and all its supplies (especially heavy equipment) are purchased by the moshav, then rented out to members. Each family purchases necessities (these are not provided) in the settlement cooperative stores. A semblance of uniformity is achieved by the allotment of specified parcels of land to each family (usually according to family size), but there is ample opportunity for individual initiative within the framework of the moshav ovdim. Whatever control is deemed necessary is exercised by the elected central committee. Not all of those living in the moshav ovdim are members of the settlement. On the average, about 20 per cent are nonmembers (nonvoting) engaged in services the moshav cannot provide for itself—teachers, doctors, artisans, social workers. Some of them are employed by the village itself, and others sell their services directly to individual members. Occasionally these people decide to join the moshav and are then alloted a parcel of land, usually smaller than the average, for supplemental income.

The moshav ovdim is the most conservative of the collective-cooperative sector of Israel's population. It, too, started with mixed farming, although about 70 per cent of its land now grows grain. Other important products are vegetables, fruit, poultry, eggs, and honey. Paradoxically, there is less industrialization in the moshav ovdim than in the kibbutz because of the socio-economic proclivities of smallholders.

The moshav shitufi, combines the collective work principle of the kibbutz with the private family system of the moshav ovdim. Like the kibbutz it is based on collective ownership (not rental) of the means of production and on collective farming, with individual initiative limited. On the other hand, as in the moshav ovdim, the mother in the moshav shitufi is mainly engaged in looking after household chores and gardening.

Both moshav types are situated on nationally owned land with renewable forty-nine-year leases at minimum rates. Also, as in the case of the kibbutz, they receive financial and technical assistance from government and other agencies.

The moshav is linked to national coordinating bodies, the largest of which is Tnuat Hamoshavim. Socialist-labor oriented, it counts some 225 settlements with a membership of 90,000. Also, Hapoel Hamizrahi (65 religious settlements with a population of approximately 30,000), Herut-Liberals (Gahal), and Poalei Agudath Israel (ultra-religious) have their own moshav-type villages. The total number of moshavim is nearing 400, with a membership of 150,000 and growing.

Together, the moshava (represented in such independent organizations as the Farmers' Federation), the kibbutz, and the moshav in 1971 comprised some 750 agricultural settlements with a population of nearly 300,000 out of a total number of Jewish inhabitants approaching 2.6 million. The non-Jewish population of 450,000 (325,000 Muslims, 75,000 Christians, and 35,000 Druze) contained more than one-half farmers (about 240,000), concentrated essentially in private-land villages.

Since the renewal of statehood, thanks to the dedication of the people and to intensive scientific methods, farm production in Israel has increased sixfold and agricultural exports have equaled that growth. Self-sufficiency in most vegetables and in poultry and eggs was reached by 1960. To avoid surpluses and dumping, to maximize use of limited agricultural resources, and to channel exports, a system of quotas was introduced for products that could not be effectively utilized. It has not always worked out well. For instance, the 1970–71 milk quota was reached in 1967, and the same year saw a big surplus of eggs. Recently there has been a slight shift toward raising cows for meat, which Israel previously had to import from Ethiopia and South America. The government has not fully committed itself to the policy because the cost of imported feed had to be considered (some of the cooperatives now have gone into fodder production).

Israel's most important agricultural products are citrus and other subtropical fruits, ground nuts, vegetables, and, of course, eggs, poultry, and milk. Related activities are fish hatcheries and commercial fishing in the Sea of Galilee, the Mediterranean, the Red Sea, and the Atlantic. There is continued increase in the yield of cotton (introduced in 1953, it now satisfies almost all local needs), flowers, avocados, melons, beet sugar, and strawberries—pointing to cash crops for export. Also for its domestic needs the country has made tremendous effort to augment the raising of grain. While in the 1950's Israel was able to raise only 15 per cent of its wheat requirement, by 1967 the farmers produced close to 60 per cent. Similar efforts were made to coax greater quotas of barley, sorghum, hay, and silage out of the land. By 1970 the farmers produced three-quarters of the country's food. From a period of severe austerity in 1948, Israel's agriculture compared favorably with most European states, achieving 8 to 9 per cent of the total domestic economy.

As to farm exports, which have increased sixfold since 1953, citrus fruit (Jaffa oranges and grapefruits) maintained its dominant position, but no longer in splendid isolation. Until 1953, citrus fruit was practically the only agricultural item sent abroad, but since that date groundnuts have become an important marketing item. Israel's climatic conditions, coupled with scientific experimentation, made cotton, avocados, strawberries, persimmon, dates, and winter-grown vegetables (tomatoes, lettuce, melons), as well as flowers, come up weeks earlier than similar crops in other Mediterranean countries. Immediate shipping and airlifting gets crops to non-Mediterranean Europe weeks before the rival products. Israel has asked for an associate membership in the Common Market and for consequent lowering of tariffs, but it is precisely Israel's success (plus weighty political considerations) that prompts the Mediterranean partners of the "elite six" to block its affiliation and to agree only to some minor accommodations.

For puzzling reasons, the skill of processing and canning fruit, vegetables, and fish has not quite been mastered by Israel. It is still struggling with this problem, and its canned products—apples, figs, quavas, peaches, apricots, cherries, and plums—are not as well received as the fresh items. There are now limited exports of breeding cattle to Iran and to Greece, and of hatching eggs and live chicks to Italy, France, and African countries.

In 1968 Israel exported $1 million worth of goose liver and goose meat to France. Goose liver reaches Paris restaurants for conversion into pâté de foie gras within twenty-four hours of the demise of the livers' donors. The British peeled $20 million worth of Israeli oranges in 1969 (but citrus products experienced a bad year in 1970). The week before Christmas, 1969, Israel sold $300,000 worth of fresh flowers in Europe and in 1970 it sold $5.3 million worth abroad. The French in 1970 consumed nearly 1,000 tons of Israeli tomatoes and about 3,000 tons of bananas, carrots, and even grapes. However, Israeli wine, among the best in the world, is finding the competition from France and other wine-producing areas too stiff.

Israel is described in the Bible as "a land flowing with milk and honey," and for a good reason—it has no water. This has been a problem throughout the ages. There is only one fresh-water lake in the country, the Sea of Galilee. The Dead Sea is too salty for irrigation. The rivers are small and few. Rain falls only during the four winter months, and in some parts of the country—the Negev—it comes in infrequent but sudden downpours.

In the 1920's the pioneers' fine sense of the possible asserted itself and, despite British misgivings, a spectacular hydroelectric project was built on the Jordan by the Jewish engineer Pinhas Rutenberg. (During the 1948 war the plant was destroyed by the Arabs.) The British themselves laid a long pipeline, with intermediate boosters, from springs near Petah Tikvah to parched Jerusalem. In 1936 the Mekorot Water Company was established by Jewish initiative to bring water to the Valley of Jezreel and to Haifa, but the enterprise became economically significant only after the establishment of Israel. Other large-scale plans and efforts by both Jews and non-Jews for watering the land were dampened by the administrivia of the mandatory government. One example was the grand design, called the Jordan TVA, by Dr. W. C. Lowdermilk.

Upon the birth of the state, the new government launched a "water offensive" and a "man-made fertility scheme," utilizing Mekorot's experience and know-how. Several undertakings were initiated, the largest and most successful (over which there were international reverberations) being the Kinneret-Negev Project, which carries water drawn from the Sea of Galilee in the north to the arid desert in the south via the National Water Conduit. That, plus minor projects such as seeding rain clouds and sinking wells, made it possible to increase the irrigation of land fivefold since 1948, to grow most of Israel's food needs, and to introduce new industrial crops.

With all this dramatic program, why does the state have an unfavorable balance of payments in agriculture? Because Israel is practically a net importer of heavy farm machinery and such important food items as nonpoultry meat, wheat, tea, and oil seeds. Agricultural exports in 1967 amounted to about $150 million, and imports were more than $156 million. But the gap in agriculture is narrowing, and despite the aftermath of war it was nearly closed in 1970.

Because of agriculture's coming of age—even though some forms of subsidies, market guarantees, and price support are maintained to make tilling the soil sufficiently attractive financially—industry and trade now receive equal treatment. It is not without some soul-searching that the leaders of the government, mostly of the Avodah party, have decided on the new course. The psychic rewards of their socialism had to be pushed into the background in the face of the material realities of the last third of the twentieth century and the vicissitudes of a protracted quasi-war period. From time to time there are outcries from Mapam or the Communists against the dehumanizing effects of industrialization and commercialism and against the economic apostasy of the Avodah Cabinet members. The latter, while succumbing to the pressures of modern society, nurse their ideological wounds and in some way, in all sincerity, try to propitiate the spirit of A. D. Gordon.

The most important instrument of the proletariat in Israel is the Histadrut, the General Federation of Labor. Earlier, mention was made of the Lavon Affair. Until that unfortunate cloak-and-dagger incident in the 1950's, which ruined the career of the "strong man" of the labor movement, Minister of Defense Pinhas Lavon, and bedeviled the political life of Ben-Gurion, Israel was a virtual duopoly. The Histadrut was as powerful as the government, and in some instances more powerful. Moreover, the secretariat of the labor organization and the Cabinet were like interlocking directorates.

The Histadrut was formed in 1920. Among its founders was David Ben-Gurion, who served as its secretary-general from 1921 to 1935. It started with a membership of 4,500 out of a general Jewish population of 100,000. In 1971 it had a membership of more than 1 million adults out of the 3 million population.

One of the main objectives of the organization was "to concentrate and then diffuse such practical knowledge as its members possessed." It thus became not only a trade union but also an educative instrument. It was different from labor federations in other countries because of its nationalist-Zionist motivation and goal. In fact, it started as a movement first for the founding of a homeland and then for building it into a workers' socialist commonwealth.

From the very beginning it launched twin activities in addition to conventional trade union functions. The first was the extension of help to collectives and cooperatives. The other was entrepreneurship (Hevrat Ovdim), engaging in commercial and industrial profit-making undertakings, the profits to be reinvested in the labor economy. The tremendous success of the Histadrut was due to the coordination of these two principles—collectivism and entrepreneurship. No rigid dogma, no doctrinaire obsession hindered the rapid rise of the Histadrut as the most unusual labor organization in the world, which even today is considered a model for Western countries.

Because of the nature of the organization and its Zionist-socialist goal, Arabs and members of centrist or rightist political parties were at first left out of the Histadrut. Only after the establishment of the state and the formation of a labor government were Arabs and nonsocialists admitted to the organization. Now there are some 55,000 Muslims and Christians in the trade union, and workers of most political orientations are represented, either individually or in blocs—right-wing Herut, for instance. But the dominant political entity in the federation is Avodah.

The range of Histadrut activities is almost limitless. It was instrumental, for instance, in developing a governmental labor code based largely on conditions previously secured by the trade union for its workers through collective bargaining. The government extended some of the features of the prestatehood labor-management agreements, especially in the field of social insurance. New legislation prompted by the Histadrut includes laws dealing with hours and rest, paid annual holidays, employment of women, work supervision, settlement of labor disputes, national insurance, civil service, severance pay, apprenticeship, collective agreements, and many other regulations.

In the area of mutual aid, the Histadrut maintains Kupat Holim, the Workers Fund for the Sick, which was first established in pre-Histadrut days to provide medical attention to pioneer settlers in outlying districts. Now Kupat Holim has some 15 hospitals, 1,200 clinics, 20 convalescent homes and 185 mother-and-child stations. It is the largest health organization in Israel, serving 2 million people, because it is available to everyone, not only to members of the Histadrut for whom subscription to it is mandatory. From time to time demands arise from nonlabor parties that the Histadrut's medical insurance be nationalized, but Kupat Holim has become a sacrosanct institution. Despite some organizational shortcomings, it has helped make Israel, especially through its care of the newcomers, the "healthiest" country in the region.

Other mutual-aid Histadrut institutions include Mishan (welfare fund loans to needy members), Dor l'Dor (assistance to the elderly), and Matziv (help to widows and orphans).

In the province of labor economy, the Histadrut sponsors Tnuva, the cooperative center for the marketing of agricultural produce. It is the pivotal wholesale marketing association in the country, handling two-thirds of the farm output, mostly for domestic but also for some foreign consumption. Another project, Hamashbir, serves the specific needs of 550 collectives and cooperatives. Together with Tnuva, it has been instrumental in holding down speculation and price manipulation. Then there are Solel Boneh and its subsidiaries: Phoenicia Glass Works, Vulkan Foundries, Nesher Cement Works, Even v'Sid Quarries, Overseas and Harbour Works Company (operating in Africa, Asia, and Latin America). Solel Boneh is the largest construction and building materials agency in the Middle East.

The Histadrut also administers banks, insurance companies, and housing projects and provides nearly all inter- and intra-urban motor transportation in the land through Egged and smaller cooperatives. In partnership with the government and other public and private bodies, it has launched such projects as Mekorot, the water resource company, the Zim Shipping Line, and El-Al national airways.

Before 1948, and for a while even after the establishment of the state, the Histadrut operated a network of schools. Now that the government has taken over the supervision of general education, the Histadrut maintains adult education classes, folk-dance groups, and art and music courses. Other cultural activities include professional and semiprofessional dramatic groups, two daily newspapers, a publishing house, the country's largest sports organization (Hapoel), teachers' seminaries, an Afro-Asian Institute for Labour Studies and Cooperation, and a Latin American Centre for Cooperative Studies and Labour. The last two projects serve mainly students from developing countries and South America.

Merely enumerating these activities does not fully describe the pervasiveness of the Histadrut; it also reaches out organizationally to a variety of professions such as doctors, attorneys, civil servants, nurses, and university professors. In addition it has a youth affiliate numbering 100,000 workers and students under eighteen.

The Histadrut's success is due in large measure to the fact that it rushed in where others feared to tread. It implemented the basic principles enunciated by its founders in the 1920's: "concentration of knowledge and then diffusion." It applied the managerial skills gathered throughout the years and, even without adequate capital, "made the desert bloom." But Israel now has emerged from a primitive economic state. By its very success the Histadrut allayed the fears of private enterprise and encouraged greater capital inflow. When the Histadrut opened its doors to non-Jews and to nonsocialists, it weakened its position further. Whereas in the days of Ben-Gurion and later Lavon the Histadrut was the central fact of Israel's reality, it now has lost some of its glamour and influence.

One symptom of the weakening of the Histadrut is the rebelliousness and belligerency of some of its most valued members, the dockworkers and longshoremen. These men were at first the country's unsung heroes in the era of illicit immigration and the smuggling of arms. Later they kept the ports, vital for contact with the outside world—the state being surrounded on land by the enemy—open and humming. In time, their valor and indispensability gained for them special status in public life. When former chief of staff General Haim Laskov became director of the Israeli Ports Authority and began introducing new and more effective work methods, a three-sided conflict developed among Laskov, the port workers, and the Histadrut. In this bruising contest the Histadrut was defied and its instructions disobeyed. The new secretary-general of the Histadrut, Itzhak Ben-Aharon, one of the leaders and theoreticians of Ahdut Avodah, was too much of a "pedant-turned-union-boss" to command attention from all concerned. Other incidents have also pointed to fissures in the labor organization.

Although the Histadrut still dominates nearly two-thirds of the Israeli economy, the private sector in the moshavot, industry, and trade have become more aggressive. In premandate times, manufacturing in Palestine consisted of the output at the wineries built by Rothschild in Rishon LeZion and in Zikhron Yaakov and small plants for such activities as processing olive oil, making soap, and the like. Under the British, industry did not grow much, even though the worldwide depression in the late 1920's and early 1930's brought modest Jewish capital to the country. The British were afraid to expand the absorptive capacity of the land and thus cause an angry reaction from the Arabs.

Nevertheless, there were serious beginnings under the mandate in textiles, condiments, pharmaceuticals, and cement. When in 1939, on the eve of World War II, the Middle East was isolated and nearly all shipping facilities were mobilized for supply and troop transport, the Jewish penchant for private enterprise asserted itself and seized the opportunity to expand existing plants and establish new ones to meet domestic needs: clothing, food-processing, beverages, metalworking, wood production, chemicals, electrical appliances, and construction materials. Allied army orders gave the infant economy further boost.

The exodus from Europe in the 1930's brought to Palestine skilled craftsmen and experts in areas such as diamond-cutting. The staid British officials would have been astounded to learn that the backward country was to emerge also as an aspiring women's fashion center, dispensing, for instance, to the four corners of the earth, the then unknown but now widely used panty-hose.

When Israel gained its independence, the emphasis was put on consumer goods for the local market. Having overcome the food problem in a relatively short time, the economy was redirected to the manufacturing of such household appliances as refrigerators and washing machines, to car assembly, and even to making paper for the "people of the book." By the late 1960's industry became the cornerstone of Israel's economy, accounting for more than a quarter of the gross national product and four-fifths of the annual exports, most of it in the hands of the private sector.

The largest production item in Israel today still is food, and 85 per cent of it is consumed domestically. In this area the Histadrut continues to play the major role. But diamonds, "Israel's best friend," have emerged as the country's largest single export item, and it is a private enterprise. Israel in 1972 surpassed Belgium as the international diamond center.

One of Israel's most serious problems is its lack of raw materials. The scant natural resources of the country, mostly in the Dead Sea, consist of potash, phosphates, bromine, and magnesium, some of which are used for the production of fertilizers exported to Africa and Asia. Copper is another commodity found in Israel. The freakish behavior of world markets in 1970–71 and the noxious effects of certain fertilizers caused what experts believe to be only a temporary setback for the Dead Sea products, while the copper industry of Timna in the southern Negev boomed.

Another serious problem for Israeli industry is its lack of energy sources. Local petroleum and natural gas supply only 10 per cent of Israel's needs (the oil wells of Sinai, occupied in 1967, are a substantial but temporary reinforcement). In 1970 Israel completed a 42-inch pipeline, with an initial carrying capacity of 1,500 tons an hour (eventually to be more than trebled), which extends from Eilat on the Gulf of Aqaba to Ashkelon, and subsequently to Ashdod on the Mediterranean, a total distance of 163 miles, by-passing the Suez Canal and further diminishing its importance to Israel and to international shipping as well. Since the destruction of the Rutenberg power station in the 1948 war, Israel has been unable to undertake any significant hydroelectric projects. Its only power comes from thermal generating units using imported fuel.

Solar energy has not lived up to expectations and is used marginally by private individuals and a few small settlements. More significant are the plans for atomic energy, which were stepped up in 1970–71.

The necessity of importing raw material has had an adverse effect on the balance of trade, a chronic situation in the country. An Israeli Minister of Commerce, Industry, and Development once observed sadly: "Everything is increasing in Israel. Our exports are increasing, our imports are increasing, our deficit is increasing." Another Cabinet Minister also had his say: "Jews were not supposed to be good soldiers, but good businessmen. Israel proved the reverse."

Paradoxically, the defense needs—an estimated 25 to 30 per cent of the budget, among the highest if not the highest percentage anywhere—which drain the treasury, have brought about industrial growth to the extent that Israel is now producing much of its own conventional weaponry and has ventured into electronics and aviation (both transport and passenger planes). In aeronautics, the Arava category was flight-tested in 1969. It consists of two models, Arava STOL (short takeoff and landing) and the Commodore Jet "Eleven Twenty-three." In 1971 Israel Aircraft Industries won the Prix de Promotion Internationale at the prestigious Le Bourget air show in Paris, an honor accorded in previous years to America's NASA, Germany's Porsche, and others of like stature. Moreover, France, which imposed a plane embargo on Israel in 1967, has purchased from IAI the rights to produce a French version of the Arava to be called Sherpa. Also in 1971, at a Washington exhibition of Armed Forces Communications and Electronics, the United States bought from Israel $70 million worth of sophisticated electronic equipment, especially ground-to-air communication's instruments. (Military attachés of the U.S.S.R. Embassy in Washington merely walked away from the exhibit with twenty catalogues.)

The IAI employs about 14,000 people and is the largest single industrial complex in Israel. It started in 1953 (as Bedek, a plane-servicing agency) with seventy workers. Now the fledgling aircraft industry is also producing the Gabriel ship-to-ship missile and is carrying out plans for advanced jet fighters. Foreign orders for the Gabriel totaled close to $40 million in 1972. Israel is also in the process of perfecting its symbolically named Jericho Missile, positioned in the Sinai and now capable of carrying 1500 pounds atomic warheads to hit targets 300–400 miles away.

Econometricians are puzzled. All their dire predictions have been false. Since 1948, the gross national product has increased on the average of 11 per cent a year, and the per capita growth has been at 5 per cent. This means that during this period Israel, with an initial Jewish population of 650,000, absorbed more than 1.5 million newcomers, maintained a staggering military establishment, and still managed to raise the standard of living in the country to compare favorably with European states. The per capita income of the Israelis in 1971 was approaching $1,800. Income tax was levied progressively up to 62.5 per cent.

United States Jewry and Jews in other parts of the world have shared with Israel a substantial portion of the housing, absorption, and development budgets. West German reparations also helped. From 1948 through 1968 the American United Jewish Appeal provided in "unilateral transfer," that is, outright gift contributions, more than $1.1 billion for the Jewish Agency. Hadassah, the American Women's Zionist Organization, raised about $185 million during this period, mainly for health services (Hadassah hospitals, etc.) and youth settlements. Redeemable Israeli bond sales in the United States amounted to $1.077 billion. An estimated additional $600 million worth were purchased in 1968–71.

Most Jews feel that their outright contributions to Israel (bond purchases, incidentally, proved to be sound investments and may be redeemed at full value as stipulated) were merely an expression of partnership with Israel in an effort to find a home for oppressed coreligionists. They were viewed not as a matter of charity, of dollars and cents, but as a matter of moral obligation and responsibility for fellow Jews. Nonetheless, many experts viewed it as a "Via Dollarosa" for Israel's economy. Others, however, pointed to the fact that, unlike many new countries, Israel applied the money most effectively and converted it to uses that eventually will leave it on a road to economic stability.

Up to 1961 Israel was also one of the recipients to U.S. Government aid to underdeveloped countries. But in that year the United States declared that the country had outgrown this category and withdrew its allocation. Also, systematic U.S. technical assistance stopped in 1962. (Israel, like other countries in Europe and Latin America, now gets occasional and specific-purpose research grants.) Up to 1966 Washington lent Israel $475 million, of which some $275 million has already been repaid.

At least one noted American economist, Leon H. Keyserling, chairman of President Harry S Truman's Council of Economic Advisers, pointed out that "the vast preponderance of Israel's progress has come from indigenous efforts; the help from overseas, while essential, has been marginal nonetheless."

A substantiating example may be the effort to curb galloping inflation in 1969–70. The government was pleading for price and wage controls. The Histadrut brought forth a "compromise"—an 8 per cent wage increase. The private sector would go no higher than 2 to 4 per cent. The final outcome of the negotiations was 4 per cent cost-of-living compensation, calculated on total wages (leave, sickness, holidays), payable in government savings bonds linked to the cost of living index; employers' purchase of government savings bonds for an amount equaling 4 per cent of their payroll; employer agreement not to raise prices as a result of this "adjustment"; a listing by the three parties (government, Histadrut, and Manufacturers Association) of nonvital items to be taxed at higher rates; and a promise by the Histadrut to foster more efficiency and productivity of labor. The objectives of this agreement were to win for labor an 8 per cent wage increase, yet to syphon off the additional purchasing power resulting from this adjustment through buying of government savings bonds; to bring stability in labor-management relations and greater productivity; and to net the government $200 million in savings bonds!

Yet the pivotal problem of Israel, despite its successful defiance of economic laws, is that its citizens refuse to live within their means. The demand for imported goods, especially consumer durables (TV sets, for instance, at an average of $500 each), is growing. There is also an increased demand for services, such as travel abroad, in the face of punitive taxation. Foreign currency reserves have dwindled dangerously below the minimum level of $500 million set by the government. In 1969, despite record exports, the country bought abroad a staggering total of $900 million more than it sold, bringing about on August 2, 1972 a devaluation of the Israeli pound (it was devalued previously in 1965 to produce a slowdown). The Common Market continues to cold-shoulder Israel's plea for associate membership, although it has made slight tariff adjustments on some export goods.

Israel, however, banks on its transformation into an industrial society and its growing ability to attract foreign capital. It also strives—and it has evinced aptitude in this area—to integrate some of its manufacturing with larger and more experienced enterprises abroad.

With rising technical and industrial standards, the government is gradually trimming its administrative controls, subsidies, and intervention. According to some government experts, but not in the view of many university professors, the gross national product of Israel will continue to grow at a minimum of 10 per cent rate annually until 1975. By that time the country's industrial output is expected to double and by 1980 to treble, and the balance of payments to improve dramatically.

Contributing to this optimistic outlook is the steadily increasing tourist trade, emerging as a significant economic factor. In the summer of 1971 so many people flocked to Israel that they strained the housing facilities in the country. The government found it necessary to advise tourists to postpone their arrival to the autumn or winter months. Even the state of semiwar and continuous harassment from Arab commandos have not stopped the flow of visitors. On the contrary, it has become a "davka," a "spite project," prompting even larger numbers to show their solidarity with the "beleaguered state." One such tourist, who for some twenty years was active in raising funds and propagandizing for Israel, finally went up to see "the land." After a week in the country he wrote home to his friends: "Remember all the lies I told you about Israel? Well, they are true!"

11 Cultural
Self-Determination

The Prophet Zechariah conceived of the Jewish commonwealth as one to be established not by might, not by power, but by spirit. Likewise, the great Jewish philosopher of the early twentieth century, Ahad Haam, considered Palestine primarily a Jewish cultural center. Things have not quite worked out that way. The state of Israel came into being in a power struggle and has maintained its existence by military might. In the realm of the spirit it has done much in many areas, but because of the vicissitudes of the times, it has been lagging in many other spheres. Perhaps the enthusiasts who thought the country would overnight become a "light unto the nations" needed a reminder like the one uttered by an American Jewish student in Jerusalem: "We keep on forgetting that we are not only the descendants of the prophets, but also the descendants of those upon whom the prophets poured their wrath."

A Zechariah, were he to visit present-day Israel, would be much pleased but also a bit disappointed. The grand spectacle of Jewish national rehabilitation in Palestine has had political and economic repercussions throughout the world. Somewhat less significant, certainly not as explosive, were the cultural implications of Israel's return to its homeland. Although it has regained its status as a shrine for the Jewish ego, Israel, unlike the Diaspora, sometimes mistakes energy for talent. There are a lot of brilliant pages in its new scriptures, but not a coherent, robust story. For instance, no one writer has yet captured the grandeur and the misery of Israel's reality, has felt the crosswinds of Western culture and at the same time inhaled the whiffs of his ancient heritage. Nobel Prize winner S. Y. Agnon immortalized the pieties and the wonders of the past, not the dynamism of a bruised and bruising people of the present.

Colonel Mordechai Bar-On, onetime chief education officer of the army and a sabra, pointed out, as Hobbes did, that in Judaism statehood was an important element but not the only one. In Jewish history, the colonel continued, two events happened within three years of each other. The first occurred in A.D. 70. Jerusalem was besieged by the Romans, and the Temple was doomed. At a critical moment Rabbi Yohanan Ben-Zakkai, the head of a yeshiva in Jerusalem, deserted the defenders and appeared before the Romans to petition for continuation of his yeshiva at Yavneh. The second event took place three years later in Massada, where some 950 Jewish freedom warriors committed suicide rather than fall into the hands of the Romans.

"From the Jewish point of view, history proved that Yohanan was right," stated Bar-On. Had the Rabbi not done what he did, had only the warriors of Massada acted in their way, then the Jewish people would not be alive today. "Perhaps," wrote Bar-On, "only a statue in the British Museum would preserve our memory. (We have all seen the famous statue of the dying Gaul.) . . . It is worth noting that Yohanan Ben-Zakkai, the deserter, was hailed as a hero by Judaism. . . . The story of Massada is not mentioned even once in the Talmud. We know about it from Josephus Flavius—a Hellenistic [Jewish] writer." Today, Massada is a symbol to Israeli youth. It seems obvious, the Colonel concludes, that "the fortress of Massada without the values of Yohanan Ben-Zakkai would be worthless."

Israelis jest that the reason they went into Sinai in 1956 and in

1967 was to return the Ten Commandments. Most Israelis, however, with the exception of a few so-called Canaanites, would agree with Colonel Bar-On's statement. Yet the threat by neighboring Arab countries to the very existence of the state made many Jews "worship other gods," and rely on the "might of their arm." Mass immigration from non-Western countries posed a different threat— the rendering of Israel into a backward, provincial, Levantine state. However, by 1960 a fluted tower dedicated to learning and housing an atomic reactor for peaceful use was put up immediately west of the village called Yavneh, where 1,890 years before Yohanan Ben-Zakkai mobilized the remnants of Jewish hope and faith to fashion the molds of his people's future. Additionally, today, on a per-capita basis, Israel ranks third—behind the United States and Sweden—in the number of computers it employs. Its 270 yeshivot have close to 20,000 Talmudic students, and its five major universities have an enrollment of nearly 50,000.

The Western Jew's monomania for "study for the sake of study" slackened a bit in Israel—notably in the kibbutz—as he became a more "normal" human being in his homeland. At the very beginning of the modern Aliyah there was a perceptible change in the educational goals of the pioneers. While unlocking the intellect of the young was still a primary objective, it was coupled with the desire to give the youngster a "functional experience" to fit him into a remodeled, natural, and enunciated democracy.

The State of Israel inherited from the British a network of Jewish schools operated by the Vaad Leumi; a governmental system of Arab, Druze, Circassian, and Bedouin schools; private academies such as yeshivot; and Christian denominational establishments. The Jewish institutions were divided into four groupings: (1) the Labor Trend, the largest, which reflected the basic principles of Jewish socialist workers; (2) the General Trend, the oldest and nonpolitical schools, which included the Herzliah Gymnasium in Tel Aviv and the Bet Sefer Reali in Haifa (both secondary schools of exceptional quality); (3) the Mizrahi Trend, which paid equal attention to Jewish religious studies and to secular subjects; and

(4) the Agudah Trend, which placed chief emphasis on religious practice and study for the sake of study.

Although each of the trends operated autonomously under its own inspectors and supervisors, there was considerable cooperation and coordination, especially among the first three, all nominally under the jurisdiction of the Vaad Leumi. Parents had to pay tuition, and attendance was not compulsory. On September 12, 1949, the new state passed the Compulsory Education Law making attendance obligatory and universal between the ages of five and fourteen for all children, without distinction of creed, race, or sex. This was a giant step for the government in the face of the religious inhibitions against female education among the fundamentalist Muslims and Orthodox Jews. It also meant confrontation with thousands of parents who previously had sent their sons to work at the age of eleven or twelve.

The effectiveness of this law in terms of attendance was astounding. In 1969 among the Jewish children attendance was 97 per cent; among the Arabs it was 95 per cent for boys and 75 per cent for girls. There is a lingering resistance among the Arabs to female schooling. Some girls register but do not attend regularly, and the authorities, when the circumstances of a delicate situation demand it, are somewhat lenient in enforcing the law. All told, in 1970 more than 800,000 students attended the educational institutions of the land.

The 1969 reforms envisioned, in the course of six years, raising the age for free and compulsory education to sixteen. These changes were initiated in the face of the fearsome defense expenditures to counteract the tendency of the old system to create "two Israels," one consisting of the Western Jews, who feel a moral obligation to give their children at least a full secondary education, even at a very stiff tuition, and the other including the Oriental Jews and Arabs who are not similarly motivated. The 1969 regulations attempted to equalize the two groups somewhat. The hope is that in the not too distant future all secondary education will be free.

In 1971 the fees in the privately owned post-primary schools ranged from 1,225 to 1,500 Israeli lire (approximately $305 to $325) a year. But there were many scholarships, loans, and subsidies by both the national government and local authorities based on parents' income. Special consideration was given to children of newcomers. Nearly 50 per cent of secondary school children were paying only a small fraction of the tuition or nothing at all.

In addition to raising the age for compulsory school attendance, the 1969 reforms have divided the academic span into two parts: six years of elementary education and six years of secondary. The latter was split further into two periods: three years of intermediate and three years of higher departments. Students who reached the maximum age for compulsory education were nevertheless expected to continue their schooling until they were eighteen in special free late-afternoon and evening classes.

Another giant step was taken by the government in 1953, when it passed the State Education Law doing away with the ideological party affiliation of the various school trends and eliminating much duplication, waste, and political brainwashing of children. (Up until 1953, for instance, some of the labor schools would fly the red flag on special occasions.) This reform also had met with stiff resistance, especially from the Marxist Mapam and from the other extreme, the rightist, ultra-Orthodox Agudath Israel. The new law prohibited party affiliation and established unified state control and supervision. Under this system parents were free to choose for their children either a state school or a state religious school. In the latter case, it stipulated the standardization of 75 per cent of the curriculum, while the remaining 25 per cent, subject to the agreement of the Ministry of Education, could follow a religious orientation, if a majority of the parents in any one school so desired. These state religious schools were "observant of Orthodox precepts as to their way of life, curriculum, teachers and inspectors."

The Agudath Israel would not and could not accept those terms, so it opted out of the state system and continued to maintain its own schools, which received a "recognized status" and large financial help from the government. There were many other non-Jewish and recognized institutions operating on the same basis as the Agudath Israel schools. The current primary school attendance is as follows: 64 per cent in the general state schools, 29 per cent in the state religious schools, 7 per cent in the independent and "recognized" schools of Agudath Israel and others.

This system functioned remarkably well considering the tremendous influx of immigrants with variegated backgrounds, the lack of classroom space, and the dearth of teachers. Some of the schools were at first housed in tents. The benches were planks placed across stones. Inadequately trained instructors were put through an intensive program of "in-service" institutes. Many of the deficiencies disappeared by the late 1960's.

Although nursery education is not yet included in free and compulsory education, many three- and four-year-olds attend schools maintained by the government, local authorities, and private organizations such as Hadassah, Mizrahi Women, and the Women's Labor Council. More than 50 per cent of these children are exempt from tuition because of hardship. The nurseries have played an important part in unifying a diverse population. The Head Start program in the United States was inspired by the success of nursery education in Israel.

The compulsory kindergarten in the five- to six-year-old bracket is a relatively more developed institution than in most other countries. It nurtures the intellectual growth of the child, especially of Middle Eastern and North African parentage, through vocabulary enrichment and memory expansion. It also enhances the powers of the youngsters for both concentration and mathematical conceptualization.

The elementary school, usually separated from the kindergarten, also has the task, in addition to its regular syllabus of studies, of closing cultural gaps. A project with the ponderous title "Center for Aiding Schools with a Preponderance of Culturally Deprived Children" was set up to provide a differential approach to education, thus offering equal opportunity to all youngsters. The program attempted to compensate the educationally undernourished children by offering them a longer school day and an extended school year. The activities encompassed guided homework as well as art and social functions. The teachers involved in the program received additional professional training to qualify them for greater effectiveness. The center also issued more simplified textbooks and made greater use of multisensory (audio-visual, and so forth) aids. In the upper grades of some elementary schools, the interclass grouping project (somewhat similar to the track system in the United States) was introduced for below-average, average, and advanced students. Educational television is a new and pervasive factor in elementary education in Israel.

Secondary schooling was until recently nongovernmental, but in 1969 some steps were taken toward eventual free and compulsory education up to the age of sixteen. Many of the secondary schools were run privately, while others were started by public organizations or by townships and municipalities. The kibbutzim and moshavim usually sponsored their own high schools, either in their respective communities or on a regional basis. No matter how sponsored, all schools are expected to adhere to the basics of a curriculum recommended by the Ministry of Education and to come under its supervision. There are three main categories on this level: general, vocational, and agricultural. About 50 per cent of the schools are general or academic, that is, humanist in orientation. At the end of twelve years of study, matriculation (Bagrut) examinations are administered to the students. Those passing the test receive a certificate entitling them to enter institutions of higher learning in Israel and elsewhere.

Teachers in the nursery, kindergarten, and elementary schools as a rule come from seminaries maintained or aided by the state or by groups of agricultural settlements. The two-year course of study is open to graduates of secondary schools. The post-primary teachers must have a B.A. or an M.A. degree. Since so many of the secondary school graduates are drafted into the army, the military has an extensive program for potential teachers. However, the complexities of modern knowledge have prompted a rethinking of pedagogic training. There is talk in the Ministry of Education of extending the teacher education period to three or even four years.

Instruction in the Jewish schools is conducted in Hebrew, with Arabic as an optional subject on the secondary level. There is now a plan to make Arabic a required language in both the elementary and the secondary schools. Arabic is the language of instruction in the Arab school, with Hebrew taught from the third grade up (after the pupils have mastered reading and writing in Arabic) in the elementary and secondary schools. English ranks first and French second among the foreign languages offered. The government also sponsors several hundred school and neighborhood clubs, as well as playgrounds and youth centers, mostly in poorer areas.

Adult education always has had appeal in Jewish life. Even the hereafter for the pious is pictured in Hebraic lore as an exercise in adult schooling, with appetizing extracurricular activities. Paradise features rapturous bearded Jews sitting at long tables sipping vintage wine, partaking in delicacies made of leviathan meat and engaging in Talmudic disputations. In earthly, present-day Israel five autonomous bodies are concerned with cultural activities for mature people: the Ministry of Education, the Histadrut, the army, the Jewish Agency, and the universities. In addition to the formalized curriculum programs there are classes training illiterates to read and write and several thousand study circles in Bible, Talmud, literature, arts, music, dance, and the like.

Next to the army in effective language instruction for adults is the Ulpan (also based on army experience). This is a four- to six-month crash program in Hebrew for *educated* immigrants. During the period of study the enrollees are expected to give all their time and attention to the project, often accepting live-in arrangements. The Ulpan has thus enabled thousands of professionals and others to become a part of the economic, cultural, and political mainstream of the country within a relatively short time.

Higher education in Israel, at a premium in earlier years, is now within easier reach of many thousands because of government assistance; in part to stop emigration of young people to study abroad, and also because of the new needs of the rapidly developing country. The cornerstone of the Hebrew University in Jerusalem was laid in 1918 on Mount Scopus "as an act of faith," in the words of Dr. Chaim Weizmann. It opened its doors in 1925 and flourished academically until 1948, when its buildings, laboratories, and magnificent Judaica library were cut off from Israel by the Arabs. The Jews then built a new and imposing campus in the part of the city they had retained after the war of independence. In 1967, the Israelis regained full use of the old campus. The Hebrew University now has close to 16,000 students and offers instruction in a wide range of social sciences, humanities, and cognate fields, including medicine. The university staff numbers 1,600. In addition, the Hebrew University was responsible for the academic program of the Haifa University College, now independent as Haifa University, with 5,000 students, and the University of the Negev, with close to 3,000 students.

Actually the first institution of higher learning established in Israel was the Technion (Israel Institute of Technology). It was founded in 1912 in Haifa at the initiative of the Hilfsverein der deutschen Juden (German Jews' Aid Society), but before it even opened its doors the language of instruction became a subject of contention between the proponents of Hebrew, on the one hand, and those of German, on the other. During World War I the matter was settled in favor of Hebrew, but regular classes did not begin until 1924. The Technion produces most of the applied scientists and civil engineers in the country and provides technical services and guidance to Israel's industry and agriculture. Its departments include, among others, architecture, aeronautical engineering, mineral engineering and metallurgy, computer science, biomedical engineering, and town planning, all leading to the D.Sc. degree. The student population, including 11,000 part-time students in extension courses, is about 15,000. More than 1,000 are on the teaching staff.

The Weizmann Institute of Science in Rehovot, mainly a research center, is of great renown. It began as the Daniel Sieff Research Institute in 1934 and was renamed in honor of the first President of Israel, under whose direction it began functioning. Its current president is Dr. Albert Sabin, developer of the oral polio vaccine. As a postgraduate institution it engages in applied investigation of the exact sciences: nuclear physics, spectroscopy, electronics, polymer research, isotope investigations, organic chemistry, genetics, and the like. The nearly 1,200 staff members include some of the world's greatest scientists.

The University of Tel Aviv has blossomed as another great institution of higher learning. It now has a student body of close to 14,000 and a staff of more than 1,500. It, too, has a medical school, as well as a school of law and numerous departments in the humanities and social sciences.

A unique university, Bar-Ilan, is situated not far from Tel Aviv. It was founded by Mizrahi, a religious movement, and is modeled after the curricular patterns of American institutions of higher learning. It teaches secular subjects in humanities and the social and natural sciences. It also offers instruction in Bible, Talmud, and other Jewish studies but stays away from theology as such, because for the Orthodox Jew the very idea of theology smacks of heresy. There are some 8,000 students at the university and a faculty of 600. Recently it established a branch in Safad.

Close to 20,000 students attend about 270 yeshivot, where the stress is primarily on learning the Talmud and the commentaries. Only a minimum of secular subjects is offered. The main objective is study for the sake of study. The fact that these schools also produce rabbis and other religious functionaries is a secondary consideration.

Despite the tremendous energy and money expended to close the cultural gap between Oriental and Western Jews, a breach still remains. The problem in many ways is more acute in Israel than elsewhere, because on the one hand the country has superior social institutions, first-rate universities, and meticulous scientific research, and on the other hand a very large segment of the population lives in the pattern of "no-shoes" societies. The school dropout rate is still very high among the Easterners after the age of fourteen. Only 15 per cent of the Orientals attend secular institutions of higher learning. Illiteracy and cultural backwardness create difficulty in getting jobs and result in a low standard of living. The crime rate is a concomitant problem. One Yemenite child was constantly absent from school the year of his arrival in Israel. He later explained why: "I used to play truant so as to sit beside the highway, watching automobiles. I couldn't understand what made them run."

The most imaginative projects were employed to lure such youngsters into the present as well as into the future. The doubts that gnaw many educators are these: How wise is it to catapult people into the last third of the twentieth century? How much harm is done to both parents and children by abruptly detaching the youngsters from their social roots? Are many of these students being educated beyond their intelligence? How pertinent or relevant is the school curriculum to these students? Is "unity in diversity" merely organized chaos?

Israeli social scientists have now come to realize that the important point is not so much what to teach but whether teaching and learning make the student aware of his potential, with resultant self-assurance in his new environment. Thus, much of the after-school work and army experience is now fashioned in this context, with a great deal of positive results. The Ministry of Education and the Ministry of Defense have offered incentives to girl soldiers to go into the homes of the illiterate and teach the mothers reading and writing. The climate in these homes has been infused with a sense of rising expectations. While some parents from the very beginning saw merit in vocational schooling, the new atmosphere conditions them to send the more gifted children to institutions with a more humanistic or classical orientation.

In all this process the Hebrew language and the Bible have played important parts. Those who fought during World War I for the introduction of German as the language of instruction in the Jewish schools of Palestine wanted to break down the cultural barriers between Jew and Gentile. They thought of Hebrew as a form of intellectual claustrophilia, as a language embalmed in books. Had these people been more familiar with Jewish history, they would have recalled that the Haskalah (Enlightenment) movement in the nineteenth century—employing the Hebrew language—was a powerful reaction against the luridness of ghetto life and religious fanaticism and an attempt to introduce cosmopolitan, rationalistic, and scientific concepts into Jewish literature.

It was the Hebraic movement that stirred up Jewish political consciousness in Europe. The Hebrew language was charged with the emotional and spiritual group experience. Within that ancient tongue were concealed the treasures of a civilization, the legacy of a nation, the yearning of a people for tomorrow. It was only natural that a return to the national homeland meant a return to the national tongue. One man is usually referred to as the "father of modern spoken Hebrew"—Eliezer Ben-Yehudah. He wrote in 1880 on his way to Palestine: "Today we are speaking foreign languages. Tomorrow we shall speak Hebrew." On a ship from Marseilles to Jaffa he began speaking Hebrew to his wife; thus they became the first Jewish family in modern times to use Hebrew in daily life. In Jerusalem it was only with the learned Oriental Jews that he could communicate in the tongue of the Bible and Maimonides, while the European Jews in that city rose up against his "profanation of the holy language." Hebrew, according to the pious Ashkenazim, could be spoken only in study and in prayer. They had forgotten in the course of centuries what their forefathers, the Talmudic sages of long ago, had said: that the Jewish people were delivered from Egyptian bondage because they did not give up speaking Hebrew.

Ben-Yehudah, the Oriental Jews, the kibbutz *halutzim,* and even the farmers in the moshava awakened the language to a free and creative life. In the end it captured the imagination and the loyalties of the majority of the Jewish people in Palestine and later

Israel. It forged durable links among immigrants from eighty different countries, speaking perhaps sixty or seventy different languages and dialects, because it could be heard in the soft crooning of a mother's lullaby, in the pungency and precision of a stevedore's profanity, in the conciseness of scientific terminology, in the "freaky" talk of teenagers.

Even more than the Hebrew language, the Bible, written in that tongue, served as a cohesive bond among the scattered tribes of Israel throughout the days of the Diaspora, for the Bible followed the exiled into the lands of their dispersion. In the darkest hours of persecution in the *mellahs* of North Africa, in the ghettos of Eastern Europe, in the Nazi concentration camps, they found consolation and sustenance in the Book of Books. From it they drew not only spiritual and psycho-religious nourishment but also secular and culturonational identity. The Bible exuded the fragrance and the flavors of ancient glory and held out the warranty of eventual restoration: "For I will take you from among the nations, and gather you out of all the countries and will bring you into your own land," pledged Ezekiel.

When the dispersed did return, no matter how divergent the degree of their literacy and modes of behavior, they were equal partners in the legacy of the land and its promise of the future. No one segment in the Jewish community could claim superior rights to the others, even by virtue of prior arrival. The Bible thus became a vibrant factor in the Israeli's everyday life, whether he was a pious Jew, a secularist, or altogether a free-thinker. Surrounded as he was by biblical landmarks, he was constantly under the spell of its religious, moral, social, national, and humanitarian message.

The most remarkable expression of affection for the Book of Books is the Bible "match," an international contest in which thus far some twenty states have participated. Each national champion comes to Jerusalem to vie with the others and to be judged by such personalities as the justices of the Supreme Court and staff members of the Apostolic Bible Institute and of Protestant theological seminaries overseas. The winner becomes an overnight hero. Bible quizzes are held not only internationally but also locally in schools, rural settlements, the army, youth movements, and even jails. One of the winners in a recent contest in the Ramleh prison was an Arab. The two first international champions were Oriental Jews.

Language, Bible, and a common history of suffering and expectancy helped bridge some of the chasms among the Jews of many lands, but these factors could not aid in the rapprochement between Israeli Jews and Israeli Arabs, although the problems of the latter were similar to those of the Oriental Jews. In addition to the questions raised in connection with the integration of the Eastern and Western Jews, there were other dilemmas in the Arab-Jewish situation. Should the school try to obliterate or to foster Arab nationalism, pan-Arabism or pan-Islamism? Should the student be conditioned to grow into his own milieu or to outgrow it into an Israeli consensual society? What right does the state have to drag the Arab into an Israeli future?

The well-intentioned government leaders and social thinkers tried to compromise. They attempted to prepare the Arab young-ster to extract significant meaning both from his own religio-ethnic environment and from the Israeli Jewish reality. They have been only partially successful.

In the days of the mandate, most Arab schools were maintained by the British government of Palestine, whereas the Jewish educa-tional system was under the administration of local Jewish au-thorities and the Vaad Leumi. To equalize the position of the two sectors, the government of Israel in 1948 transferred the Arab schools to the jurisdiction of local Arab Councils, investing them with the right to levy rates in their respective places for educa-tional purposes. Israel assumed the same financial obligations and pedagogic supervision it exercised over the Jewish school system.

This autonomy was well received by the Arabs. They were con-siderably less enthusiastic in 1949 about the Compulsory Education Act, which insisted on coeducation. Since there is a direct link between the educational level of parents and the progress of their children, a campaign against illiteracy among adult Arabs was begun, with some modicum of success even among women, who were lured to classes in handicrafts, sewing, and cosmetology at Nazareth, Haifa, and other areas of large Arab concentration.

The language of instruction in all Arab schools is Arabic, offering students the opportunity to be culturally creative in their own tongue. Hebrew is taught from the third grade up, as indicated, after the pupils have mastered reading and writing in their native language. English and French, and occasionally another foreign language, are electives. Arab history and Islamic thought and practice are also a part of the curriculum, as well as the usual secular subjects; modern textbooks in Arabic are used. The Hebrew University is engaged in a special project of translating Hebrew works into Arabic and Arabic classics into Hebrew.

Some 85,000 Arab students attend about 400 Arab government schools (kindergarten, primary, and post-primary), and about 16,000 are enrolled in 90 nonstate institutions, supported mainly by religious groups, with subventions from the government. Registration for boys is near 95 per cent and for girls 75 per cent—a dramatic jump since 1948, when only 20 per cent of the girls attended school. The Druze have progressed even more strikingly. Only 900 were enrolled in the Druze schools in 1948; close to 9,000 attended in 1970, a tenfold increase, while the Druze population barely doubled from 16,000 to 35,000.

The initial difficulties of finding qualified instructors are being painfully overcome through pedagogic seminaries, special courses, and in-service training. Nevertheless, the quality of instruction, although improved, is still below that of the Jewish schools. Graduates of Arab secondary institutions attending colleges and universities find it difficult to compete with the graduates of Jewish secondary schools. This, coupled with the peculiar problems of an Arab minority tied emotionally to the vast Arab community outside Israel, threatening the very existence of the state of which they are citizens, makes it extremely difficult for Arab students to function normally on Israeli campuses, as we have seen in an earlier chapter. A little-known fact, though, is that many hundreds of Arab students, some sources say many thousands (this is impossible to ascertain for obvious reasons), from Israeli-occupied areas, as well as from Israel itself, were allowed since 1967 to go to Egypt to study at its universities and to return to their respective communities.

Not only the Oriental Jew and the Arab but also the kibbutz has its problems. The kibbutz provides for all the needs of its members "from razor blades to housing, from window curtains to concert tickets, from full medical care to honeymoons, from education to financial aid to dependents outside the kibbutz, from plants for the garden to trips abroad." This is a description by Moshe Kerem, a member of a kibbutz in Galilee, who is known to many as Murray Weingarten, the author of *Life in a Kibbutz*. In a government pamphlet Kerem points out that most of the kibbutzim came to believe that dormitory experience is the best way to teach individuals habits of community living and cooperation from the very earliest age. They feel that the psychological tension between parents and children, which is so pronounced in current society, can thus be relieved. The children stay together, eat together, and study together. As they grow older they conduct their own affairs with the guidance of their teachers and group leaders. Nursing mothers are naturally with their infants during the first months. Parents of older children may visit their youngsters during the day. The evening, of course, is spent with father and mother at home until bedtime.

In recent years a dozen kibbutzim or more, affiliated with the former Mapai, have allowed children—claiming that this fosters psychological security—to sleep in the homes of their parents, thus occasioning much debate. There are variations in this permissiveness. In some instances the children stay home until the age of three; in others, until they enter secondary school.

Children's houses, Kerem says in his excellent and concise description, are usually built as units and contain facilities for youngsters of a particular age group. They include sleeping quarters for four or five children, play areas, dining accommodations, and washrooms. Children "graduate" from one house to another as they advance in age. Adults working with them are trained in kibbutz-sponsored courses and in teachers' colleges. Kibbutz federations employ consulting psychologists and operate special classes for difficult children. Often secondary schools, sometimes even primary institutions, are established on a regional basis. The educational system emphasizes agriculture, but its most important pedagogic principle is that the school is an extension of the children's society, and that consequently there is a different, less formal relationship between student and teacher.

Kerem adds that the kibbutz movement does not accept government stipends for individual children but prefers to receive a lump sum based on the percentage of children who have passed the national examinations and to apply this sum to the education of all its children. Formal achievement (as evinced in grades) is discounted in an attempt to develop the child in accordance with his ability, through the establishment of personal relationships between him and his fellow students, and between him and his teachers. Kibbutz schools, therefore, also exclude the government-sponsored senior matriculation (Bagrut) from the curriculum. Students who want to go to the university—their number is increasing—prepare for the examination after graduation from the secondary school. Kerem concludes his discussion of education in the collective settlement: "One criticism made of the Kibbutz school system has been that in common with progressive educational systems generally it suffers from lack of discipline and, as a result, children know less than they should." Kerem thinks, though, that the fault, as in the case of progressive education, is with mediocre teachers and not with the system.

This is not the only adverse criticism of the kibbutz which has been subjected to much analysis. The noted psychologist Dr. Bruno Bettelheim wrote *Children of a Dream*, in which the kibbutz youngsters often appear as the children of a nightmare. He claims that youngsters separated from their parents in infancy suffer irreparable damage. Viscount Samuel, the son of the first British High

Commissioner in Palestine, took the noted psychologist's arguments gently apart in an article published by *Jewish Frontier* in October, 1969. Unlike Dr. Bettelheim, Edwin Samuel speaks and writes Hebrew fluently and once lived for many years in a kibbutz. He pointed out that American theories about child-rearing are not universally true for all places and all times.

Bettelheim observed that the founders of the kibbutz "rejected" the traditional Jewish family and the typical "momma." It seems, he declared, that the kibbutzniks did not trust themselves to raise their children to become the creators of a new society. Lord Samuel's contention was that kibbutz founders were returning, after years of wandering, to the warmth of family life, not escaping from it. Bettelheim's argument that the community dining hall represented a "massive psychic rejection of the former eating customs" is laughed off by Samuel. The kibbutznik was not rejecting "momma's" cooking, either consciously or subconsciously. A common hall was the *only* way in which cooking for a group could be done economically. Every lumber camp in America is run on the same principle. "Lumberjacks would be surprised to know that they were expressing a massive psychic rejection of anything." As to child care, Lord Samuel adds, conditions in the early kibbutz were extremely rough: Malaria was prevalent, as were dysentery and other diseases. The parents could not afford to build barracks or houses for themselves. They lived in tents for years, but for their children they managed to erect wooden huts and to screen the windows against mosquitoes and flies. While they themselves ate "rough," they had food especially cooked for their offspring.

Having segregated the children for hygienic reasons, Samuel added, they found that this gave the members of the collective an unexpected double bonus. First, one mother could look after several children, releasing the others to work in the fields. Second, it allowed a full night's sleep to most of the women. The kibbutz then discovered to its amazement that the children were thriving both physically and intellectually.

There is little doubt that group achievement reduces anxiety about failure and strengthens the ability to cooperate. However, another stricture sometimes advanced against the kibbutz is its in-group thinking and egocentricity: Like-minded people produce like-minded children. There is something dehumanizing in intellectual conformity, which often causes intellectual unemployment. The kibbutz movement in Israel is now considering the establishment of a university for its own students, and this further points to sociocultural isolation. This project is contemplated seriously, even though an amazing 80 per cent of kibbutz children who spend, on the average, four years away from home—army and other duties—return to their own or other collective settlements, despite the enticements of the outside world. Many writers, painters, and musicians who receive their training elsewhere at the expense of the kibbutz come back and pursue their creative activities, turning over their royalties—sometimes considerable amounts —to the collective treasury.

The kibbutzniks today, sometimes infatuated with their own ideological rhetoric, are an elite group, making up not quite 4 per cent of the total population but providing, together with the moshavniks, almost 30 per cent of the army and government leadership. Their cultural life is selective but rich in the areas of their choice, because of their own copious inner resources and because of the massive libraries they have assembled and the extensive adult education courses, lectures, and activities in theater, music, and art that they have organized. Many of the world's greatest performers are delighted to appear before the discerning and appreciative kibbutz audiences.

Those who are not members of a kibbutz, who do not share in the amenities of collectives or cooperatives and are not even affiliated directly or indirectly with the Histadrut, are the beneficiaries of many social and educational services dispensed by governmental and private agencies. Among the most prominent individuals contributing to Jewish community welfare in Palestine was Henrietta Szold. Born in Baltimore, she was the founder of Hadassah, the American Women's Zionist Organization. In the 1920's she formulated mother-care programs, child welfare centers, youth-training institutes, and a School for Hygiene Service. In this work she was helped by WIZO (Women's International Zionist Organization) and Hadassah. In 1931, when she was seventy-one years old, Henrietta Szold inaugurated the Vaad Leumi's social welfare department, which later became Israel's Ministry of Social Welfare. The ministry extended its activities to include, in addition to mother-infant care and child-youth programs, aid to the aged, retarded, and blind. It also maintains service for juvenile and adult offenders.

The government operates a National Insurance Institute for long-time citizens and newcomers alike. Financed by employer, employee, and self-employed persons, the plan in 1970 guaranteed pensions (at the age of sixty-five for men and sixty for women) to some 900,000 people. In 1969 close to 23,000 elderly persons who were not legally entitled to insurance nevertheless received special old-age allowances. The ministry supports eleven homes for the rehabilitation of delinquent youth and a haven for homeless Muslim children. Especially effective is the work with the blind in cooperation with Christian churches in Jerusalem and Nazareth. The programs training the sightless to operate IBM machines and spin cotton show great promise. Similar projects are conducted for the deaf and mute in the Helen Keller House in Tel-Aviv.

Non-Israeli organizations, supported by Jews the world over, continue to render health and social service supplementing governmental efforts. These agencies are the ORT schools, operating vocational training centers; Joint Distribution Committee, sponsoring Malben, a network of homes for the aged; WIZO, supporting seventy-five day homes for infants and toddlers, thirteen agricultural schools, and other projects; Hadassah, conducting, in addition to hospitals and clinics, electronics schools, printing shops, and youth guidance projects; and the Pioneer Women Organization (together with the Women's Labor Council of the Histadrut), maintaining 500 nurseries and kindergartens, clubs, and summer camps, as well as agricultural schools. Mizrahi Women and the

Council of Jewish Women also contribute significantly to care and welfare in the country.

While the government and outside agencies were hard at work to solve Israel's domestic problems, the country's scientists were busy investigating the mysteries of the universe and the potentialities of nuclear power. It was logical for the Jewish community to rely from the very beginning upon science and technology to alleviate one of the country's major problems—paucity of natural resources. Thus the Haifa Technion, the Hebrew University in Jerusalem, and the Weizmann Institute in Rehovot were called into being by the prestate Yishuv. The government in the post-1948 period proceeded to establish other scientific units, such as the Institute for Research on Fabrics and Forest Products, the National Physics Laboratory, the Institute for Biological Research, the Institute for Arid Zone Research, the Oceanographical and Limnological Research Institute, the Atomic Energy Commission, and the like. To coordinate all of these activities, a National Council for Research and Development was formed. The Academy of Sciences and Humanities, an organization of scholars independent of the government, was founded to maintain contact and exchanges with the outside world.

Israelis, who ordinarily are not accused of understatement, did not publicize their achievements, especially in the sensitive fields of nuclear and aeronautic studies. Because of common tendencies among Jewish scientists, and because of the suspiciousness of the British government in Palestine, research at first was of an abstract and pure nature. Later the new state's needs demanded that the academicians turn to applied science.

Among the notable accomplishments of the Israeli scientific community were those in the field of hydrology. It was a "natural" pursuit, since the best-known hydrologist in antiquity was Moses, who tapped water out of a rock. His descendants some 3,300 years later perfected new drilling techniques and used radioactive isotopes to label and trace the passage of water along aquifers. The Arid Zone Research Institute employs electric currents to filter the salt water in the Negev. The desalination projects at Eilat and at other sites have been less successful for lack of money, originally promised by the United States.

Israel is among the few countries that recently made great strides in atoms for peace programs by experimenting in industry, agriculture, and science in general. The Isotope Department of the Weizmann Institute came up several years ago with enriched oxygen, described as "heavy water," and is the chief supplier of it —about 90 per cent of the world demand. By virtue of its "weightier" atoms, the heavy water contains labeled oxygen and can be detected, as a tracer, wherever it goes. A physician, by injecting the liquid into a living body, can follow its path by taking blood samples. It is also of significant value in nuclear studies. Another example of Israeli atomic research is the development of a means to eradicate insects by sterilizing them with gamma radiation. In fact, it is suspected in many diplomatic and scientific quarters that Israel can produce and has produced the device for total eradication—the atomic bomb.

There is also major research in cancer. Israel was one of the contributors to the distinction made between the dormant and active stages of this killer. In the Six-Day War the most advanced methods of emergency treatment of soldiers in the field; of surgery in hospitals; of skin, nerve, and bone grafts; and of withdrawing splinters from eyes were used—all contributing to a remarkable rate of recovery.

In the field of aeronautics unique progress has been made in getting foreign craft flown by Israeli pilots to perform beyond their original capacity. Moreover, the Israelis are well on their way to producing their own jet fighter planes. They already have launched a twin turbojet transport airplane, the Arava, capable of carrying a payload of two tons or twenty passengers. It won for Israel several international prizes. As early as 1961 Israel sent up meteorological rockets. It now also makes its own ship-to-ship missiles and highly sophisticated communication instruments.

The idea of science-based industries was given a tremendous

boost by the Prime Minister's Economic Conference in 1968. As the character and substance of man's daily needs rapidly change, one method of meeting new demands is through electronic projects. The Conference addressed itself to this problem because Israel developed a bottleneck in the lower-level of production—shortage of technicians. The impetus provided by the Conference resulted in both short- and long-range planning. Thus the Histadrut and ORT schools expanded their services to train mechanics, while several companies, along with Yeda of the Weizmann Institute and Miles Laboratories, formed a subsidiary to sell plastic coatings for oranges, new types of insecticides, fine chemicals, fragilographs (which test blood cells to combat leukemia), and other products. Elron Electronics, founded by the graduates of the Technion, has had phenomenal success. It has even produced a low-cost computer, the Mosshauer Spectrometer. Plantex, backed by the Rothschilds, produces and markets alkaloids, glucocides, and vegetable extracts.

There is extensive use of computers in Israel. One of the first was named Golem after the famous robot reputed to have been created in the sixteenth century by Rabbi Judah Loewe of Prague; a monument was erected to this subject of many literary works in the capital of Czechoslovakia.

Oddly enough, the Jews, who have produced literary luminaries in the Diaspora, such as Heinrich Heine, Franz Kafka, Arnold Zweig, André Maurois, Boris Pasternak, Ilya Ehrenburg, Elmer Rice, Arthur Miller, and Norman Mailer—to name a few—have failed to come up with a really great Israeli writer. Hayim Nahman Bialik, generally accepted as the foremost modern poet in Hebrew literature, wrote his magnificent poetry in Russia and in other European countries before settling in Palestine. S. Y. Agnon, the 1966 Nobel Prize winner, captured the best of yesterday but not the reality of Israel today.

Poetry, on the whole, has fared somewhat better than prose. Itzhak Lamdan, in his work *Massada,* expressed the struggle of the Third Aliyah, the yearning of the pioneers for a homeland, and their resolution, having regained their birthplace, never to abandon it. Uri Zvi Greenberg at times conveyed the thunder and the wrath of the prophets of old. Avraham Shlonsky, rebellious "breaker of the tablets," introduced a new literary style. However, by their own admission, none of these poets has measured up to Bialik.

Perhaps the storm and stress attending Israel's rebirth, the drama of a people's return to an ancient land, were too big and too close to encase in literary testimony. Besides, non-Israelis of great talent have tried to do it and failed—Sholom Asch and Arthur Koestler, for example. Among the more notable novelists in Israel are Hayim Hazaz (some Israeli critics felt he was more deserving of the Nobel Prize than Agnon) and Moshe Shamir, who succeeded in taking some sharply focused snapshots of Israel's actuality.

For a while it appeared that a new group of young writers, the Canaanites, would usher in some originality. Mostly sabras, they trivialized or completely ignored Diasporic experience. They considered themselves the inheritors of ancient Hebrew and Canaanite legacy and sacrificed totally at the altars of Chemosh, Tammuz, and Ashtoreth. Long- and curly-haired, they looked like Samson but acted like Philistines. As one reads their works now, one finds in them a remarkable congestion of nonsense.

The quantitative factor of Israel's literary production is more apparent than the qualitative. Per capita, the country ranks second in the world in the number of titles it published in the last several years.

In the humanities and the social sciences, Israel has impeccable scholarship and sound research, but again no glittering personalities, pathfinders, theoreticians, ideologists, or philosophers. A. D. Gordon, Berl Katzenelson, and Martin Buber were transplants, although they were nourished in the culturally fertile soil of the Bibleland, especially Gordon and Katzenelson. Among historians, Jacob L. Talmon of the Hebrew University is outstanding, and Benjamin Akzin is a brilliant political scientist, although he, too, is not an Israeli product. But there is a great deal of promise in the recent graduates of the country's universities. Among Talmudic scholars there is profound knowledge of, and deep insight into, the Jewish religious heritage, but no giants who can be mentioned in the same breath with a Rabbi Akiva, Maimonides, or the Gaon of Vilna, as, let us say, Ben-Gurion's name may be associated with those of Joshua, and Judah Maccabee, and Bar Kokhba.

The story is somewhat different in archaeology. It is a national pastime, especially for the sabras who are so anxious to associate themselves with the glories of the past. Love of the Bible, not always in the religious sense, is one manifestation of it. Even the abortive Canaanite literary movement is evidence of it. For the immigrants, archaeology means a personal identification with the country. They are not newcomers to a strange land; they are returnees seeking and finding their roots—sometimes in crannies, cracks, or crevices of rocks, sometimes in the dry and drifting sand of the desert. While amateur archaeologists abound and pose great danger to methodical, scientific procedure, there are also first-rate and meticulously trained scholars such as Yigael Yadin, the son of Eliezer Sukenik of the Dead Sea Scrolls fame, Binyamin Mazar, and Yohanan Aharoni.

Scholars with patience, tact (a most valuable asset in a land holy to three major religions), and brilliance have delved into a past awaiting discovery. They have searched also the more "recent" paleolithic, neolithic, and chalcolithic periods; the beginnings of the Jewish commonwealth; the nascence of Christianity; and the arrival of Islam. Among the current projects are digs around the Western (Wailing) Wall, which was part of a structure surrounding the Temple in Jerusalem. The various museums in the country display some of the Dead Sea Scrolls, the Bar-Kokhba letters, and other significant relics.

In the arts, Israel's performance has been less spectacular. Great hopes and modest funds were invested in the country's theaters. Habimah, the National Theater, which had its Hebraic birth in Communist Moscow in 1917–18 and was guided by such personalities as Stanislavsky and Vakhtangov, lost its creativity and magic when it was transplanted to Palestine in the late 1920's. It is still powerful in the presentation of its earlier successes, *The Dybbuk* and *The Wandering Jew*, but it falters when it comes to Greek and more modern classics or avant-garde plays. The Cameri is an Israeli product of much promise but lacks the means to fulfill its potential. The Haifa Municipal Theater, a more recent project, is doing better than expected. There are scores of other professional and semiprofessional companies, "little theaters," and drama groups.

No original Israeli play of real substance had been staged yet. Thus far pieces of more than ordinary quality have been *Cazablan* (in the *West Side Story* genre), *King Solomon and the Cobbler*, *He Walked the Fields*, and *Sodom City*, the last a reproduction of Dodge City (a kind of biblical Western). Most plays produced are translations from the classics—Shakespeare, Strindberg, Ibsen, and Shaw. Among the recent productions are *Who's Afraid of Virginia Woolf?*, *Mother Courage*, *Measure for Measure*, *My Fair Lady*, *Man of La Mancha*, *Fiddler on the Roof*, and *Hair*.

The problem is that the original Israeli plays are amateurish and the audiences are professional, among the most professional in the world. Despite recent television, the Israelis are still fanatical theatergoers. Initially the Histadrut—through its excellent Ohel (Tent) Dramatic Company—and the kibbutz and the moshav, then the government, and later the municipalities nourished and encouraged the theater habit. While in most other countries large segments of the population never have the opportunity to see a quality stage production, in Israel there is no "peasant" class, certainly not in the agricultural kibbutzim and moshavim. If there is some cultural marginality it is in the cities among the Eastern Jews, and it is fast disappearing. Moreover, the Israeli theater is mobile, and its mobility, if not its other requirements, is subsidized by the government and several public bodies. Nearly 40 per cent of the Tel Aviv and Haifa theaters' performances are given on the road.

Cinema is the particular fare of the Oriental Jews. While television has affected attendance in the movie houses, Israel still ranks high in the boxoffice calculations of Hollywood and other film production centers. Hollywood has lately discovered Israel for film-making purposes. There are now also several Israeli companies experimenting with avant-garde movies.

Music fares only a little better than the theater. There is modest talent with a great deal of good will among the Israeli composers. Again, the audience is professional and the indigenous serious music writers are still amateurish. Israel is a singing and dancing country, whose folk songs draw from biblical themes, liturgic origins, pioneering motifs, army life, and other inexhaustible sources of Jewish expression across many centuries and from all continents of the world. There are literally thousands of choral groups, dance circles, bands, and orchestras. The country has a first-rate philharmonic orchestra of international repute. Founded by Bronislaw Huberman, it has played under the batons of Toscanini, Mitropoulos, Ormandy, Markevitch, Koussevitzky, Sargent, Bernstein, and Mehta. Some of the most talented artists in the world have performed many times in the little country on the far end of the Mediterranean: Casals, Rubinstein, Heifetz, Stern, Menuhin, Peerce. The cities do not enjoy a monopoly, and visiting virtuosi and conductors are pleased to appear in kibbutzim and moshavim.

The many music schools and dance studios in the country have produced a number of young violinists and pianists who already have made their mark internationally. But as yet there is no specific Israeli style and no great composer. German-born Paul Ben-Haim attempted to create a Mediterranean style, but it is too early to judge its development.

Painting, drawing, sculpture, and kindred art forms are well advanced in the country. Somehow more than in the other creative branches of Israeli culture, the painter has been able to combine the biblical idiom, the Oriental touch, and Western influence into a meaningful whole. Intoxicated with the beauty of Israel, some of the artists have managed to shake off Paris and Rome and express *sui generis* the reunion of the Jewish people with their homeland: Reuben Rubin, Mané Katz, Marcel Jancu, Mordekhai Ardon, Nahum Gutman, and several younger people.

There are artist colonies in Ein Hod near Haifa, in Safad, and in Jaffa. Art galleries in the major cities exhibit private collections and world masterpieces. Museums and art schools are scattered all over the country. The better known are the Bezalel School of Art, the Billy Rose Art Garden of Modern Sculpture—both in Jerusalem and both part of the Israel Museum—and the Tel Aviv Museum.

Israel's architectural shortcomings are due primarily to haste and lack of resources in a country that trebled its population with refugees in less than twenty years. Yet there are some lovely and pleasing exceptions in Jerusalem and in Haifa.

The land of the kibbutz now has scuba-diving in the Red Sea, golf in Caesaria, yoga on Tel Aviv beaches, and frustrated soccer and basketball teams in Olympic competition. It has many other activities: tennis, cricket, rowing, handball, wrestling, fencing, volleyball, track, hikes, and skiing on Mount Hermon in the Golan Heights area, occupied in 1967. All sports are amateur. The most popular spectator game is soccer; next is basketball, followed by volleyball. Teams in these sports play in fiercely competitive leagues, supervised, as are other organized physical activities, by the Sports and Physical Culture Authority.

Israel participates in the Olympic games without noticeable success. It belongs to the Asian sports federations, as well as to European associations—as befits a country situated on the crossroads of three continents. In addition, it hosts an international Jewish Olympiad, called Maccabiah, every four years. There is also an annual three-day gala march from the coastal plains to Jerusalem in which thousands participate. In marching, more than in any other sport, Israel has gained international recognition, winning several contests held in the Netherlands in recent years. Much of the physical fitness of the country, though, is due to a highly efficient calisthenics program in the schools and in the youth movements. There is a daily newspaper devoted completely to sports.

The mirror of Israeli life is the press. It reflects the heterogeneity of the population and all phases of its socio-economic, psychoreligious and political views. In 1972 there were twenty-three dailies: thirteen in Hebrew, two in Arabic, one in Yiddish and seven in foreign languages—English (*Jerusalem Post*), German, Hungarian, French, Polish, Bulgarian, and Romanian. The Hebrew-language dailies fall, theoretically, into two categories, the press of opinion and the press of information. The press of opinion is the organ of political parties, such as *Al-Hamishmar* (Mapam) and *Hatzofeh* (National Religious Party). The press of information is independent of parties. There are three such papers: *Haaretz, Maariv, Yediot Aharonot.* But the independent press really reflects the centrist point of view. *Haaretz,* a *New York Times*–like morning daily, has a weekday circulation of about 40,000. Friday and holiday editions reach about 60,000. *Davar,* the other morning daily, is the organ of the Histadrut and enjoys a circulation equal to that of *Haaretz.*

The mass circulation papers are the afternoon dailies, *Maariv* and *Yediot Aharonot,* both tabloid, claiming a weekday circulation in excess of 150,000 and more than 200,000 for weekend and holiday editions. There were more than 400 periodicals in 1972, about 300 in Hebrew, 50 in English, and the rest in Arabic, Yiddish, Bulgarian, Romanian, Spanish, Ladino (Judeo-Spanish), Hungarian, Polish, and Persian. As a result of increased immigration from the Soviet Union, a Russian-language weekly was launched in 1971.

The larger dailies have their own correspondents abroad (sometimes sharing them with French, British, or American papers). But foreign news coverage is highly preferential in that it focuses on events relating to Israel. Other foreign items are of secondary importance. There is also skimpy coverage of Jewish life outside the country, unless it pertains to Israel. The partisan publications are not free from occasional vituperative items and overstatements, especially around election time. Even the apolitical independents do a lot of inkletting and once in a while will engage in exposés. Journalism in Israel, on the whole, is zestful, fairly accurate, and highly readable. Ephraim Kishon, of *Maariv,* is perhaps the best-known writer in and out of Israel, having had his *feuilletons* published in book form in several languages, including English. He is delightfully irreverent, painfully logical, and supremely humorous.

In pointing out the less successful aspects of Israel's culture, one needs to remember that the small country was bedeviled by a war and burdened with absorption problems. It could not possibly explode in all fields of creativity, no matter how gifted its people. It would appear on balance, and as a matter of priority, that the most significant advance of the country has been in military preparedness and in economics. Moreover, there was fear that in sprinting ahead culturally a large segment of the population would be left behind, without the inner resources to catch up later.

Typical of the desire of most Israelis to "drag everybody into the future without abandoning the past" was the incident in which Jossi, teaching at the Bezalel School of Art, was trying to motivate a young Arab "to find his roots, to express his native Nazareth in his painting." But the instructor had a hard time with his student. In Jossi's words: "He wants to be the Picasso of Nazareth, not the Arab from Nazareth."

12 Membership in the Family of Nations

"Victory is the greatest tragedy in the world, except defeat." These words, uttered by the Duke of Wellington more than a century ago, applied to Israel since the United Nations called it into being on November 29, 1947, by partitioning Palestine into two states, Jewish and Arab. The Jewish community accepted partition reluctantly as a compromise solution. The Arabs of Palestine and surrounding countries rejected it out of hand. Earlier in 1947, when Britain turned the Palestine problem over to the world organization, some members of the United Nations favored a federal state, composed of Jewish and Arab autonomous entities. The majority voted for partition and complete sovereignty for the two states. Israel proclaimed its independence on May 14, 1948, a day before British withdrawal from the country.

Among the big powers, the U.S.S.R. was the most ardent supporter of Israel. "It would be unjust to deny the right of the Jewish people to realize their aspiration to establish their own state," said the then head of the Russian delegation to the United Nations, Andrei Gromyko, on April 16, 1948, at the Security Council. Gromyko rebuked the Arabs who opposed partition of any kind in the hopes of gaining all of Palestine: "The Soviet delegation cannot but express surprise at the position adopted by the Arab states in the Palestine question, and particularly at the fact that these states—or some of them at least—have resorted to such action as sending troops and carrying out military operations aimed at the suppression of the national movement in Palestine." Then Gromyko added: "We do not know of a single case of invasion of the territory of another state by the armed forces of Israel, except in self-defense, when they had to beat off attacks by the armed forces of other states on Israeli territory. That was self-defense in the full sense of the word."

The Kremlin's support of Israel stemmed from the desire to gain a foothold in an area coveted by the Russians from the days of Peter the Great. It was a logical effort in the attempt to eliminate Great Britain from the Middle East. It was purely situation ethics, a calculus of risk. A great many Israelis were Russian-born or came from satellite countries such as Poland, Hungary, and Czechoslovakia, the last being a main source of arms supply for Israel in its struggle with the Arabs. Moreover, the country's progressive workers made collectivism thrive. Moscow thus figured that the new state could be drawn into its orbit. However, things did not work out to the Kremlin's liking. Even the socialists in Israel were mostly non-Marxist. When the Communist and associated elements in the country were not strong enough to swing Israel into the Russian vortex, Moscow became increasingly disappointed. As Great Britain and France began losing their moorings in the Arab world, the Soviet Union seized the new and unexpected opportunities to ingratiate its way into the much more promising area surrounding Israel, and in time it evolved a kind of Monroeski Doctrine in the region.

Another of the great powers voting for Israel was the United States, but its policy at that time was not clear. President Truman was a stanch supporter of the idea of Jewish self-determination, but the State Department was less than enthusiastic about Jewish statehood. This somewhat unsympathetic attitude continued when Israel became, in the eyes of the American diplomats, an *enfant terrible*, upsetting carelessly devised plans and rebutting "bold old answers" to emergency problems. Before the United Nations vote on November 29, 1947, they made many attempts, sometimes without the knowledge of the President, to dodge a final decision by declaring Palestine a U.N. trusteeship. However, in view of the Presidential position and of the Russian intentions, which became suddenly clear to the State Department, the United States voted for partition. Since adoption of the plan required a two-thirds majority in the Assembly, the United States, having committed itself to the idea of a Jewish state, used its influence, especially among the Latin American countries, to secure the necessary support. The vote was 33 to 13, with 10 abstentions.

The entire Soviet bloc was for the resolution, except Yugoslavia, which abstained because of its significant Muslim minority. Also abstaining was Great Britain, very much piqued by the whole affair but still hoping that in the ensuing hostilities between the Jews and the Arabs the former—outnumbered 30 to 1—would come begging for help. Neither the Jews nor the Arabs paid much attention to the sulking Englishmen.

Of the remaining two great powers, China abstained, but France voted for the resolution, partially out of a desire for *revanche,* because Great Britain two years earlier was instrumental in evicting France from Syria and Lebanon. The United States, stealing a diplomatic march on the Soviet Union, recognized Israel minutes after receiving word of the Jewish declaration of independence, on May 14, 1947, being the first country to do so. The U.S.S.R. was second.

The Arabs declared that the United Nations vote was unfair, because it meant the sacrifice of their rights for the solution of the Jewish problem. The Israelis countered that in 1922 two-thirds of historic Palestine was detached to create an Arab state, Transjordan (now Jordan), and that even in 1947 they were allotted by the United Nations only 55 per cent of the remaining third with full civil rights to the Arabs living in the area. The Arabs also felt betrayed by the United States because, they insisted, the American

Presidents Roosevelt and Truman promised them that no basic decision regarding Palestine would be taken without agreement of both Arabs and Jews. Again, the Israelis replied that they made every effort to elicit Arab cooperation but the Arabs completely rejected the idea of conferences and agreements.

The Arab League, formed by the United Kingdom in 1945 to bring about Arab unity and continued British hegemony in the Middle East, was a failure. Only in one area was it heard—its univocal denunciation of the new Jewish state. Soon after the declaration of independence, the regular armies from Syria, Lebanon, Transjordan, Iraq, and Egypt and token contingents from Saudi Arabia and Yemen challenged Israel's existence. The new state had a Jewish population of 650,000. Egypt alone had more than 20 million. The Arab Legion of Transjordan was a well-trained force commanded by Brigadier John Bagot Glubb and forty other British officers. The Israeli Army was headed by Brigadier Yakov Dori, chief of staff, and Colonel Yigael Yadin, chief of operations. The underground Haganah now surfaced as the mainstay of the national army, but Palmah continued as an elite force and the Irgun and the Stern Group also maintained separate identities, sometimes clashing with Haganah over policy and operations. Nevertheless, there was over-all cooperation. Thanks to far-sighted and meticulous planning by Ben-Gurion and his aides, military equipment began arriving from Western Europe, Czechoslovakia, and the United States, much of the arms being smuggled out of those countries.

The high morale, exemplary leadership, personal courage, and Western efficiency of the Jews brought stunning defeats of the Arab forces, except the Transjordan Legion, which occupied the Old City of Jerusalem (East Jerusalem), with most of the holy places, and the bulk of Samaria and Judea regions, incorporating 2,200 square miles into Transjordan. (Having accomplished that, the name of the country was changed from Transjordan to Jordan, since it gained control over territory on both sides of the river.) Israel added, as a result of the conquest, 2,400 square miles (including the Negev, but not the Gaza area, which was occupied by

Egypt) to the original 5,600 allotted to it by the United Nations partition plan. It also retained control over the new and modern section of Jerusalem.

During the hostilities the United Nations made desperate attempts to bring about peace between the belligerents. It appointed Count Folke Bernadotte, head of the Swedish Red Cross, as its mediator. Bernadotte worked out a new partition plan, its main feature being reassignment of the Negev area to the Arabs and the internationalization of Jerusalem. This infuriated the desperados of the Stern Group, who assassinated Bernadotte. Dr. Ralph Bunche succeeded him and, with the aid of an Anglo-American Conciliation Commission, initiated armistice talks on the island of Rhodes between Israel, on one side, and Egypt, Syria, Lebanon, and Transjordan, on the other. Iraq, Saudi Arabia, and Yemen did not border Israel, so they did not feel impelled to sign an armistice with the new country. The North African states and Sudan were not yet independent, nor were they considered part of the Middle East. It was only in the late 1950's and in the 1960's that they became enmeshed in that area.

The talks on Rhodes were indirect, the Arabs refusing to meet Israel formally. Dr. Bunche shuttled from one headquarters to the other. (Finally, though, according to some accounts, they met face to face, surreptitiously.) It took more than six months, from January to July, 1949, to get the belligerents to sign the armistice. There were no peace treaties. Basically the agreements maintained the territorial dispositions resulting from the war operations. Jordan by and large held on to the territories it occupied, Israel kept the territories it acquired, and Egypt continued to control the Gaza strip. The Arabs ever since the Rhodes talks were too weak to make war and too weak to make peace. Israel thereafter never lost a war and never won a conference.

The Israeli-Arab clash resulted in a history of "grief agreed upon"—the refugee problem. How this situation arose and how many victims it has affected are not clear and will remain wrapped in the miasmic mists of 1948–49.

The Arabs contend that the refugees were expelled or fled in panic as a result of Jewish threats or terrorist activity. A retaliatory massacre of the civilian population of Deir Yassin by the Irgun in April, 1948, is cited as prime evidence of Jewish atrocities. The Arabs point out that the flight of refugees was deliberately fomented to make room for Jewish immigrants and that the possessions of the fleeing Arabs were promptly appropriated by the Jewish authorities.

The Israelis claim vehemently that Deir Yassin was one of a very few incidents in a bloody confrontation and that the Arabs fled at the exhortation of the Arab League and of the neighboring Arab governments, who promised them that they would return with the conquering armies to share in the division of captured Jewish property. Moreover, the Israelis ascertain that the bulk of the Arabs left before the Deir Yassin incident, which appalled most Jews to the point that Ben-Gurion felt impelled to telegraph apologies to King Abdullah of Transjordan. Jewish residents of Haifa to this day insist that they had urged their neighbors to stay. Finally, the Israelis say that all wars inevitably result in refugees, and that it was the Arabs who declared war on Israel. When war is born, truth dies. Even the number of fleeing refugees is not certain. It is variously estimated at between 600,000 and 1 million.

Be that as it may, the creation of the state of Israel caused the refugee problem. Many Israelis feel a moral if not a political or legal obligation toward the victims. This feeling lost much of its intensity when the Arab states started using the refugees as political pawns. When the neighboring governments began insisting that all deported Palestinians be repatriated and their possessions fully restored before any negotiations with the new state could take place, the Israelis replied that this would mean bringing back a large "fifth column," infused with hatred of the Jews and working with the enemies of Israel to annihilate the fledgling state. In short, it would have meant suicide. The Israelis agreed to accept approximately 100,000 refugees to rejoin relatives among the 200,000 Arabs who remained in the country, and to compensate the balance of the Palestinians for resettlement in the neighboring lands. Perhaps Israel's most convincing argument was that it took in as many Jewish refugees from Muslim countries as there were Arab refugees and settled them in Israel with the help of some 13–14 million coreligionists the world over. It could see no reason why the Arabs, numbering almost 100 million (or the larger Muslim community of 600 million), rich in oil and in other natural resources, could not do as much for their brothers. It pointed to a population exchange, involving close to 2 million persons, between Turkey and Greece after World War I. Israel held that a settlement of the refugee problem should be bound up in an over-all peace arrangement envisioning full recognition of Israel's sovereignty.

There the matter rested. Hundreds of thousands of human beings, who during a period of little more than two decades have almost doubled in number, were confined to intolerable camps. Often disease-ridden and hungry, they were stripped of dignity and of hope, while neither their brothers, the Arabs, nor their cousins, the Jews, budged from their positions.

On November 19, 1948, the U.N. General Assembly created the United Nations Relief for Palestinian Refugees (UNRPR) to provide immediate help in the form of food, clothing, tents, fuel, and medical care to any resident of Palestine who had lost his home and livelihood as a result of war. As there was then a prospect of a solution to the problem, the General Assembly established in December, 1949, the United Nations Relief and Works Agency (UNRWA) to provide on a temporary basis, in addition to physical care, also schooling, vocational training, and special hardship assistance. Following the armistice agreements, it was widely assumed that peace would soon be concluded. But this had not eventuated, and so the UNRWA mandate had been extended from one U.N. session to another.

Confusion as to the number of refugees has been compounded by considering the entire pre-1948 Palestine Arab population, without taking into account that large stretches of Palestinian territories—Samaria, Judea, and Gaza—were occupied by Arab countries, and that refugees from Israel merely swelled these overpopulated areas. The problem was further complicated by duplicate registration, nonrefugee poor, and other ineligible people. Thus U.N. figures in 1949 listed the number of Arabs entitled to aid as follows: Lebanon, 127,800; Syria, 78,200; Transjordan, 94,000; "Arab" Palestine, 375,400; Israel, 3,700; Gaza strip, 245,000; other, 15,900; total, 940,000. Transjordan, when it changed its name to Jordan, incorporated "Arab" Palestine (Samaria and Judea) and had the largest number of refugees.

Some of the people had become refugees a second time and a few a third time as a result of the 1956 and 1967 wars. Even with UNRWA help (a minimum of 1,500 calories a day, supplemented by what the refugees raised themselves), they were plagued by chronic illness and a burning desire for revenge, nurtured by Arab governments with a dream of pan-Arabism. Attempts to rehabilitate the camps and to provide more and better facilities were usually met with the admonition: "If you are going to build permanent houses, it will signify your relinquishment of rights to your Palestine possessions."

The 1948–49 defeat inflicted deep and unhealable wounds on Arab pride, and Arab tradition cried out for revenge. Despite the armistice agreements with Lebanon, Syria, Jordan, and Egypt, sporadic frontier incidents occurred in the early 1950's, mostly on the Jordanian border. Israel retaliated, but in 1952 it suffered 147 casualties. The United Nations truce supervisory agencies could not stop the clashes and found it difficult to investigate and to assess blame. The Arab incursions and killings became more numerous, and Israel's reprisals, although less frequent, were more massive, for example, in Quibya, where apparently innocent civilians lost their lives. Israel was censured by the Security Council, but when a bus in the Negev desert was riddled with bullets and eleven passengers were killed, the United Nations Mixed Armistice Commission was unable to find evidence of Arab sabotage. The Israeli delegation then boycotted the sessions of the U.N. supervisory agency.

In the meantime, Egypt had its revolution and Gamal Abdel

Nasser came to power. By 1954 the Sinai border was heating up. An economic boycott sponsored by the Arab League began hurting Israel. In addition, Egypt not only blocked passage of Israeli boats through the Suez Canal but also stopped vessels of other nations carrying goods to Israel.

When the first instances of restricting shipments occurred in 1951, Israel protested to the United Nations. The Security Council called on Egypt to cease interference and to observe the international conventions regarding the freedom of passage through the canal. Cairo disregarded the council's resolutions and extended the blockade to the Gulf of Aqaba. In 1954 an Israeli boat and its crew were seized on Nasser's orders. The Security Council met again and instructed Egypt to release the boat and its complement. After some hesitation Egypt complied, but it continued to harass, detain, and confiscate vessels carrying goods to and from Israel. Border incidents increased in number and in ferocity. Israel's strong retaliatory action was deemed by many a device to compel the Arabs to come to terms.

If that was the case, it did not work. The small country's growing superiority stiffened the attitude of its adversaries. Egypt's military rulers abandoned most of their plans for internal reforms to concentrate on a "second round" with the "Jewish intruders," and for that they needed arms. Enter Czechoslovakia—again—but this time through Egyptian portals. Toward the end of 1955 Prague and Cairo completed an arms deal, and Israel began thinking seriously of a preventive war.

On July 26, 1956, Nasser announced the nationalization of the Suez Canal. This brought Egypt into confrontation with France and Great Britain as well. The three countries apparently coordinated their efforts for punitive action against the offender. But Israel "coordinated" better than either Great Britain or France, and within 100 hours reached the Suez, while the United Kingdom and France got bogged down after the initial bombing of Port Said and landing of troops in the Canal Zone.

In separate forceful protests which had the effect of cooperative performance, both the U.S.S.R. and the United States warned Britain, France, and Israel against further action. Moscow threatened to send "volunteer" soldiers and to employ "frightful weapons." Washington announced that if Russia intervened, it would meet Soviet forces with its own "frightful weapons." The U.N. General Assembly passed two resolutions calling for a cease-fire and withdrawal of all invading forces under the supervision of a special U.N. Emergency Force (UNEF) to be made up of nations from small and medium powers. Great Britain and France complied, but Israel (which had also gained control over Sharm el-Sheikh along the Straits of Tiran, leading to the Gulf of Aqaba) was reluctant.

Israel insisted on guarantees that the Sinai Peninsula would not be used by Egypt for incursions into its territory and that Israeli ships would have freedom of passage through the Suez Canal and the Gulf of Aqaba. Neither the United Nations nor any of the big powers was ready to give such guarantees. The U.S. Secretary of State John Foster Dulles sent Ben-Gurion a bitter caveat that if the prime minister did not order withdrawal of his soldiers from Egyptian soil, Washington would stop all financial and technical help to Israel and would not object to Israel's expulsion from the United Nations. President Dwight D. Eisenhower added, however, that it could be assumed that Egypt would not prevent Israeli shipping from using the canal and the Gulf of Aqaba. Dismayed, Israel gave in and by March 1, 1957, recalled its troops with the declaration that it reserved the right to take action if Egypt should revert to sorties into Israel and to interference with Israeli freedom of navigation. There was also a presumption that UNEF would act as a buffer between Egypt and Israel.

A man of lesser stature than Ben-Gurion would have been driven out of office by his countrymen in 1956–57. Popular resentment of the United States was high in Israel. Short of achieving its full purpose, the Sinai action nevertheless brought tangible and positive results for Israel. It neutralized the Gaza Strip; it stopped Egyptian *fedayeen* (trained commando) infiltration into the Negev, allowing a faster pace of development in the area; it stilled the hopes of Cairo for an early "second round"; most important, while it left the Suez Canal problem unresolved, it opened up free navigation in the Gulf of Aqaba and the sea routes to Africa from the Israeli port of Eilat, thus weakening dramatically the Arab boycott.

But the Sinai action necessitated a revolution in Israel's foreign policy. The country found itself politically isolated. From the very beginning its internal and external policies seem to have been given prophetic expression by Hillel, a first-century sage, who said: "If I am not for myself, who will be for me? and being for my own self, who am I? and if not now, when?"

The Kremlin, until the Suez crisis, talked from both sides of its mouth. It supported the creation of Israel in 1948, but once the British were out and the Israelis were intent on keeping a neutral position between East and West, it began looking around for oases in the Arabian deserts. But in August, 1949, the U.S.S.R. concluded an agreement with Israel stipulating that all former Russian Orthodox properties (encompassing churches, convents, and hospices in Jerusalem and elsewhere) would be taken over by the Soviet-controlled Russian Orthodox Church. Moscow went so far as to appoint a central religious authority in Jerusalem.

The erosion of relations between the two countries became evident in 1952–54 when waves of anti-Semitism swept Russia, featuring the alleged Doctors' Plot against the life of Stalin and other Soviet leaders. Trials of Jewish Communists in Czechoslovakia and Hungary suggested further proof of a change in the Kremlin's attitude. On February 9, 1953, a bomb exploded in the U.S.S.R. Embassy in Tel Aviv, leading to a temporary suspension of diplomatic relations between Russia and Israel. By the end of 1955 the Soviet bloc began supplying large amounts of arms to Egypt and to Syria. In December, Khrushchev, then the Communist Party First Secretary, said that "from the very first day of its existence, the state of Israel has been taking a hostile, threatening position toward its neighbors. Imperialists are behind Israel, trying to exploit it against the Arabs for their own benefit." From then on the dithyrambic outbursts against the Jewish state were prominent aspects of Soviet foreign policy, whether they originated in Moscow or at the United Nations. Repression of Jews in the U.S.S.R. ranged from imprisonment on trumped up charges to returning letters to senders because the stamps bore the likeness of Theodor Herzl, the founder of political Zionism.

The Kremlin never advocated the annihilation of Israel but seemed interested in "controlled turmoil" in the Middle East, which would enable it to pose as the champion of the Arab cause. Indeed, Russia could legitimately claim to be Muslim power, since about one-fifth of its population—from 40 to 50 million people in its Central Asian republics—are Muslim. There are more Muslims in the U.S.S.R. than in the largest Arab state, Egypt. There are only 3 million Jews in the Soviet Union.

The original Russian plan was to set up Egypt as a showcase for the Middle East, but Nasser was not pliable enough. When tension between Syria and Israel increased in the 1960's, the Kremlin apparently provided the catalyst for the crisis by producing facts before they occurred, supplying spurious intelligence reports that Israel was preparing to attack Syria. Nasser demanded and got the removal of UNEF from Sinai and closed the Straits of Tiran on May 22, 1967, to Israeli shipping. This caused confrontation with Jerusalem and international consternation. On June 5, Israel took the offensive and again proved its superiority over the combined Arab forces of Egypt, Syria, and Jordan. The Arab defeat in six days enabled the Russians to entrench themselves even more in Egypt, though under Sadat the Russians have their problems.

With the exception of the John Foster Dulles period, Israel throughout its existence has been the recipient not only of American technical and financial aid but also of verbal felicities. In the early days of the Jewish state, when things were really tough economically, a visitor from Germany suggested facetiously that Israel declare war on the United States. Defeated, Israel would enjoy unlimited American support and become as prosperous as Germany. Replied a disgruntled Israeli: "With our luck we would win the war."

Even when Israel tried to stay out of the East-West tug-of-war, it never lost sight of the fact that in the final analysis America, with its 5 to 6 million Jews, would come to Israel's rescue when its existence was threatened. In May, 1950, a tripartite declaration of the United States, Great Britain, and France had "guaranteed" the territorial integrity of the Middle East states against external aggression. This declaration included Israel and is held valid to this day by the Jerusalem government, although some authorities on international law feel that Israel nullified the declaration by its Sinai action in 1956 and the Six-Day War of 1967.

The shift in Soviet policy made it even harder for Israel to maintain a neutral position in world affairs. It attempted some feeble moves to assert its independence of action when, for instance, it recognized the Mao regime and voted consistently for the admission of Communist China to the United Nations. In the meantime, the United States began to worry about its own interests in the Middle East as the Russians initiated serious penetrations into the Arab world. An American rapprochement with Nasser's Egypt in 1953–57 was completely botched by the United States, especially in the matter of the Aswan Dam, when Secretary of State Dulles reneged on the promise to help Egypt finance the project. The Baghdad Pact, inspired by the United States, brought together Iraq, Iran, Turkey, and Pakistan in 1955 as a northern line of defense, intended as a barrier to further Russian incursions. Iraq dropped out of the organization in 1958 after its king was deposed by Abdel Karem Kassem, and the pact was then renamed CENTO. All the agreement succeeded in doing was to infuriate Nasser, who saw in the pact a counterweight and a menace to his regime.

Similarly, the Eisenhower Doctrine of 1957 was formulated to keep the Russians out of the area by promising military help against aggression to any Middle East government requesting it. Lebanon, fearing a Nasser takeover, did ask for help in 1958, and the United States complied, further alienating the Egyptian ruler.

Yet, curiously, throughout this period and in the years following, Washington deemed Nasser the most stabilizing factor in the Middle East and the chief bulwark against Communist penetration into the region. Part of the American problem was that it did not understand that to Arabs, mistakenly or not, Israel appeared more dangerous than Russia or Communism.

The events leading to 1967 caught the United States totally unprepared. Three months preceding the May crisis there was no American Ambassador in the United Arab Republic (Egypt became part of the U.A.R. in 1958 when it "coalesced" with Syria. The union was dissolved in 1961, but officially Egypt remained the U.A.R. until 1971, when it resumed its original name, Egypt). Other diplomats and the United States chargé d'affaires, David G. Nes, sent clear warnings of the impending dangers, but they were disregarded. Washington had no contingency plans, no comprehension of what its responsibilities in the situation were. It was only on May 21, after Nasser began mobilizing, that an inexperienced ambassador, Richard Nolte, arrived in Cairo. Reportedly, when questioned about the crisis he asked, "What crisis?"

Israel won a stunning victory in the Six-Day War of 1967. It destroyed most of the Egyptian air force, occupied the Sinai Peninsula, overran the Palestinian areas of the West Bank of the Jordan, seized the Golan Heights, from which Syrian snipers and infiltrators had harassed Jewish settlements for years, and joined the Old City (and East Jerusalem) with the New City of Jerusalem.

The Russians, however, replenished the Egyptian air force and added surface-to-air missiles of the most advanced types for U.A.R. defense and offense. Moreover, Soviet technicians were manning these sophisticated installations and Russian pilots were flying some Egyptian planes. Israel, which previously was getting its aircraft (Mystères and Mirages) from France, no longer could obtain them because of a French embargo. It therefore turned to the United States for the purchase of Skyhawks and Phantoms, the latter an advanced American jet. Washington consented to sell some of these planes to Israel, but not all that the country needed.

In fact, the United States reneged on some future sales pursuant to a so-called even-handed policy, prompting an Israeli diplomat to exclaim in exasperation: "What we are getting from Washington are not Phantoms but mirages." However, in 1972 President Richard Nixon had a change of heart and the sale of aircraft to Israel increased dramatically.

The United States has vital interests in the Middle East's oil and other natural resources. The area is also of tremendous importance strategically. As one U.S. journalist, Clayton Fritchey, put it: "Where would the United States be in that area if Israel collapsed, and the whole region was taken over by hostile Arabs and their great patron, Soviet Russia. The answer suggests that our ties to Israel rest as much on self-interest as on anything else."

Fearing an escalation of hostilities in the Middle East and eventual confrontation between the two superpowers, Washington, with tacit Moscow agreement, in the summer of 1970 launched a peace offensive in the area resulting in a renewal of the cease-fire agreements in 1971, and in preliminary negotiations for stabilizing the situation in that part of the world.

The other two great powers directly concerned with the Middle East were the United Kingdom and France. Together with the superpowers they made up the Big Four, meeting off and on since the 1967 war in search of a solution to the Middle East dilemma. On the whole, Great Britain's relations with the Yishuv during the mandate had not been very cordial, and diplomatic contacts after the birth of the state were ambiguous on both sides. Israel kept its suspicion of English pro-Arab attitudes, while London could not forgive Israel for its 1948 victory, which pointedly marked the beginning of the decline of the British Empire. The Suez fiasco of 1956, when England could not knock out the Egyptians while the Israelis rushed across Sinai to the Suez Canal in a matter of days, was another degrading experience, perhaps the *coup de grâce* to lingering colonial ambitions.

Despite the chill in the diplomatic realm, Israel and Great Britain soon realized that their economic interests did not have to suffer from residual peeves or injured pride. England held relatively significant investments in Israel and imported large quantities of citrus fruit from that country. Notwithstanding political difficulties, the two states normalized their foreign affairs. During the U.N. debates regarding the June, 1967, war, when the Soviet Union assumed a pro-Arab position and the United States spoke up for Israel, Great Britain tried to be neutral. Its Foreign Secretary, George Brown, meted out his indictments in all directions, but his favorite target was Israel. In the period following 1967, Israel had some difficulty in getting the tanks it wanted from England, but neither did the Arabs get all they asked.

France and Israel started out like a pair of lovers. Then Paris not only cooled its ardor, but rudely rejected its suitor. While Russia in a sense was Israel's midwife, it was the United States that helped nourish the infant state. But little Israel did not want to appear as the "lackey of American imperialism," so it turned also to France. Paris was delighted by this boost to its slowly rising morale, down after World War II to the lowest ebb since Charlemagne. It was a gracious compliment from a country such as Israel to French *élan vital*. Quai d'Orsay's ambassadors in Israel learned to speak Hebrew and the Israelis started studying the French language more diligently in their schools. Israeli military heroes were adulated in Paris. The 1956 Suez tidbit was probably cooked up in the French cuisine of Guy Mollet, the then Premier, with the help of the Israeli chef, David Ben-Gurion. The Anglo-French showing in Egypt made the Israeli military feat look even better. Later, French aircraft piloted by Israelis seemed to prove French technical skills.

There was also scientific cooperation in the production of the atomic bomb, enabling France to enter without invitation the nuclear club. Even when Charles de Gaulle came to power, France continued its affection for Israel. The pair, short and stocky Ben-Gurion and the elongated French leader, called David and De-Gauliath, developed a very cordial relationship until Paris settled the Algerian problem.

One of the reasons for France's inordinate interest in the little country on the other end of the Mediterranean was Arab (especially Egyptian) help to rebellious Algeria. When that North African state gained its independence in 1962, a noticeable veering away from Israel and drawing closer to the Arabs began. France was Israel's main supplier of jet planes. In 1967 Jerusalem had fifty Mirages on order. When Nasser blocked the Tiran Straits, Israel warned the Egyptian ruler that this was *casus belli* and that it would go to war to clear the waterway for passage. Abba Eban, the Israeli Foreign Minister, flew to Paris to see de Gaulle. The French President, perceiving an opportunity to act as arbitrator and to re-establish his country as a major factor in the Middle East, cautioned Israel not to wage war, because he would see to it that peace was restored. Israel was unconvinced because of its experience with similar promises regarding both Suez and the Gulf of Aqaba after its 1956 retirement from those areas. When Israel launched its military offensives, there was no fury like that of a de Gaulle scorned. France imposed a complete embargo on jet planes to Israel and impounded those ready for delivery, despite the fact that they were paid for.

Neither the French military nor the general population liked the reversal of policy toward Israel. The public hailed the 1967 victory of "our comrades in arms and spirit." French newspapers, with few exceptions, wrote editorials against de Gaulle's action, which was continued by his successor, Georges Pompidou. The embargo was to apply equally to all warring parties in the Middle East, but Paris found plausible excuses for selling jets to Iraq, Libya, and other Arab countries. Israel deemed it lethal legalism and refused to take back the $200 million it paid for the Mirages.

German–Israeli relations understandably were uneasy. In March, 1951, Jerusalem submitted to Bonn a claim for $1.5 billion in restitution for losses suffered by Jews during the Nazi regime. This action by the Israeli Government elicited fierce opposition from both the extreme right and the radical left, resulting in demonstrations against "Jews who would deal with bloody Germany." There was also opposition in West Germany, but less volatile. Cooler heads prevailed in an attempt not to expunge the memory of the nefarious Nazi deeds, but to make some amends to the state that received the seared remnant of the victims. The final amount agreed upon between West Germany and Israel was about $850 million in cash and in goods, over a period of twelve years. It was later extended for an additional short period. This sum was apart from the indemnities to be paid to individual survivors of the holocaust. Israel later established full diplomatic relations with West Germany on an ambassadorial level. East Germany and Israel have never been able to get together, nor has there been a perceptible desire for a rapprochement on either side.

Israel enjoyed most cordial relations with all West European countries, especially the Netherlands and Belgium. Some of the desperately needed spare parts for the French Mystères and Mirages somehow found their way from the Benelux countries to Haifa and Lydda (Lod)—the latter being the main Israeli air base. Despite the assassination of Swedish Count Bernadotte, there was lively communication between the Scandinavian countries and Israel in many social, economic, and cultural areas.

Warm contacts between Israel and Latin American countries existed ever since 1948, when many of these countries helped bring Israel into being. Some Latin American statesmen, especially Jorge Garcia-Granados of Guatemala and Enrique Rodriguez Fabregat of Uruguay, became ardent advocates of the Zionist cause at the United Nations. This friendship ripened into reciprocal gestures by Israel, such as supplying expertise, notably in agriculture, to several countries on that continent. A Centre for Cooperative Studies and Labour for Latin America, founded in Israel in 1962, has had more than 600 students engaged in projects. In addition, close to 700 people participated in mobile courses held in Latin America by the center.

A number of Muslim countries (not to be confused with Arab states—not every Muslim is an Arab and not every Arab is a Muslim) have recognized Israel. Among them are Turkey and Iran. The former went so far as to exchange ambassadors with the

Jewish state and to court technical aid. However, the frequent bloody conflicts between Israel and its Arab neighbors and a Turkish rapprochement with the Soviet Union led Ankara to suspend diplomatic relations with Israel several times. Iran, on the other hand, has never sent an official representative to Israel and has consented only to an Israeli diplomatic mission in Teheran, but it has consistently pursued a friendly policy toward Jerusalem, making full use of Israeli know-how and scientific advice.

A fascinating phase of Israel's foreign affairs is its tie with Afro-Asian countries. In 1955, U Nu, the Burmese chief-of-state, visited his friend Ben-Gurion and was deeply impressed with the frontier collectives. At U Nu's request, a group of Israeli kibbutzniks soon arrived to set up Burmese collectives on the border with Red China. The Namazang Region experiment was later adopted in the Majaguas Region of Venezuela.

But it was the opening up of the Gulf of Aqaba that offered Israel the opportunity to build bridgeheads with Asia and Africa and to shake off the Arab boycott. By constructing a modern economy from scratch, with a minimum of natural resources, Israel could very well serve as a model for new and developing states. Its hard-won expertise in agriculture and industry, cooperative organization, health, education, and social services was made available to the emergent countries. They were ready to accept the help extended because Israel did not aspire to colonial expansion; did not preach ideology, either Communist or capitalist; and did not attach political strings to its aid, as was usually the case with Eastern or Western powers. Whenever a host country felt that the Israelis had finished their project, there was no problem. The Jews merely "folded up their tents" and moved to another place or went home.

Also, the problems of the new states were more similar to those of Israel than to the ones encountered by Western lands: molding nations of divergent tribal groups, combating disease, mastering an inhospitable climate, weaving new social patterns, and imparting modern techniques to culturally undernourished people.

The most important factor in this aid was Israel's recognition that it was not enough to come in, perform a chore, and then leave. Rather, it trained local workers on the spot or in Israel. When a task was completed, it left a cadre of trainees to proceed with similar projects, often with the infectious dynamism of the teachers. Very few Israelis were allowed by their government to go to Africa to make profit for themselves. Nor did the Jewish technicians look down upon the "natives" but mixed easily with them.

In what specific ways did the Jews help the Africans? Israel has sent many medical teams to various parts of the world. A doctor's arrival has an immediate effect. A dying man may be saved on the first day of the physician's work. But the objective of the medical missions was long range. The Ichilow Hospital in Tel Aviv, for instance, adopted the Ilongwe Hospital in Nyasaland (now Malawi). A nine-man team was sent out to Africa to lay the foundation of several medical programs, some of its members remaining on a loan basis. The entire Ichilow staff was available to Ilongwe doctors for consultation and special services. At the same time fourteen nurses from the African hospital were studying at the Hadassah Nursing School in Jerusalem.

Eye disease has long been a pernicious ailment in Africa. The head of the Ophthalmology Department of the Hebrew University started comprehensive work on the problem in Liberia years ago. A pilot thirty-bed clinic was established in Monrovia, and Liberian doctors and nurses were sent for advanced training in Jerusalem. Similar schemes were initiated in Tanzania and Rwanda and later in about ten other African countries. While medical personnel were at work in these states, native students were undergoing special training in Israel; some of the new doctors are now taking over from their Jewish colleagues.

Israeli seamen inaugurated and for several years guided the Ghanaian Navy. The Kilimanjaro Hotel in Nairobi was constructed by Jews. The University of Addis-Ababa and other institutions of higher learning in Africa were planned or expanded by Haifa and Jerusalem academicians; collectives, cooperatives, and Nahal- and

Gadna-like movements were started by kibbutzniks; police in Nigeria and elsewhere were trained by Israeli law enforcement officers; roads cutting through African wastelands and skyscrapers in booming cities were built by what a Latin American described as the Israeli "development mafia."

By the early 1970's, more than 11,000 people from Africa, Asia, the Mediterranean basin, Europe, and even the United States (the Southwest Alabama Farmers Cooperative Association, for instance), were trained in Israel at such schools as the Afro-Asian Institute for Labour Studies and Cooperation, established in 1960 (which already served some 2,000 students from 80 countries); the aforementioned Centre for Cooperative Studies and Labour for Latin America, founded in 1962; and the Mount Carmel Training Centre, which graduated more than 1,000 women with majors in community development, food and applied nutrition, adult studies, consumer education, cooperative marketing, and home economics.

Not all projects in the developing countries have been successful. (Incidentally, a measure of Israel's tact is that the phrase "developing countries" was apparently first employed in the Afro-Asian Institute in deference to African sensitivity to the term "underdeveloped countries.") Politicians in host communities sometimes interfered and demanded high-paying jobs and favors for themselves. At times people refused to work as hard as the Israeli staff. In joint businesses, when branches were formed outside the large cities and manned by local personnel, service usually was poor. Governments frequently expected both immediate and continuing positive results. Also, Israeli efforts at times were too spontaneous, daring, and occasionally ill planned. Large Israeli contractors, like Solel Boneh or Mekorot, now and then pressed for profits at the expense of local needs. But, generally speaking, the programs were very successful. In the words of the President of Mali, a mostly Muslim country, "Israel has become an object of pilgrimage for African peoples who seek inspiration on how to build their own countries. Israel has become a human approach to building a new society of 200 million Africans."

What benefits did Israel derive from it all? In addition to the propaganda value of negating Arab League boycott boasts, Israel gained markets, sources of materials, and badly needed support at the United Nations. After the Six-Day War, fifteen Afro-Asian nations voted for the pro-Arab resolution, but seventeen African states, twenty-two Latin American countries, and two Asian governments voted for the Western resolution, which was more favorable to Israel.

Although it was the decision by the General Assembly of the United Nations on November 29, 1947, that created Israel, the new state derived little comfort from most subsequent U.N. action. While the attacks on Israeli settlements from Arab territory were frequent and resulted in killings, the burning of fields, and the wrecking of buildings, they were small-scale operations and did not command headlines in the world press, nor did they elicit much censure from the United Nations. Israeli reprisals were less frequent but more destructive to life and property. They usually captured front-page coverage and resulted in condemnation from the Security Council. Jerusalem complained that the U.N. response was Pavlovian and insisted that the Security Council (the U.S.S.R. and its satellites, France, China, the Muslim states) was stacked against it. The Soviet representative in particular developed a lusty taste for verbal assaults.

Whenever a new crisis developed in the Middle East, the United Nations was fresh out of answers and left the solution, if any, to the Big Two or to the Big Four. In the crucial days of 1967, when Nasser closed the Tiran Straits, the Arabs and Israelis were mobilizing, and the lightning and thunder of war were clearly visible and audible, U Thant, Secretary General of the United Nations, withdrew the UNEF forces that were serving as a buffer between Egypt and Israel, prompting Abba Eban, the Israeli Foreign Minister, to remark that the Secretary General was like a man who carried an open umbrella for days but, the moment it started to rain, folded it.

U Thant bristled and made the unusual move of defending himself as a person. In simple justice to the Secretary General, it must be said that when he withdrew UNEF the situation on the border already was beyond control because the United Nations failed to act. Several UNEF units were by then behind advancing Egyptian elements, and eighteen members of the emergency force were killed in the initial crossfire between U.A.R. and Israeli troops.

The Security Council debates during this period were furious and frustrating. Jerusalem, however, once again showed its mettle on the diplomatic field. One of the good fortunes of the new state was its very fine foreign service, with superb representatives in the major capitals of the world and, especially, at the United Nations. The U.N. mission was often headed by Foreign Minister Abba Eban, acclaimed as the anointed spokesman of Israel. These diplomats engaged in brilliant rear-guard action to gain valuable time for their military during the 1967 war. Israel, it now appears, was pushed into a preventive conflict with Egypt by an ill-advised move on the part of the U.S.S.R. and Syria, which supplied Cairo with the spurious intelligence that Israel was about to invade Syria. Egypt, the largest of the Arab powers and the champion of pan-Arabism, presumably acted out of a compulsion to divert the Israelis from their northern neighbor. Israel, challenged by Egypt, had no choice but take on the United Arab Republic and its ally Jordan.

In the ensuing war, Israel swiftly destroyed the Egyptian air force and overran Sinai. It also captured East Jerusalem and occupied the West Bank of Jordan. Syria, in the meantime, began making warlike noises and initiated a push into Israel. The delaying tactics of the Israel diplomats at the United Nations allowed their military forces to turn northward and to take over the Golan Heights. On June 10 (New York time) the Israeli representatives at the United Nations ran out of maneuvers and consented to a cease-fire, stopping further penetration into Syria. Nonetheless, by then Israeli forces were in control of strategic points, which reduced Israel's vulnerability by shifting the line of defense into Arab territory. All this created a new balance of power in the region.

Through the hot summer of 1967, the United Nations debated

the new realities in the Middle East, and in the fall the Security Council had another go at the problem. The Arabs and the Russians wanted a complete withdrawal of the "aggressors" from the occupied areas. Israel insisted on direct negotiations with their adversaries, resulting in "contractual agreements." In an address at the twenty-fourth session of the General Assembly, Eban said: "It is an error to regard the United Nations process as a substitute for direct settlement; that is precisely the opposite of what the organization is meant to be. The United Nations is supposed to be an instrument for ending conflicts, not an arena for waging them." Then he added:

> The alternative to a directly negotiated settlement would, at best, be the formulation of vague, ambivalent, unchecked arrangements open to continuing interpretations—like the arrangements of 1957 which fell down like a house of cards within a few hours in 1967. . . . We also learned a stark, unforgettable lesson in 1967 about the inherent fragility of international guarantees and Security Council safeguards in the present state of the world's power balance. We carry this lesson forward into our future history.

But the Security Council did exactly what Eban warned against. On November 22, 1967, a much-tortured resolution, put in final ambiguous form by the United Kingdom, authorized the dispatch of a special representative to negotiate with the Arabs and the Israelis and to achieve a peaceful settlement of the Middle East conflict. That representative, selected later, was Gunnar Jarring, Sweden's Ambassador to Moscow. The resolution also listed the principles that were to guide the special envoy, but they were deliberately vague, permitting each party to make its own interpretations. It called for the "withdrawal of Israeli forces from territories occupied in the recent conflict." It did not say *all* the territories, but the Arabs read it this way, while the Israelis insist that it refers merely to certain areas.

The 1967 conflict added 350,000 more refugees, more pawns for the politicians whose dreams of pan-Arabism rest factually on only one adhesive—hatred of Israel. Islam considers itself a community-state and hopes for an eventual worldwide well-defined Muslim society—with pan-Arabism leading to that desired end—but an Oxford professor, H. A. R. Gibb, a noted Arabophile and authority on Islam, wrote long ago:

> Pan-Arabism . . . constitutes wishing for thinking . . . it has no grasp of the problems of government, administration and finance of the economic structure of the world, and the economic poverty of the Arab countries, of the discipline, training and scientific tradition that underlie technical progress. Its leaders may perhaps not be quite so ignorant but in their own supposed interests they are ready to exploit the passions and the instincts of the mob.

Pan-Arabism has a littered past. While feeding the homeless and the suffering masses in the refugee camps with euphoriants, the various Arab countries engage one another in feuds of varying intensity, ranging from assassination plots to squabbles at summit meetings, where nothing much is accomplished except an occasional rearrangement of desert sands. The self-proclaimed "socialist" and "people's governments" of Syria and Iraq have each conspired to overthrow the regime of the other. Hundreds of Syrian Baathists (socialists) languish in the jails of Iraq. Hundreds of Iraqi Baathists are incarcerated in the prisons of Syria. Libya and Algeria have recently joined the "revolutionary" Arab regimes.

To fan the fires of insurgency, Arab chiefs of state have each organized pet guerrilla or commando groups in their respective refugee camps. Thus Nasser sponsored a "Palestinian military entity" under General Ahmed Shukeiry, a boastful and thoroughly incompetent rabble-rouser. At the same time Syria had its own pet resistance band. No fewer than ten recognizable militant organizations have functioned among the refugees, often engaged in fratricidal warfare, which caused dissipation of their power in the 1970's.

The feline diplomacy of Nasser, an accomplished loser, who so skillfully contrived excuses for his failures, had lost some of its appeal among the Palestinians who had forged hitherto a mythical but more recently a substantial political self-identity, bordering on genuine nationalism. "Who are the Egyptians and the Syrians who presume to talk in our behalf? Have we, the prime victims of this tragedy, been consulted in declaring a cease-fire?" a moderate leader of the occupied West Bank complained.

Authentic Palestinian national leaders have also emerged, although relying on help from various Arab and non-Arab sources friendly to their cause or interested in unsettled conditions in the area. One of them was Yassir Arafat, and another was Dr. George Habash. Arafat, the commander of the larger group, Al-Fatah, lacked the social ideólogy, decisiveness, the charisma of a folk hero. Habash had all three attributes but was enmeshed in a Maoist brand Marxism, a not too popular cause in the part of the Muslim world that still has kings. Moreover, he was a Christian Arab. Financial support for his movement was not as munificient as that for Arafat. Both have suffered irreparable damage at the hands of King Hussein of Jordan, whose regime they wanted to topple.

For Israel these elements did not pose a military threat, since they lacked the know-how and the modern tools of warfare (jet planes, for one thing). Strutting and saluting made for impressive television documentaries, and spectacular jet hijacking massaged the Arab ego somewhat. But neither of these counted much against the well-disciplined, highly trained, better equipped, and technically sophisticated Israeli Army. Still, the commando elements were not to be dismissed lightly, because they had serious nuisance value as perpetrators of grave border incidents, often resulting in loss of life and destruction of property. In a sense the commando groups were of greater menace to tottering Arab regimes, as the old leadership failed to propose substantial, workable solutions.

Be that as it may, the "guerrilla diplomacy" of the Arab liberation movements propelled them to the fore as a residual factor in any settlement with Israel. They became the very center of the struggle against the Jewish state. "We are the new Diaspora," proclaimed a young Palestinian journalist, referring to the Jewish dispersion. "We, too, tell one another, 'Next year in Jerusalem.'" There was a new sense of "manifest destiny" among the Palestinians, which rejected the "Ibn Monroe Doctrine" of Nasser. Paradoxically, this newfound confidence and self-esteem may prompt the Palestinians to take matters into their own hands and work out a plan, agreeable in its broad outline to Israel, that would give them autonomy in a new Jordanian setup, on the one hand, and would forge an economic link with Israel, on the other.

The occupation policy of Israel has made such an arrangement feasible, especially since the death of Nasser in 1970. It has not been heavy-handed. It has allowed the Arabs to administer their own local institutions, so long as there is no threat to Israel's security. There is freedom of movement from the West Bank to the East Bank and vice versa for Palestinians to sell their products in Jordan and in Saudi Arabia. Tens of thousands have commuted daily to work in Israel proper. Palestinians have been the beneficiaries of improved methods for the cultivation of soil and for the management of business. They have enjoyed freedom of journalistic expression, extending even to criticism of the occupying authorities. However, the moment acts of subversion are discovered in a given area, buildings suspected of hiding terrorists are razed, and sometimes entire city blocks are obliterated. The people deemed guilty are arrested, and offenders are punished severely, but not executed. The first death sentence for saboteurs, pronounced in August, 1970, against two Arabs who killed two other Arabs on orders of a commando organization, was later commuted to life imprisonment.

The silent majority of the Arabs in the occupied area is in an awful bind. To cooperate or even acquiesce in Israeli occupation goes against the ethnic and religious pride of most Arabs, and also brings down upon them the wrath of the extremists. To stop the normal ebb and flow of life in order to rebuff Israel means self-inflicted economic deprivation and sanctions from the occupying authorities. More and more demands are voiced for solving the problem along the lines of the aforementioned autonomous existence within Jordan and an economic linkage with Israel, even with the possibility of a corridor through Israeli territory for a Jordanian window onto the Mediterranean.

Peaceful municipal elections in some of the largest West Bank cities were held in April and May of 1972, despite threats of reprisal from the guerrillas. This was taken as another sign of West Bank movement toward autonomy and a possible link with either Israel or Jordan, or both.

Israel's bid since 1948 for direct negotiations with the Arabs once evoked this remark from General E. L. M. Burns, former chief of the United Nations Truce Supervision Organization: "I do not know what grounds the Israelis had for this confidence in their own charm and persuasiveness at the conference table." It may not be their charm but their greater readiness through direct negotiations to roll back from the Suez Canal in exchange for free passage (although the canal is no longer the rich-ditch it was); to evacuate the Sinai Peninsula, except Sharm-el-Sheik, and have it demilitarized; to leave the West Bank (with some border rectification and autonomous existence); to give up the Golan Heights, with ironclad guarantees for its demilitarization; to agree to the internationalization of the non-Jewish holy places in Old (East) Jerusalem, perhaps with some kind of nominal Jordanian presence in that area, but no division in its administrative entity; to consent to take in some Arabs within a family-reunion plan and help resettle the remainder in the autonomous part of Jordan or in any other country.

Before his death in 1970 Nasser appeared to be more inclined toward some kind of "arrangement" with Israel, if only to escape complete submission to the U.S.S.R. Anwar Sadat, Nasser's successor, also has indicated from time to time a desire for settlement. However, both he and Israeli Prime Minister Golda Meir have been too ambivalent and too cautious. It could be that both missed an excellent opportunity in 1970–71 to work out a pattern for peace.

Peace may help Israel resolve the dilemma bothering so many of its citizens: Will the country remain a Western enclave in the region, or will it enmesh itself in Middle East society? Israel, it would seem, has the gift to weave a distinctive Western pattern into the rich and colorful fabric of the area.

13 Perils and Promise

A chosen people, or like unto all the other nations? Sinaic morality or contingency ethics? Which of these have cradled Israel into statehood?

Summing up the comments of Jeremiah Ben-Jacob, a writer on Jewish nationalism, it appears that Nazism created for the Zionist movement a revolutionary lever that it had never possessed in its previous seventy years of activity. The impact of the experience was in many ways paradoxical. It led to bitterness against the world but also to a sense of special mission; to complete distrust of Europe but also to a spiritual response made vivid by the light of the conflagration; to corroding cynicism about human nature but also to stirring comradeship and fraternity; to a tragic conviction of the failure of normal political methods and moral persuasion but also to a revival of the Messianic yearning and the belief in the unique destiny of Israel; to a struggle against the decrees of a hostile world but also to a furtive insight into the twilight of Western civilization.

With such an insight, "the saving remnant" of the Jews became an extraordinary power—a force out of all proportion to its numerical strength. Its vigor was fed by an overwhelming sense of urgency, by the abandonment of traditional defensive Jewish attitudes and the adoption of a defiant outlook and militant action. Not quite free of vituperative urges after centuries of persecution, the Jews in Israel nevertheless built altars—but on volcanoes.

One of the initial problems encountered by the early pioneers in the 1870's and 1880's was what Professor Amitai Etzioni of Columbia University calls "colonial temptations." To begin with, the Jews claimed to have returned to their homeland, and not to have come into Palestine as occupying strangers. While contemporary Israelis are aware that Zionism meant the movement of Europeans into the Middle East, they stress that it did not follow the colonial pattern of exploitation of the natives. The potential of exploitation, however, *was* there at the beginning, when the Jewish farmers employed Arab labor and servants. "At that stage," Etzioni says, "a Jewish-owned and managed vineyard or orchard did not look very different from a French one in Algeria or a British one in Kenya." Etzioni may have read Ben Gurion's remarks that in those days Jewish workers as well had to submit like slaves to the indignity of having a Jewish farmer feel their muscles and tap their chests to see whether or not they would be hired for a day's work in the field.

The Second Aliyah nipped this "Jewish colonialism" in the bud. A. D. Gordon and his followers established new social patterns and a new type of collective settlement, the kibbutz, which to this day is still the core of many values in Israel.

The initial Jewish struggle in Palestine was against Ottoman and British colonialism, not against the Arabs. In that struggle the leaders of the Yishuv—Ben-Gurion, Ben-Zvi, and others—hoped the Arabs would join the Jews and together throw off the yoke of imperialism for a common future.

Over the years an ultra-nationalist and militant movement developed—the Revisionists of Vladimir Jabotinsky, which later became the Herut party of Menahem Begin—but its aim was expansionism rather than colonialism; more important than this casuistic distinction, the movement always remained a minority. Until 1967 its views were so unacceptable to the majority that in ten coalition governments until the Six-Day War, it and the Communist Party were excluded from the Cabinet. During the 1967 emergency, Herut (as a part of the Gahal alignment) joined a broadly based national government, only to leave it in 1970 because Herut insisted on Israel's keeping all areas occupied in 1967. Again Etzioni points out: "Whatever course is followed, it is difficult to believe that Israel will renounce its anti-colonial tradition. It will find a way—if there is only minimum cooperation from the other side—to provide for its security without running the lives of another people or keeping them as second-class citizens in Israel."

While the kibbutz was an important deterrent to "Jewish colonialism," it also evolved as an elite group, a socio-economic and psychopolitical aristocracy. It is difficult to foresee the future of the movement now that "the individual bathroom has triumphed, along with refrigerators, electric ranges, coffee breaks and private apartments with more square feet of space per occupant than the average flat of the city workers who are not burdened with idealism."

Hal Lehrman, an astute observer of the Israeli scene and the author of the above remarks, also elicited both a question and an answer from a veteran kibbutznik: "Is comfort an ideological surrender? Yes, if the comfort kept my son from accepting the hardships I accepted when I was young. . . . I gave up very little to accept this suffering. My son does more—he gives up all the new comforts when he goes out to fight or joins a Nahal garrison in an exposed position."

The crucial problem is whether the children raised in the kibbutz who leave it for military duty or for study will return to it. The overwhelming majority of them do, perhaps because the collective offers *both* comfort and ideology. Austerity, in the view of many kibbutzniks, is not a prerequisite for pioneering, nor is prosperity an indication of a "thaw in idealism." Comfort, rather, is a vindication of utopia.

The fact that many kibbutzim have become entrepreneurs engaged in employer-employee practices, thus violating a cardinal socialist tenet, causes sleepless nights to many veterans of the movement. They hope, though, that with the passing of emergencies and the coming of peace to the Middle East the collectives and the cooperatives no longer will be compelled morally to contribute to the defense economy of the country, nor to the solution of unemployment or surplus manpower problems. The kibbutz and the moshav, they presume, will return to normalcy, to the principles of self-labor.

Many social analysts, however, now look upon the kibbutz, and even the moshav, as the products of the mythological, epic, or heroic age of the Jewish experience in Palestine and foretell its eventual disappearance in the more mundane, prosaic days of an established state. However, others feel that as an elite group, typically closed-in and uncommunicative, imbued with the notion that its mode of life is vigorous, comfortable, *and* idealistic, the kibbutz, despite obvious and foreseeable philosophical and ideological difficulties, is not headed for oblivion. It may not envelop the majority of the population in the country, as it once hoped to, since more Israelis are prone to admire it than to join it, but as one kibbutz leader put it: "We don't believe any more that the collective is Zion's only instrument."

Even the nonsocialist elements of Zionism did not view the nationalist movement merely as a theology of survival. Nearly every returning Jew in the twentieth century saw in Zionism a promise to establish a just or at least a humane society in the ancient homeland. The early pioneer rejected the ghetto but not its warmth, its love for learning, and its other positive values. The first kibbutzniks discarded much of the Jewish religious traditions but substituted a creed and a cult of their own, no less institutionalized than those of their parents. The Israeli-born, post-1948 generation, flushed with victory, trivialized the Diaspora; some even exhibited an organic revulsion against the *shtetl* (East European small town) and against the gilded ghettos of West European and American Jewry.

But the 1967 events demonstrated to every Israeli Jew that, without its ties to the Diaspora, their country was a small Middle

Eastern state, neither economically sound, militarily secure, religiously self-sustaining, nor scientifically self-sufficient.

Terribly isolated and horrified by an indifferent or hostile non-Jewish world, the Israelis discovered the depth of the reservoirs of Jewish ethnicity, religious culture, and political activism along with the financial resources in the Diaspora. All these have come to the rescue of the beleaguered ministate to nurture its economy, staff its scientific institutions, and bolster its population with an ever-increasing Western Aliyah.

The growth of immigration from the "lands of prosperity"— Great Britain, South Africa, South America, France, and the United States (close to 9,000 from America in 1970)—has changed somewhat the temper and the tempo of the population. But as 1967 fades into history, it is still possible to trace the streams of the various Aliyot in Israeli society, since each Aliyah brought its own variations and its own problems of absorption. It is still possible to discern the obeisance to paternalism on the part of the East European and the Oriental Jews. Thus the pious look for guidance to the religious authorities not only in matters of faith. The secularists in the kibbutz and in the moshav turn to the "ideologues" for enlightenment on codes of socialist behavior, including the extent to which they may return to religious sources and observances as "symbols of identity with the totality of the Jewish people." Members of the multifarious parties seek direction from their respective political oracles.

Thus the sociopolitical acculturation is not as smooth as was hoped in a country where more than 50 per cent of the population was already native-born. Some of the problems between the Orientals and the Occidentals remain, as evidenced by the demonstrations of the Jewish Black Panthers, however small and unrepresentative the group is. Even less promising was the psychoreligious climate. There was a great deal of compromise on the part of both the secularists and the religionists, despite acrimonious public discussion and vocal denunciation, because neither side wanted to split the country at a time when the very existence of the state was menaced. Nevertheless, there were many protests for and against Sabbath and holiday observances, often resulting in mayhem and arrests. Should the external dangers to the physical being of the state disappear, there is some likelihood of a *kultur-kampf*, a struggle between "clericalism" and "anticlericalism," between radical free-thinkers and religious zealots, which may assume serious dimensions.

While the devout Jews and the secularists may have their differences, the vast majority, even in the free-thinkers' camp, feels that Israel must have a "Jewish" character. Hence the complete rejection by most Israelis of a binational or multinational state in which eventually they would find themselves an ethnic minority. Such an idea was adopted by some Arab commando groups as a "compromise solution," because they found it impossible to dislodge or to obliterate Israel. The New Left and some Western intellectuals, for more honest reasons, saw in the polyethnic state a just settlement of the problem of competing nationalisms.

Most Israelis and many other observers find this plan impractical in view of the political and economic instability of the Arab countries. If the Arabs cannot live in peace among themselves, they ask, how could they coexist with Jews in a binational state? Besides, the problems of binational and multinational existence manifested in Cyprus, Nigeria, Pakistan, Canada, and Yugoslavia are hardly encouraging examples. More significantly, the Israelis and their sympathizers reject the idea because it would do away with the Jewish character of the new political entity. When a Jewish state was voted into existence by the United Nations on November 29, 1947, it was conceived not only as a haven to solve Jewish homelessness but also as a religious, spiritual, and cultural center for the fruition of unique Jewish creativity.

"Hatikvah," the national anthem of Israel, which vows that the Jewish hope of redemption will perish only with the last breath of the last Jew, is also the hymn of many Jews the world over. But Rabbi Jack J. Cohen, director of the Hillel House at the Hebrew University in Jerusalem, asks what "Hatikvah" can possibly mean to an Israeli Arab. He further points to "the almost complete identification of the State of Israel with its Jewishness, which is understandable as an historical stage but unjustifiable as a philosophical position for democratic and liberal minded Jews." Rabbi Cohen himself seems to envision a pluralistic State of Israel (not a multinational entity), somewhat after the manner of a Christian American or a Christian British state, as a solution of the problem.

Still another subject that occupies the director of the Hillel House is the eventual confrontation of Israel with Islam and Islamic culture, and with the Arab world and Arabic culture. It makes no difference whether the Islamic or Arab civilizations are advanced or not: Judaism and the Israeli way of life will most assuredly be affected by interaction with them. A primary and edifying example of this is the current tortured process of accommodating, integrating, and synthesizing Western Jews and the Oriental Jews who have emerged from the Arab world.

However, the major task of Israel's foreign policy has been to bring about peace in the Middle East without compromising the Jewish character of the state. The crux of the problem as viewed from Jerusalem and from Tel Aviv is not borders but the constant attempt by Arabs to eliminate Israel, whether or not it returns to its 1948 or 1967 boundaries. It is the recognition of Israel as a state and its security within a contractually defined area that worries the Jewish government leaders. Thus, Israel in the years following the Six-Day War was ready to demilitarize Sinai and even the Golan Heights—wrested from Syria—a most strategic area from which Arab snipers could continually harass Jewish border settlements. Israel, as pointed out in the preceding chapter, was also ready to return most of the occupied West Bank to Jordan, or to acquiesce in an autonomous state in that region under Jordan, or to an independent entity—adding on to it the populous Gaza Strip —separated from Jordan. Even the problem of Jerusalem, an emotional and delicate issue, could, in the view of some Israelis, be solved by internationalizing the Christian holy places and handing over the sacred Muslim shrines to Jordan; Jordan would thus have some presence in Jerusalem without affecting too much the administration of the city as a whole. The Suez Canal and the Tiran Straits would be open to free international passage, including Israel.

The fruitless U.N. discussion regarding the Middle East conflict reminded one moderate Israeli diplomat of the story of a man who arrived breathless at the railroad station. Noticing the train he was to take still on the tracks, he became very agitated. Asked why he lost his temper, since he came before the train's departure, the man replied: "I was certain that I would miss it, so I did not bring my luggage." Both sides, added the diplomat, usually arrive at the U.N. on time, but without their luggage.

The death of Gamal Abdel Nasser may have induced the Arabs and the Israelis to bring their luggage and to board the peace train. Nasser's image could not be duplicated by any of the Arab leaders who survived him for use in forging an all-enveloping pan-Arab union. Guerrilla diplomacy and commando "propaganda of the deed" had lost most of their luster. To obliterate Israel was no longer deemed practical in the eyes of many Arabs. There was also evidence that Nasser himself before his death was ready for peace negotiations. At the age of fifty-two, he had developed a generation gap with the young Egyptians. He got caught in a Russian roulette game and realized the only way he could neutralize the Kremlin was to make peace and to introduce a greater American presence in the Middle East.

Israel, too, was tarnishing its moral image in the international community by its adamant stand. Inside the country small groups of university professors and students were staging demonstrations against Israeli militancy. Thus the peace train, halted on the tracks, was almost ready to take on passengers for a purposeful run.

Many of the war refugees, whose intellectuals spoke of their own dispersion as the Arab Diaspora, have discovered that the vague notions of Palestinian identity have realistic foundations and that the "New Jerusalem" may be the West Bank of the Jordan. A comparatively benign Israeli occupation ("comparatively," because no foreign occupation can be completely humane), has contributed much to material prosperity, the raising of educational standards, and the welding of the people in the region into a closer economic and political entity. The Jordanian civil war in September, 1970, between King Hussein's forces and the guerrillas weakened the Arab militants, preparing the ground for moderate leadership in the West Bank for peace settlement, self-determination, and the solution of the refugee problem, with the help of both Israel and sympathetic outsiders. The orderly municipal elections in the West Bank in 1972 are another sign of new times.

In a peaceful Middle East, how would Israel fare? Karl Marx once said that "the Jew lives on the pores of gentile economy." The situation is quite different for the Jew in his homeland. Israel's economic performance in the past bodes well for the future, despite dire "professorial" predictions both in that country and abroad. The fury of the academicians was aimed at the Israeli nonscientific approach, called by two scholars, Professor M. Gross of Wayne State University and the Israeli researcher Itzhak Galnoor, a "plan-as-you-go" system with a strong commitment to ideology as a guide in socio-economic action.

The whole thrust of the early Zionist movement was nonmaterialistic, with an emphasis on pioneering, self-sacrifice, and collectivism. The political and administrative elite that has been charting the Israeli course since the birth of the state in 1948 has remained bound to this ideology and its nonplanning orientation. Thus Israel never reached out for economic power for its own sake but has often harnessed its growing strength for social purposes, making the welfare of the people the fundamental principle of its conduct. As a result, the country's progress since independence has been marked by both pragmatism and vision. Theories, plans, charts, and statistics have played a modest role in the Israeli scheme of things. Intuitive approach, action, meeting deadlines, and mastering crises have been standard procedure not only for the government but also for the private sector of the country.

On the other hand, some writers, including Gross and Galnoor, have feared that Israel, moving into the industrial world, will take the "professors" and the "econometricians" too seriously, emulating the complex systems of the more "advanced" countries and relying almost entirely on statistics and projections to the exclusion of ideological principles and instinctive reaction to complicated problems. Recalling that Israel, per capita, was the third-largest user of computers in 1970–71, there was some basis for this fear. There was also the dread that Israel might cease to experiment and fall into the trap in which other new states found themselves—putting all its economic eggs into one basket. The strength of the state has been that it accommodated various ideologies—those of the collectives and those of the private sector—so that the failure of any one of them posed no fatal risks to the country as a whole. Such accommodation may have brought occasional recessions or even reverses, such as those of 1962–65, but Israel was able to recover from them because of its diversified and flexible system.

Leon H. Keyserling, adviser to President Truman, said:

> No economist with any claim to realism or objectivity can fail to marvel at the scope of Israel's economic goals during the past two decades and the miracle of their attainment. . . . The record of real economic growth has been virtually unprecedented. . . . To date, the vast preponderance of Israel's progress has come from indigenous efforts. . . .
>
> The genius of Israel has been its dominant recognition that economic and social progress reinforce each other and that there is no valid dichotomy between the two. This approach has been a major contribution of Israel to mankind. The accent upon this approach in the future, the realization that Israel above all must remain true to itself, will fortify its progress in the years ahead.

In the cultural and scientific fields, Israel's future also looks bright. In the Diaspora, Jews are mostly in the middle class, in the professions or services. Few are in the blue-collar or hard-hat jobs. An increased Aliyah from the Diasporic countries would, therefore,

pose a tremendous problem for Israel. But it need not be so, concludes Arie L. Eliav, former Secretary General of Avodah, the
Israeli Labor party. According to him, the tremendous technological
progress made during the recent past—which may be expected to
continue in the future—in cybernetics, automation, electronics,
chemistry, biology, agrotechnology, and medicine has turned the
social-professional pyramid upside down. Israel can and must "con-
vert the great professional reservoir of the Jews in the Diaspora
from a historic burden into a spur for a greater future."

For instance, the tens of thousands of doctors among the Jews cannot be asked to change their profession when they come to Israel, but
they can make the country an international medical research center. The land, lacking natural resources and raw material, has and
will continue to have high-quality manpower. In the scientific era,
Eliav claimed, the importance of skilled manpower is greater than
that of raw material. Just as Israel pioneered in agriculture, it can
lead the way in biochemistry and synthetics. It can be in the
vanguard of nuclear research, missiles, and computer science and
can continue to advance in areas it cultivated years ago. However,
not only its accomplishments in the agricultural and scientific
fields but also its contribution to the solution of social problems
of town and village can be increased and made available to other
countries. Lying along two prominent waterways, the Mediterranean and the Red Sea, and along intercontinental air routes, the
country can become a significant international link and a leading
maritime and aerial shipping power. Like the kibbutz in Israel, the
Jewish state may itself pioneer in a sociopolitical and economic role
in the world at large. First, though, it will have to prove itself by
making durable peace with the Arabs. It showed what a ministate can do to defend itself; it also has the capacity to demonstrate
what a small nation can do to develop life values.

In what politico-ideological context can modern Israel function?
The Six-Day War proved beyond doubt that the democratic regime
of Israel is far superior to the authoritarian-totalitarian systems of
its adversaries in the Middle East. In many ways it is similar to the

Western democracies, especially the United States, but in many other ways it is vastly dissimilar.

An American journalist who settled in Israel, Eliezer Whartman, pointed out the "differing approaches to freedom" of Israelis and Americans. The divergence between the younger and smaller democracy, on the one hand, and that of the United States, on the other, is that unlike the average American, the average Israeli has a fairly clear idea of what his country is trying to achieve (despite acrimonious party exchanges) and, what is more important, identifies himself intimately with that aim. Every effort to reach the national goal is viewed by the individual citizen as a personal accomplishment.

In the area of human relations, most Israelis truly feel that they are their brother's keepers. As an example Whartman compares America's attitude toward its immigrant Puerto Ricans with Israel's to its immigrant Yemenites. The hostility, overt and passive, that the Puerto Rican senses in the continental United States stems from almost all strata of society, including other oppressed minorities. By contrast, in Israel, despite many shortcomings and failures, there is a collective effort to see that the immigrant is fed, clothed, housed, and provided with work so that he can integrate quickly into society. This, however, should not be confused with conformity. Israel is notoriously nonconformist. No one in that country is expected to change his political views to suit his neighbors when he moves up in the income brackets. College students tended to individual dress and to criticism of their teachers long before it became fashionable in the United States. Nor is there the hysterical fear of Communism in Israel that prevails in America. This is all the more significant in a land where the threat of the Soviet Union is much more real than it is in the United States.

Whartman, however, sees Israel's shortcomings and chides the friends of the country for suppressing honest evaluation because of Israeli sensitivity to criticism and because of its precarious international position. One of the problems plaguing the country has been its party setup. A fundamental precept of democracy is that government is an instrument of the people, by the people, and for the people, and that it is always responsible to the people, *not* to the parties. Coming from an East European background, where there was no democratic interplay between the people and its rulers, influenced by the mandatory government, which did not pay much attention to the wishes of the Palestinian subjects, and entrapped in factional politics, which demanded party loyalty, the Israeli civil servant simply has not possessed a Western approach to democracy.

Another point made by Whartman is that a democracy demands that its people be good citizens not only of their country but of their communities as well. In Israel there is a strange imbalance—the people are highly conscious of national goals, but they possess only the barest understanding of municipal and neighborhood responsibility. It is difficult for the average non-kibbutz, non-moshav Israeli to understand that, in addition to his national duties, he has continuing duties toward his fellow townsmen, and that not everything can be left to the whims of governmental agencies. Thus, for instance, Tel Aviv has few public parks or playgrounds, simply because the Tel Avivians cannot grasp the Western concept that if people want something strongly enough, they can organize themselves and go out and get it. They leave it to their parties.

While political parties are still the most prominent fact in Israeli political life, there is some evidence that the pervasiveness of this reality is being mitigated. First, there are the municipal reforms, mentioned in an earlier chapter. Second, there is the new phenomenon influenced by Western immigration of alignments of alliances involving several parties. Thus, Avodah, the Labor party now in power, is not as homogeneous as its predecessor Mapai was; like an American party, it is a catchall for a variety of groups and individuals who differ on many issues. Yet, because of Avodah's continued pre-eminence and power, Israel also resembles somewhat the one-party system in Communist countries in that a single political grouping is always in control, exercising vast economic and ideological power, which can be employed to perpetuate itself. Unlike the Communist states, Israel, of course, has many opposition parties, but they do not possess the material means, the discipline, or the leadership of Avodah. It is to the vast credit of the Labor party that it is now amenable to national electoral reforms, which may take away some of its hegemony.

The struggle between the Old Guard and the Young Turks of the labor movement lost some of its bitterness after 1967, largely because the Young Turks were placed in responsible positions in the national coalition government. Also, the Young Turks are now not so very young—most were in their middle forties when the Six-Day War broke out.

Slowly but noticeably, a shift away from East European political concepts has taken place in the past several years. This process may have far-reaching consequences. The seasoned "ideologues," the word-intoxicated theoreticians of the older generation, are fading away, and a generation even younger than the Young Turks—university graduates, nuclear physicists, technicians, and "sociocultural engineers"—has discarded the verbal culture not only in the laboratory and the workshop but also in journalism, literature, and philosophy. The social goals remain primarily the same, but the methods of achieving them are changing.

It was feared that the succession of wars and the climate of violence would do irreparable damage to the young; it would create in Israel a Middle East Sparta, a Little Prussia. Most social scientists do not see evidence of scarring residual effects in present-day Israel caused by the ongoing conflicts with neighboring countries. In fact, an element of Israeli students has identified itself with the peace movements of young people the world over. Also, the sudden onrush of "hipsters" and "freaks" in the late 1960's and early 1970's left its imprint on some Israeli youngsters, although in the eyes of most of the country's university students they were "lovable nonentities who sit around and ignorantly discuss Hindu religion."

To be sure, jeans, guitars, hard rock, and country music have made the scene in Israel, especially during the summer, but mostly these are not popular with the sabras but with the 50,000 or more foreign students who inundate the country during the vacation months. Also, the drug culture has not sapped the vitality of Israeli youth. While some have been experimenting with hash, hard narcotics have been largely controlled and are mostly prevalent among foreign students. In fact, Israeli leaders think that their country's achievements as a social innovator, not its military success, may guide alienated Jewish youths in Europe's and America's New Left.

However, Professor Jacob L. Talmon, a renowned Israeli historian, is "uneasy about the commonly held view of Israel as the 'bastion of the free world,' " and as the home of democracy. Dr. Talmon sees Zionism as *sui generis*. "Its values are unique and special, derived neither from the Right nor the Left." In that, probably, he is correct.

Israel does not aim at a people's democracy, Soviet style, because the country's concern is not with overthrowing capitalism, or with the "expropriation of the expropriators," or with the "dictatorship of the proletariat," but with the nurturing of Israel's economy and with the building of a just and equitable society for *all*. Also, the affluent society in America, derogated but envied by many despite its shortcomings, is not ideologically alluring to most Israelis.

The welfare state, as it developed in the recent past, is much more attractive to the average Israeli and more adequately meets his needs, but in his eyes it still does not measure up to the goals and potentialities of his country. Israel adopted many features of the welfare state and in some instances made improvements in them, such as care for, and integration of newcomers. In other cases the country has not done as well, such as in free education on the secondary and higher levels. But Israel's current leadership, be it the Old Guard or the not-so-Young Turks (for that matter, the upcoming generation as well), is not willing to base its welfare program primarily on the financial resources of a bourgeois society.

Since the beginning of the Second Aliyah in the early part of the twentieth century, the Jews have generated a threefold *bloodless* revolution: a nationalist revolution, re-creating a peoplehood through the "ingathering of exiles"; an economic revolution in agriculture and technology; and a social revolution in which the role of money management has never been confused with the responsibilities of economic and social policy, and where the recognition has been strong that economic progress and social responsibility are interdependent.

The uniqueness of Israel is that its "glorious revolution," unlike so many other revolutions, has not come at the expense of the masses or at the expense of the capitalists. Hence the labor movement—the workers' parties with a majority in the parliament—which still possesses the power to impose socialist patterns on the entire country, has never used this potential. While it has fostered and developed its own ideological design, it has also encouraged the private sector to nurture its life style as a complement to what one may call a *mutualist* society or state.

Selected Bibliography

GENERAL

BEN-GURION, D. *Israel: Years of Challenge*. London: Anthony Blond, 1964.
BERMANT, C. *Israel*. New York: Walker, 1967.
BONDY, R. *The Israelis*. New York: Funk and Wagnalls, 1969.
ELON, A. *Israelis: Founders and Sons*. New York: Holt, Rinehart and Winston, 1971.
FEIN, L. J. *Israel: Politics and People*. Boston: Little, Brown, 1968.
LOUVISH, M. *The Challenge of Israel*. Jerusalem: Israel Universities Press, 1968.
NAAMANI, I. T., RUDAVSKY, D., and KATSH, A. I., eds., *Israel Through the Eyes of Its Leaders*. New York-Tel Aviv: New York University-Institute of Hebrew Studies, 1971.
PRITTIE, T. *Israel: Miracle in the Desert* (revised edition). New York: Praeger, 1968.

GEOGRAPHY, ARCHAEOLOGY, FLORA AND FAUNA

AHARONI, Y., and AVI-YONAH, M. *The Macmillan Bible Atlas*. New York: Macmillan, 1968.
ALBRIGHT, W. F. *The Archaeology of Palestine*. London: Penguin Books, 1949 (paper, 1960).
HOLLIS, C., and BROWNRIGG, R. *Holy Places: Jewish, Christian and Muslim Monuments in the Holy Land*. New York: Praeger, 1969.
KOLLEK, TEDDY, and PEARLMAN, M. *Jerusalem: A History of Forty Centuries*. New York: Random House, 1968.
ORNI, E. *Geography of Israel*. Jerusalem: Israel Universities Press, 1971.
VILNAY, Z. *The New Israel Atlas: Bible to Present Day*. New York: McGraw-Hill, 1969.
YADIN, Y. *Masada: Herod's Fortress and the Zealots' Last Stand*. New York: Random House, 1966.
YADIN, Y. *The Message of the Scrolls*. New York: Simon and Schuster, 1957.

233

JEWISH HISTORY AND ZIONISM

BEN-GURION, D., ed., *The Jews in Their Land*. London: Aldus Books, 1966.
EBAN, A. *My People*. New York: Behrman House/Random House, 1968.
HALPERN, B. *The Idea of a Jewish State* (second edition). Cambridge, Mass.: Harvard University Press, 1969.
HERTZBERG, A., ed., *The Zionist Idea: A Historical Analysis and Reader*. New York: Atheneum; Philadelphia: The Jewish Publication Society, 1970.
HUREWITZ, J. C. *The Struggle for Palestine*. New York: Greenwood, 1968.
LITVINOFF, B. *The House of Their Fathers: A History of Zionism*. New York: Praeger, 1965.
PATAI, R., ed., *Encyclopedia of Zionism and Israel* (two volumes). New York: Herzl Press and McGraw-Hill, 1971.
SACHAR, A. L. *A History of the Jews*. New York: Knopf, 1965.

POLITICS AND GOVERNMENT

ARIAN, R. *Ideological Change in Israel*. Cleveland: Case Western Reserve University, 1968.
BADI, J. *The Government of the State of Israel*. New York: Twayne, 1963.
BAKER, H. E. *Legal Systems of Israel*. Jerusalem: Israel Universities Press, 1968.
FREUDENHEIM, Y. *Government in Israel*. Dobbs Ferry, N.Y.: Oceana, 1967.
KRAINES, O. *Government and Politics in Israel*. Boston, Houghton Mifflin, 1961.
LANDAU, J. M. *The Arabs in Israel: A Political Study*. London: Oxford University Press, 1969.
ZIDON, A. *Knesset: The Parliament of Israel*. New York: Herzl Press, 1967.

FOREIGN RELATIONS AND INTERNATIONAL COOPERATION

DRAPER, T. *Israel and World Politics: Roots of the Third Arab-Israeli War*. New York: Viking, 1968.
EBAN, A. *Voice of Israel* (revised edition). New York: Horizon, 1969.
EYTAN, W. *The First Ten Years: A Diplomatic History of Israel*. New York: Simon and Schuster, 1958.
FRANK, M. *Cooperative Land Settlement in Israel and Their Relevance to Afrian Countries*. Basle: Byblos-Verlag, 1968.
KREININ, M. E. *Israel and Africa: A Study in Technical Cooperation*. New York: Praeger, 1964.
LAQUEUR, W. *The Israel-Arab Reader: A Documentary History of the Middle East Conflict*. New York: Citadel, 1969.
LAUFER, L. *Israel and the Developing Countries: New Approaches to Cooperation*. New York: The Twentieth Century Fund, 1967.

THE ARAB-ISRAELI CONFLICT

ALLON, Y. *The Making of Israel's Army.* London: Vallentine-Mitchell, 1970.
Associated Press, *Lightning out of Israel: The Six-Day War in the Middle East.* New York: 1967.
CHURCHILL, R., and CHURCHILL, W. S. *The Six-Day War.* Boston: Houghton Mifflin, 1967.
HAUER, C. E. JR. *Crisis and Conscience in the Middle East.* Chicago: Quadrangle Books, 1970.
HUREWITZ, J. C. *Middle East Politics: The Military Dimension.* New York: Praeger, 1969.
KHADDURI, M. D., ed., *The Arab-Israeli Impasse.* Washington: R. B. Luce, 1968.
KHOURI, F. J. *The Arab-Israeli Dilemma.* Syracuse, N.Y.: Syracuse University Press, 1968.
LORCH, N. *The Edge of the Sword: Israel's War of Independence, 1947–1949.* New York: G. P. Putnam's Sons, 1961.
MARSHALL, S. L. A. *Sinai Victory.* New York: William Morrow, 1958.
MARSHALL, S. L. A., the Editors of the American Heritage Magazine and United Press International. *Swift Sword.* New York: 1967.
SAFRAN, N. *From War to War: The Arab-Israeli Confrontation, 1948–1967.* New York: Pegasus, 1969.

SOCIETY AND ECONOMY

AKZIN, B., and DROR, Y. *Israel: High-Pressure Planning.* Syracuse, N.Y.: Syracuse University Press, 1966.
BEIN, A. *Return to the Soil.* Jerusalem: Zionist Organization, 1952.
BETTELHEIM, B. *Children of the Dream.* New York: Macmillan, 1967.
COHEN, A. *Arab Border Villages in Israel: A Study of Continuity and Change in Social Organization.* Manchester, England: Manchester University Press, 1965.
EISENSTADT, S. N. *Development and Integration.* London: Pall Mall, 1969.
HOROWITZ, D. *The Economics of Israel.* London: Oxford University Press, 1967.
KANOVSKY, E. *The Economy of the Israeli Kibbutz.* Cambridge, Mass.: Harvard University Press, 1966.
KLAYMAN, M. *The Moshav in Israel.* New York: John Day, 1970.
LEON, D. *The Kibbutz: A New Way of Life.* New York: Pergamon Press, 1969.
MALKOSH, N. *Histadrut in Israel: Its Aims and Achievements.* Tel Aviv: Histadrut, 1961.
PATINKIN, D. *The Israel Economy: The First Decade.* Jerusalem: The Falk Project for Economic Research in Israel, 1967.
RABIN, A. I. *Growing Up in a Kibbutz.* New York: Springer, 1965.

SAMUEL, E. *The Structure of Society in Israel.* New York: Random House, 1969.

SPIRO, M. E. *Kibbutz: Venture in Utopia.* New York: Schocken Books, 1963.

STOCK, E. *From Conflict to Understanding: Relations Between Jews and Arabs in Israel Since 1948.* New York: Institute of Human Relations, American Jewish Committee, 1968.

WEINGARTEN, M. *Life in a Kibbutz.* New York: Reconstructionist Press, 1955.

WEITZ, R., and ROKACH, A. *Agricultural Development Planning and Implementation: An Israeli Case Study.* New York: Praeger, 1968.

CULTURE

BENTWICH, J. S. *Education in Israel.* Philadelphia: Jewish Publication Society, 1965.

COLBI, S. *Short History of Christianity in the Holy Land.* Tel Aviv: Am Hassefer, 1965.

GRADENWITZ, P. *Music and Musicians in Israel.* Tel Aviv: Israeli Music Publications, 1959.

KOHANSKY, M. *The Hebrew Theater—Its First Fifty Years.* Jerusalem: Israeli Universities Press, 1968.

PENUELI, S. Y., and UKHMANI, A., eds., *Anthology of Hebrew Short Stories* (two volumes). Tel Aviv: Institute for the Translation of Hebrew Literature and Megiddo, 1965.

PENUELI, S. Y., and UKHMANI, A., eds., *Anthology of Modern Hebrew Poetry* (two volumes). Jerusalem: Institute for the Translation of Hebrew Literature and Israel Universities Press, 1966.

TAMMUZ, B. and WYKES-JOYCE, M., eds., *Art in Israel.* Tel Aviv: Massada, 1966.

Index

Weizmann Institute of Science, 10, 168, 179, 181
Welfare state, 134, 231
West Bank (of Jordan), 202, 211, 213–16, 223, 225
Western Wall, 9, 58, 73, 183 (*see also* Holy places)
West Germany (*see* Germany)
Whartman, Eliezer, 228 ff.
White Paper (British) of 1939, 41 ff., 128 (*see also* Royal Commission [British] of 1937)
"White Russian" territory (religious holdings), 76
"Who Is a Jew?" controversy, 64 ff., 112
Wilson, Woodrow
Wingate, Orde Charles, 126
WIZO (Women's International Zionist Organization), 178
Women's Equal Rights Law, 62, 85
Women's Labor Council, 164, 178
World War I, 19, 25 ff., 40, 50, 58, 59
World War II, 29, 41, 52, 127, 152
"World workshop," xii–xiii, 227, 231–32

Yaari, Meir, 103
Yadin, Yigael, 16, 183, 192
Yarkon River, 137

Yavneh, 17, 160, 161
Yellin-Mor, Nathan, 115
Yemen, 192, 193
Yemenites, 42, 46 ff., 115
Yeshayahu, Yisrael, 50
Yeshiva (plural: yeshivot), 68, 114, 160, 161
Yiddish, 33, 49, 92, 118; press, 187
Young Israel (Sephardic), 115 (*see also* Parties, political)
Youth Aliyah, 41 ff.
Youth Corps (*see* Gadna)
Yugoslavia, 43, 191

Zahal (*see* Defense Army of Israel)
Zealots, 16
Zechariah, 159
Zevi, Sabbatai, 20–21
Zhdanov, Andrei, ix
Zim Shipping Line, 150
Zion, Mount, 9 (*see also* Holy places)
Zion Mule Corps, 122, 125
Zion, yearning for, 19–28
Zionim Klaliyim (*see* General Zionists)
Zionism, 19, 22 ff., 80 ff.
Zionist Congress, First (1897), 24, 32; Fifth, 140; Twenty-eighth, 69
Zionist World Organization, 81 ff., 90, 128
Zuabi, Abd al-Aziz, 117